THE HOME FRONT

THE HOME FRONT

*Derbyshire in the
First World War*

Scott C. Lomax

PEN & SWORD
HISTORY

First published in Great Britain in 2016 by
PEN AND SWORD HISTORY
an imprint of
Pen and Sword Books Ltd
47 Church Street
Barnsley
South Yorkshire S70 2AS

ISBN 978 1 47383 440 8

Printed and bound in England
by CPI Group (UK) Ltd, Croydon, CR0 4YY

Typeset in Times New Roman by
CHIC GRAPHICS

Pen & Sword Books Ltd incorporates the imprints of Pen & Sword
Archaeology, Atlas, Aviation, Battleground, Discovery,
Family History, History, Maritime, Military, Naval, Politics, Railways,
Select, Social History, Transport, True Crime, Claymore Press,
Frontline Books, Leo Cooper, Praetorian Press, Remember When,
Seaforth Publishing and Wharncliffe.

For a complete list of Pen and Sword titles please contact
Pen and Sword Books Limited
47 Church Street, Barnsley, South Yorkshire, S70 2AS, England
E-mail: enquiries@pen-and-sword.co.uk
Website: www.pen-and-sword.co.uk

Contents

ACKNOWLEDGEMENTS

This book is the culmination of a vast amount of original research, in which I have been assisted by the following people: staff at Chesterfield Local Studies Library; Derbyshire County Record Office; Nick Tomlinson (Picture the Past); Aidan Haley (Assistant Archivist at Chatsworth); Peter Collins (Collections Curator at Rolls-Royce); Chloe Mason (granddaughter of Winnie Mason and great granddaughter of Alice Wheeldon); and I am also grateful to Michael Briggs for his kindness in providing photographs and information about the 5th and 6th Battalions Sherwood Foresters (Notts and Derby Regiment).

I would also like to thank Eloise Hansen and the staff of Pen and Sword Books for publishing this detailed account of one of the most important periods of Derbyshire's twentieth-century history. Finally, thank you to my wife and son for their patience and support.

The following sources have been invaluable in my research:

The *Derbyshire Times,* The *Derby Mercury,* The *Derby Daily Telegraph* (together these three newspapers provide coverage of most events that occurred within the whole county during the war years and form the main source of information for this book).

The Link (a quarterly publication for employees of Robinsons and Sons Ltd, first produced in June 1918 and available at Chesterfield Local Studies Library).

Basson, S., *Chesterfield: The Official History 1867 – 2000* (Harefield: Yore Publications, 2000).

Brittain, V., *Testament of Youth* (London: Virago Press, 2014).

Cooper, G., *Glossop in the Great War* (Barnsley: Pen and Sword Books Ltd, 2014).

Gayler, M., *Derby: Remembering 1914-18* (Stroud: The History Press, 2014).

Giles, E., *Chesterfield: A History of the Spireites* (Southend-on-Sea: Desert Island Books, 2013).

Kirk, Felix and Bartnik, *The Bombing of Rolls-Royce at Derby in Two World Wars* (Derby: Rolls-Royce Heritage Trust, 2002).

Lloyd George, D., *War Memoirs of David Lloyd George* (London: Odhams Press Ltd, 1938).

Mark, G., *Prisoners of War in British Hands during World War One: A Study of their history, the camps and their mails* (Wiveliscombe: The Postal History Society, 2007).

Norton History Group, *Norton in Wartime: An account of life during wartime in a village on the southern boundary of Sheffield* (Sheffield: Norton History Group, 1995).

Marsden, B.M., 'How Bradbourne Became Derbyshire's only Thankful Village.' *Reflections Magazine*: January 2015, p. 46-48.

Phizackerley, G. (Ed), *The Diaries of Maria Gyte of Sheldon, Derbyshire 1913-1920* (Cromford: Scarthin Books, 2008).

Reid, A., 'The effects of the 1918-1919 influenza pandemic on infant and child health in Derbyshire', *Medical History* 49(1) 2005, pp. 29-54.

Taylor, K. and Brown, T., *A Derbyshire Parish at War: South Darley and the Great War 1914-1919* (Bakewell: Country Books, 2000).

Taylor, K., *Matlock and the Great War 1914-1919: The sacrifice Made by the Families of a Provincial Town.* (Bakewell: Country Books, 2010).

A number of original documents held by Derbyshire County Record Office have also been studied. Where they are used as a source, the archives reference number is cited. However, a large number of documents not referred to in the text were also studied for general background research.

PREFACE

'We are making history every day. And some of our local history will be by no means the least interesting for the future generations to read', read part of an article in the *Derby Mercury* on 1 February 1918.

How true those words are. The following chapters show the more interesting aspects of the history of the county of Derbyshire during one of the most important periods of recent centuries.

Much has been written about the First World War and the involvement of the people of Derbyshire on the Front Line. Comparatively little, however, has been written about the efforts of the civilian population of Derbyshire. It is apt that during the centenary commemorations of the Great War, whilst paying our respects to those who were killed serving our country, we recognise also the impact that the war had on those at home and the civilian efforts which made victory possible.

Of course, it is necessary to include information about those brave men who hailed from Derbyshire and found themselves on the battlefields or on the seas. However, this is largely confined to the recruitment process, ending when the men left the county, although some information about their conditions, morale and, occasionally deaths, is provided in a bid to show the impact on those back home.

The book *The Home Front: Derbyshire in the First World War* provides detailed information to form the first definitive account of the role and experiences of Derbyshire folk during the Great War. It details: the run up to war; the war fever which led to thousands of Derbyshire's men answering their country's call; work in the factories, with tools and weapons being manufactured; the role of the miners in obtaining coal for use on the war front and at home, to keep the home fires burning; the efforts, and difficulties, faced by the county's farmers in feeding the nation; the county's role in treating wounded servicemen; the role of women; defence of the county; a Zeppelin raid which caused damage, destruction and loss of life in parts of

Derbyshire. For the first time in the county's history, Derbyshire's citizens realised that the horrors of war were not confined to overseas battles but could be witnessed and experienced in their own neighbourhoods; Belgian refugees and how they were looked after; conscientious objectors; an alleged plot by a Derbyshire family to assassinate the Prime Minister; prisoners of war held in the county; food shortages and the use of rationing; the Armistice and peace celebrations; the influenza epidemic which killed thousands of people in Sheffield as the war came to an end; and the social and economic legacy of the war, which helped mould the county into what it is today.

Above all this book details the human experiences, thoughts, concerns, fears and hopes of Derbyshire people during one of the most important periods in recent history.

CHAPTER 1

The Run Up to War

On Thursday 25 June 1914, several mining communities in North Derbyshire experienced pomp and ceremony as King George V and his Queen, Mary, graced the county with their presence.

As reported in the *Derbyshire Times*, the royal couple were met with 'scenes of enthusiasm', heard the 'cheers of thousands' wherever they passed and witnessed the 'fluttering of flags' waved by tens of thousands who gathered in the streets and open spaces to watch the royal car pass through their neighbourhoods.

On that Thursday morning the car passed through the village of Creswell but did not stop, leading to 'feelings of disappointment.' The car then travelled to Clowne where there were 'handsome decorations' in the streets,

The Market Place in Shirebrook, well decorated for the royal visit. *Courtesy of Derbyshire Libraries and www.picturethepast.org.uk*

and adorning buildings. Disaster almost occurred when a police horse bolted as the royal car arrived in the village and nearly charged into the crowd, but it was brought under control without causing damage or injury. The King and his wife stayed only five minutes in Clowne, in what was described as a 'flying visit' but this did not dampen enthusiasm. There was 'a rousing reception' for the royals, and later the children were presented with medals to mark the occasion.

From Clowne the entourage moved to Bolsover where there was 'extraordinary enthusiasm', with a day of festivities held, and many parties continued several hours after the royals left.

At Shirebrook there was so much excitement that the crowd began pushing to get to the royal car as it came to a halt, resulting in part of a barrier, separating the crowd from the road, collapsing and large numbers of people were crushed. Thankfully there were no serious injuries.

A brief exodus from Derbyshire occurred, as the royals visited Mansfield and Newstead Abbey, before returning to visit Ilkeston and Heanor. In Ilkeston there was a procession of the 5th Battalion Sherwood Foresters

Bath Street, Ilkeston, decorated to greet the arrival of the King and Queen. *Courtesy of Derbyshire Libraries and www.picturethepast.org.uk*

The royal car containing King George V and Queen Mary, arriving in Market Street, Heanor. *Courtesy of Derbyshire Libraries and www.picturethepast.org.uk*

(Notts and Derby Regiment) and 8,000 school children, and the blasts of the colliery sirens heralded the arrival of the royals. The market place was a 'blaze of colours' and it was remarked there was not a single building without flags and decorations. Enterprising shopkeepers removed goods from their windows and provided space for people to view the festivities, at a price. The King and Queen were also greeted with many thousands of well wishers in Heanor.

Also visited that day were Whaley and Whaley Common, Shuttlewood and Stanfree, Palterton and Scarcliffe. There was no visit to Chesterfield, where that same day trials of motor buses took place over several routes with buses having been introduced to the town in April, and on that same day the market clock was illuminated by electricity for the first time. There was also no visit to Staveley and its mining communities. Despite not being visited, Dronfield held its own festivities with its annual feast. Services, processions and maypole dancing, kept the residents in high spirits.

13

The above events were largely described in lengthy articles featured in the edition of the *Derbyshire Times* which went on sale on Saturday 27 June 1914. The following day, as the people of Derbyshire were still reading of the royal visit, there were events of a royal nature occurring approximately 1,100 miles away in a place few had heard of, that would have very grave consequences for their own lives.

On Sunday 28 June Archduke Franz Ferdinand, heir to the throne of Austria-Hungary, and his wife Sophie inspected the army at Sarajevo. The soldiers were not the only ones with arms in the city, however, that day. A group of seven young Bosnian Serbs, in a gang known as the Black Hand had planned to assassinate the Archduke as he drove along the Appel Quay; the main road in the city. One of the men threw a bomb at the car but it missed the vehicle and that man was arrested. The visit was then abandoned, with the intention that the Archduke would return home, but the driver of the car was unaware of that plan and so the journey continued along a route which had been well publicised. As the car turned into Franz Josef Street, there stood Gavrilo Princip, gun in hand. Princip pulled the trigger and the bullet hit the heir in the neck, rupturing his jugular. A short struggle followed during which Sophie was shot and killed. Within a short period of time the Archduke had bled to death.

Back in Derbyshire, where relatively few knew of the events described above, there was concern about the weather and its effects on the crops, livestock, roads and housing. Following a period of intense heat which had dominated June, horrendous storms brought havoc across Derbyshire, and further afield, with thunder, lightning, hail and rain on 21 June. On that day a man was struck by lightning at Grange Mills. The storms continued into July. On 1 July a 'terrific thunderstorm' hit the county, which was described in the press as being 'one of the largest storms experienced in some time' lasting into the night. In Chesterfield between 6pm until after 11pm there was almost continuous lightning and the three telephone lines between the town and Nottingham were cut off. In Matlock a man was struck by lightning although he was not seriously injured. A woman in Weston-on-Trent was less fortunate, being killed when struck. In North Derbyshire a woman was also struck by lightning whilst holding a pair of scissors. In Tideswell a bus was overturned.

The following day, 1 July, there was hail and even sleet, with miniature blocks of ice falling from the sky. In Ashbourne, it was described as a storm of exceptional violence. There were further similar storms over the course of the following three weeks. Isaac Barnes, a Castleford miner, was struck by lightning and was blinded. Lightning does sometimes strike twice; the following day he was struck yet again and it was claimed his eyesight returned.

The storms, especially that of 1 July, left a trail of damage and destruction across the county with horses laying dead in fields and many houses badly damaged.

Whilst local thought and opinion was at this time concentrated on the weather, few considered the fear of 'European war', with the Derbyshire newspapers entirely devoid of references to growing tensions, but the superstitious may have believed the weather was an omen, a sign of things to come, as storm clouds began to gather in both a literal and metaphorical sense.

CHAPTER 2

The Outbreak of War

Following the assassination of Archduke Ferdinand few could have predicted the speed and extent of its consequences. There was little mention of the aftermath in the local newspapers and any discussions in the county about events outside Derbyshire were dominated by the 'Ulster Situation'. Vera Brittain, a native of Buxton who served as a nurse for part of the war, recalled in her book *Testament of Youth*, 'I entirely failed to notice in the daily papers of June 29th an account of the assassination, on the previous morning, of a European potentate whose name was unknown to me, in a Balkan town of which I had never heard.' Yet she recalled the prayers and concerns for Ulster.

The Ulster Situation related to the issue of Home Rule in Ireland. In March 1914 the Curragh Mutiny had occurred, with the British army in Ireland showing disloyalty. Weapons were brought from Germany the following month and would later be used in bloodshed. In July matters came to a head when arguments took place to decide whether four or six Ulster counties should be excluded from Home Rule. The Home Rule legislation was passed in the House of Commons and was due to come into force in September 1914.

A conference was held at Buckingham Palace, addressed by the King, to try and resolve the situation. When the conference ended, three days later, it was widely recognised it had been a failure.

Whilst the conference was in progress, Austria-Hungary sent a note to Serbia accusing them of being involved in the assassination. The note demanded that Serbian officials, under Austro-Hungarian supervision, arrest all those on Serbian soil who made the assassination possible. Germany announced it had no part in the writing of the note, but would support its ally Austria-Hungary if another power got involved (the anticipated power being Serbia's ally Russia). The deadline for a response to the note was 25 July and as the deadline approached the Russian army began to mobilise.

Although those who read the daily national newspapers and took an interest in current affairs may have had a partial understanding of the developing situation across the English Channel, and therefore would have been aware that the Prime Minister, Herbert Henry Asquith (who was Prime Minister at the start of the war until 5 December 1916), had described the situation as 'very grave', there was general apathy.

At this time the editorials of the *Derby Mercury* and *Derbyshire Times* were solely about the king's conference. With regards to that matter the country was 'brought to the brink of fratricidal strife', with a civil war 'inevitable' unless immediate action was taken. The writers of letters to the *Derbyshire Times* at this time focussed on Stanfree Spa Bath, the National Union of Clerks and the quality of music performances at Queens Park. Those who wrote to the *Derby Mercury* were most concerned about the appointment of the Art Gallery curator and the council's reluctance to pay for a qualified curator.

On 25 July, less than two weeks before Britain became immersed in what was first described as the 'European War', the territorial forces of the 5th and 6th battalions of the Sherwood Foresters (Notts and Derby Regiment), who hailed from Derbyshire, headed to their annual training camps on the Yorkshire coast, with many hundreds of tents being dubbed 'canvas city'. Little did they know how soon, and to what degree, their training would be required.

It was not until 31 July that the possibility of war was raised in the Derbyshire newspapers. In the *Derby Mercury* that day 'a sensational week' of dramatic and momentous events were described, which had been 'startling in suddenness and grave indeed in possibilities'. The paper described Austria declaring war on Serbia and how 'All Europe has been roused in a twinkling'.

The following day, in an account of the Territorials' training camp in the *Derbyshire Times*, a correspondent reported, 'The war cloud of Europe is the big theme of conversation and the healthy appetites of the terriers are whetted. I have no hesitation in saying if the command came Colonel Clayton would lead the Battalion full of enthusiasm and ready to go anywhere required.'

Again, the *Derbyshire Times* editor focussed on the problems in Ireland, with problems in Europe considered a complication and a distraction that caused the Buckingham Palace conference's failure. There had been bloodshed in Dublin when gunrunners fired on British soldiers, who retaliated killing three and injuring a further thirty-eight. However, by this time there had been attacks by Serbians against Austrians, with shots fired at troops and a bridge over the Danube blown up, leading to war.

Mentioning war for the first time, the editorial continued:

'The European War has long been dreaded and long foretold, and today one of the great Powers of Europe is actively engaged in war and Europe is an open powder magazine with a conflagration raging in proximity to it. The people of this country may well be alarmed that through the pledge of International alliances the whole of Europe is entangled in the issues that arise out of the conflict between Austria and Serbia and that Great Britain, with the other great powers, is as likely as not to be drawn into the conflict. Our word is our bond in such a crisis as this, and even at the cost of a war, which would probably be the most exhausting and ruinous in our history, Great Britain will have to hold to her pledged word … '

Letter writers appeared to be less concerned with the prospect of a great war; Chesterfield races and yet again music in Queens Park were the issues of contention.

On 2 August the Territorials hurried back to Derbyshire after their training camps were closed in anticipation of mobilisation.

Although the *Glossop Chronicle* wrote of the possible approach of 'Armageddon' in its 3 August edition, across Derbyshire that day people enjoyed the Bank Holiday (which at this time was celebrated at the beginning of August), in a relatively carefree manner. There were train trips to the coast, and for those who stayed in the county there were walks, picnics and sports, such as in Matlock were athletic sports were held on the cricket ground, with 3,500 spectators. The day was generally sunny, with just a few showers in parts of Derbyshire, and most people made the most of an infrequent break from work.

Vera Brittain later recalled not minding playing tennis, 'particularly as the events reported in the newspapers seemed too incredible to be taken quite seriously'. In her diary at the time she recorded, 'I do not know how we all managed to play tennis so calmly and take quite an interest in the result. I suppose it is because we all know so little of the real meaning of war that we are so indifferent.' The indifference was seemingly shared by the majority of those in Derbyshire who did not believe Britain would be affected.

The reason for the indifference was that for a population that rarely, and in some cases never, ventured beyond the Derbyshire borders, talk of events in a country that they had never heard of seemed of little relevance to them. Derbyshire men had been involved in wars, most notably in South Africa, but only a minority were involved. As Brittain wrote, 'To me and my contemporaries, with our cheerful confidence in the benignity of fate, War

Derby's Cornmarket prior to the war. It was soon to become the scene of much military activity. *Courtesy of A.P. Knighton and www.picturethepast.org.uk*

was something remote, unimaginable, its monstrous destructions and distresses safely shut up, like the Black Death and the Great Fire, between the covers of history books.' Current affairs, she added, were 'something that must be followed in the newspapers but would never, conceivably, have to be lived'.

What a difference a day makes; the day after leisure and recreation Germany invaded Belgium; and failing to respond to a British ultimatum, Britain declared war on Germany. The carefree days of summer were over.

CHAPTER 3

Joining the Colours

It was now necessary to assemble a formidable army to combat what was called the 'arrogance and madness' of the German government.

Appeals for recruits appeared in the local and national newspapers, and were posted where ever they might be seen, including on the sides of trams and in all entertainment venues. A prominent advertisement in the *Derby Daily Telegraph* on the day following the declaration of war read:

> Your King and Country Needs You.
> Will you answer your country's call? Each day is fraught with the gravest possibilities, and at this very moment the Empire is on the brink of the greatest war in the history of the world.
>
> In this crisis your country calls on all her young unmarried men to rally round the Flag and enlist in the ranks of her army.
>
> If every patriotic young man answers her call, England and her Empire will emerge stronger and more united than ever.

Anyone interested in enlisting was urged to visit their nearest recruiting office.

People were warned the war would create difficulties that had not been experienced in a hundred years, and that it was a war 'at our doors' unlike that fought in South Africa and so to protect the nation all should do their bit.

Each town in Derbyshire, and most villages, had at least one recruiting office and men were encouraged to visit in order to put their names forward.

In Derbyshire, there were military units already established, including regular and territorials. The 5th Battalion Sherwood Foresters were based at the Royal Drill Hall on Becket Street, Derby. The 4th North Midland (Howitzer) Brigade, Royal Field Artillery (Derbyshire Artillery), made up of the 1st and 2nd Derbyshire (Howitzer) Battery, the 4th Midland (Howitzer)

New recruits outside the recruiting office in Hayfield in 1914. *Courtesy of Mrs J. Sidebottom and www.picturethepast.org.uk*

New recruits outside the Infants' School at Killamarsh, used for recruitment during the early days of war. *Courtesy of V. Green and www.picturethepast.org.uk*

The first three men to enlist at the Matlock Recruiting Office in 1914. *Courtesy of Beverley Toone and www.picturethepast.org.uk*

Ammunition Column and the Derbyshire Yeomanry, had their headquarters at Siddals Road, Derby. The 1st North Midland Field Ambulance, Royal Army Medical Corp (RAMC) which formed part of the 46th (North Midland) Division had their headquarters at St Mary's Gate, Derby.

In Chesterfield, the 6th Battalion Sherwood Foresters had their headquarters at the Drill Hall on Ashgate Road.

The 5th Battalion consisted largely of men from Derby and the south of the county, whilst the 6th Battalion was based in Chesterfield and was predominantly formed of men from the north of the county. These two territorial battalions formed the main body of Derbyshire's volunteer warriors and formed the focus of Derbyshire's county efforts in terms of recruitment and providing money and comforts. Both battalions were formed of a number of companies, with each company representing men from a particular part of the county.

Three days after the declaration of war, Lord Kitchener called for 100,000 men for what was popularly called the 'New Army', with the famous poster stating 'Your Country Needs You'. In order to meet this figure, which was soon found to be insufficient, men who had volunteered in peace time and during earlier conflicts, particularly in South Africa, were urged, if they had not already done so, to pledge themselves to their country and to embark on active military service in the European War. However, in order to meet the required number of men, new battalions had to be formed and more men sought for the long established ones.

The 9th (Service) Battalion was formed in Derby in August 1914. The 10th (Service) Battalion was created in Derby in September 1914. The 11th (Service) Battalion was established in Derby in September 1914. The 12th (Service) Battalion (Pioneers) was formed in Derby on 1 October 1914.

Other battalions were created in the county during the course of the war as the military required men in ever increasing numbers. The 16th (Service) Battalion (known as the Chatsworth Rifles) was formed in Derby on 16 April 1915 by the Duke of Devonshire. The 18th (Service) Battalion was formed in Derby on 27 July 1915. The 20th (Labour) Battalion was formed in Derby in May 1916.

When it was realised the war was not going to be as short lived as it had originally been hoped, and casualty numbers would be high, it was recognised that reserve battalions would be required in order to ensure, as much as was possible, that battalions had their full quota of men. Key reserve battalions for the Sherwood Foresters in Derbyshire were the 2nd/5th Battalion formed at Derby on 16 October 1914, the 3rd/5th Battalion formed in Derby in March 1915, the 2nd/6th Battalion formed in Chesterfield on 14 September 1914 and the 3rd/6th formed in March 1915. With the creation of the reserve battalions, the original battalions became known as the 1st/5th and 1st/6th.

During the autumn of 1914, a Yeomanry Reserve Regiment was established with training at Chatsworth and a reserve Army Service Corps trained at Ashgate in Chesterfield.

These formed the main military units with whom Derbyshire's men fought during the First World War, and enabled recruits to be part of battalions made up of people from their own county and often people they knew. However, Derbyshire men feature in the rolls of honour of battalions across the country and frequently soldiers would change battalions. For example, Patrick Kelly, a brother of my great grandmother, was a member of the 1st/6th Battalion Sherwood Foresters prior to the outbreak of war. He went with the battalion to France in 1915, was poisoned in a gas attack the following year and was discharged, returned to Britain and after recovering he joined the 6th Battalion Leicestershire Regiment.

The appeals made by the government and local authorities were joined by religious men. The Venerable Archdeacon Crosse, of Chesterfield, said men were duty bound to respond to the nation's call: 'I appeal to the men and the women of the land. Mothers you must bravely give your sons, wives give husbands. On the women of England a great responsibility rests. If the women are brave and true, patient and strong, then the men will do the right.' As will become clear in the chapters that follow, religious ministers on the whole supported the war and regularly justified its orchestration; and made appeals for more men and money.

Single men were particularly targeted. It was believed married men had responsibilities such as wives and often children, whilst single men often had no reason to stay.

To encourage men to join, by alleviating concerns about how their loved ones would cope, allowances were provided whereby employers paid a proportion (usually a half) of their employees' wages to their wives or partners. However, there were concerns in Derbyshire about the effects the allowances were having on businesses who could not afford to carry on paying the wives. The Derby Chamber of Commerce argued in August 1914 that the government should pay rather than the employer, although it was accepted that employers should keep the jobs open for the men to return to following the war. The government soon began to pay a separation allowance for the dependants of soldiers and sailors.

'Creswell recruits receive a hearty send-off' in 1914. *Courtesy of Derbyshire Libraries and www.picturethepast.org.uk*

There was a 'fine response' in Derbyshire for the call to arms as men experienced what has become known as 'war fever', with such enthusiasm to experience war and a sense of urgency to join before it ended.

There were some unexpected volunteers; the cowboys performing at the Wild Australia Show in Clay Cross volunteered themselves. The show consisted of more than 100 cowboys who were experts in horse riding and shooting.

The Vicar of Creswell, W. B. Soole, volunteered himself and his motorbike but his bishop thought he should stay to serve his parishioners' needs.

The Territorials who had given the pledge to serve, having recently returned from their annual camps, were instructed to mobilise in preparation of war. One man of the 6th Battalion, was down Maltby colliery when he was notified of the mobilisation by the police. He travelled to Chesterfield as quickly as he could, leaving the pit with his colleagues cheering supportively.

The men of the 5th and 6th Battalions headed to Derby and Chesterfield respectively, with the streets in the outlying districts lined with well wishers.

The Ashbourne Company marched sixteen miles to Matlock and spent the night in the Town Hall. Along with the Matlock contingent they gave the town 'the appearance of a military centre'. The following day, thousands lined the streets in Matlock to see off the men as they marched to Chesterfield, and the Derbyshire Imperial Yeomanry left for Ipswich.

The mobilisation of the territorial forces gave Chesterfield 'a spectacle which it has never before experienced', with the town 'suddenly transformed into a garrison town'. From morning to night the streets were 'thronged with khaki clad figures'.

During the enlisting process, military doctors were busy giving medicals and kit was inspected, with equipment replaced if necessary. Upon it being supplied they were expected to wear their khaki uniform to show that they had joined up.

During and following recruitment, the Drill Hall in Chesterfield accommodated most of the 6th Battalion, whilst its officers had quarters at the Portland Hotel and other licensed houses. The men of the ASC Mounted Transport and Supply Column stayed in tents in a field near Ashgate Lodge

On the eve of their departure from Chesterfield, the 6th Battalion, consisting of 1,000 men, marched to the Crooked Spire where they 'solemnly' deposited their colours placing them on the altar during a service which opened with the hymn *O God Our Help in Ages Past*. After the colours were laid, Archdeacon Crosse told those present, 'Officers and men of the 6th Battalion Notts and Derbyshire Regiment. I receive your colours into the church of God, and we will guard them and honour them. So may God guard you and your country honour you.'

Earlier that day, the troops had attended Sunday afternoon service and heard the Archdeacon read from the Epistle of St Paul to the Romans: 'I beseech you, brethren, present your bodies a willing sacrifice, holy and acceptable unto God.' The men were asked to use it as their motto.

The following day, Monday 10 August, Chesterfield gave the men a hearty send off, with flags visible everywhere and thousands lining the streets. Following a band, the troops, largely wearing full battle kit with the exception of the newest recruits who were yet to receive uniform, marched from the Central School playground to the Market Place. Two field guns and approximately twenty horses were amongst the men, who were followed by the mounted Derbyshire Yeomanry. The recruits were in cheery spirits, singing *It's a Long Way to Tipperary* as they passed along Saltergate.

When the market clock boomed 2pm the soldiers arrived in the Market Place, 'heralded by tremendous cheers'. So many spectators had come that by 1pm it was difficult to walk along Burlington Street and through the market.

Leaving Chesterfield, the men set off for Derby, first heading to Ripley (passing through Alfreton where they were greeted by huge cheering crowds)

Men of the 6th Battalion Sherwood Foresters preparing to leave Chesterfield on
10 August 1914. *Reproduced courtesy of Michael Briggs*

Men of the 6th Battalion Sherwood Foresters heading to the Midland Railway
Station in Chesterfield; and then on to   Derby, 10 August 1914. *Reproduced
courtesy of Michael Briggs*

Soldiers marching across Ripley Market Place in August 1914. *Courtesy of Wood Collection and www.picturethepast.org.uk*

where they spent the night at the Town Hall, Drill Hall, schools and other public buildings. In Ripley they would have been wary about drinking water because there were concerns, first raised in June 1914, regarding the 'filthy' water supply. Indeed it was believed livestock were contaminating it, although by the start of the war some measures had been introduced to improve the supply.

The Yeomanry, Mounted Territorials and the Transport Corps left Chesterfield on 12 August.

There were also mobilisations in towns including Wirksworth, Bakewell and Belper, where bands paraded the streets.

At Bakewell, the bishop of Derby, Dr Abraham, gave an address wishing God speed to the men and urging them not to make any mistake about the position England was in. He stated his belief that the war would create a strain which would test the manhood and endurance of their country like never before.

JOINING THE COLOURS

In Belper, soldiers of the Lincoln and Leicestershire Army Service Corps and the 2nd NM (North Midlands) Field Ambulance were quartered in the River Gardens, Public Hall, schools and anywhere else that was willing to accept them. A YMCA marquee was provided in Belper for troops to have recreation and comforts.

In Belper the men who had departed for Derby had left a great, 'Now they are gone', the *Derbyshire Times* remarked regarding their brief stay, 'and Belper people have much food for thought and remembrance in years to come over that stirring week in August 1914 when the first experiences of war were felt in the town'.

The men of the 5th and 6th battalions of the Sherwood Foresters, along with their Nottinghamshire comrades in the 7th and 8th battalions, converged on Derby prior to heading to their camp. Derby was also host to the Northampton Yeomanry, the Notts and Derby Army Service Corps and Royal Engineers. Whilst in Derby they found recreation at the YMCA premises at the Victoria Hall where between 11-14 August, 5,000 soldiers passed through its doors and 2,645 letters were sent. Women offered to mend any damaged

Men of the 5th Battalion Sherwood Foresters in Derby in August 1914. *Reproduced courtesy of Michael Briggs*

clothing while they were in the town (it was not until 1977 that Derby became a city and so the term 'town' will be used throughout this book).

Whilst in Derby, men stayed in the Drill Hall, schools, public halls and in the spare rooms of the many people who wanted to do their bit by providing accommodation. The officers stayed in finer public buildings such as the Town Hall and in hotels.

When the troops began to leave Derby early on Saturday 15 August it was remarked the railway sidings at Osmaston Park had become a mecca of mothers and wives, brothers and sisters who converged to give tearful farewells to their loved ones.

The mood was generally jovial with singing, cheering and whistling. The men of the 5th Battalion, who had deposited their colours at All Saints' church for safekeeping, paraded at the Drill Hall. Few people were around to see them march to the station because their early departure had not been anticipated, but the men had to wait for several hours due to heavy demands on the available trains and when it was learnt the men were to leave that day news spread quickly. During the wait enterprising fruiterers did a 'brisk trade' selling large quantities of fruit to the soldiers. In total approximately 16,000 men left Derby on the eighty trains requisitioned for the transportation of soldiers and equipment, with the final train leaving Derby on the Sunday night. They first headed to Luton and from there to their training camps, with the 5th and 6th Battalions based at Harpenden.

At this time so many men were heading to war and to the camps that 104 troop trains passed through Chesterfield in one day and night

In addition to troops and auxiliary staff, transport was needed. Horses and motor wagons of good calibre were requisitioned by the army, in towns and villages across the county. Many farmers took horses and traps to Bakewell Show but had to find other means of returning home because their horses had been taken. By the end of August 200 horses had been requisitioned in Bakewell. The Brampton Brewery had two of its lorries requisitioned and Stretton's Derby Brewery had most of its horses and all its motor vehicles requisitioned.

There were calls for ambulance men to accompany an expeditionary force to France and Belgium. Deputy Commissioner S.C. Wardell of Dee Hall House, Alfreton, who was in charge of the No. 5 district St John's Ambulance Brigade covering Derbyshire, Nottinghamshire, Leicestershire and Staffordshire, appealed for men. By 15 August 1914 there were approximately 6,000 ambulance volunteers across the country, with 1,200 from the No. 5 district.

Commandeered horses being led away in Duffield. *Courtesy of Bromby Collection and www.picturethepast.org.uk*

On 11 September 1914, the regular soldiers of the 2nd Battalion of the Sherwood Foresters landed at St Nazaire and were soon to engage in battle.

Men of the 1st Battalion Sherwood Foresters (also among the regular army) were hurriedly brought back from India where they had been serving. On 10 October approximately thirty such men from Chesterfield hastily returned to the town still clad in their regimental Indian dress, including Pith service helmets and short calico knickers. They had very little time back in Derbyshire before being rushed to join their fellow comrades, before being sent to France, arriving in Le Havre on 5 November 1914.

A 'loud, long and lusty cheer' was heard when the 5th and 6th Battalions of the Sherwood Foresters were told that they, along with their Nottinghamshire comrades of the 7th and 8th battalions, together forming the 46th (North Midland) Division, had been accepted for service, according to a correspondent for the *Derbyshire Times*. The men, who were at their camp at Harpenden, were glad they would have the chance to show what they could do for their country. They would be among the first territorial soldiers to head to war.

A.E. Hopkins visited the men at Harpenden and remarked he had never known 'a brighter, happier, prouder, or more courageous lot of men.' After three months at Harpenden the men moved to a camp in Braintree.

Their departure from England would not be until February 1915 and it was quickly realised they would need to be joined by many more men if victory was to be ensured.

Recruitment meetings took place in almost every town and village in Derbyshire. Typically, bands played patriotic music prior to 'rousing speeches' by speakers which usually included local dignitaries who were keen to state they would have joined up themselves but alas they were too old, and if available military representatives were present. Often a local clergyman played a key role. The crowds were told stories of German brutality against the Belgians, especially women and children, and against British soldiers. An appeal would then be made for men to come forward and pledge themselves to their country, with promises of receiving a hero's welcome upon their return. A few examples of such meetings will suffice.

Mr F.C. Arkwright of Willersley Castle spoke at a recruiting event at Matlock Town Hall on 24 August 1914. He urged men to come forward and hoped Matlock would not disgrace itself. Almost fifty enlisted during the meeting. Arkwright paid their train fare to Derby and other expenses the following day.

On 4 September 1914 'stirring speeches' provided the people of Chesterfield with 'every reason to feel proud of their town', according to the *Derbyshire Times*, when efforts were made to recruit more men.

A meeting was held at the Chesterfield Market Hall, convened by Mr Locker Lampson, MP for Salisbury and former Unionist candidate for Chesterfield. According to the newspaper, 'it was heartening to witness the eagerness with which able bodied men enlisted' during the event which saw speeches and patriotic music performances to encourage men to sign up. So many people came that an overflow meeting was needed.

Speaking in the Market Hall, Captain W.B. Robinson, who had fought in South Africa, presided. Robinson was, he said, in a very happy position because he was not going to ask men to do anything he had not done.

Recognising that many in the audience were miners, Robinson asked whether they knew 'the Germans had absolutely closed down a pit and deliberately entombed the men?' Cries of 'shame' could be heard in response. Robinson continued that if the men were Englishmen they would avenge that terrible and inhumane act.

Captain Bathurst said Kitchener had sent him to Chesterfield to help with the meeting and to provide information about the current situation. Kitchener was convinced it was the 'bounden duty of every able bodied man to join the Army' to fight for their existence. The Germans were fighting hard, Bathurst told the crowd, and a large number of men were needed 'to thrash them'.

A man in the audience asked a question that was a prevalent thought amongst older men: 'What do you keep refusing us older men for?' He was told that as long as men were wanted it was believed there would be sufficient volunteers, and so no older men were needed.

Alderman C.P. Markham said he was too old but that he was trying to ensure funds were available for the maintenance of the volunteers. He added he had given his boat to the government and if he had any money left they could have that too.

Archdeacon Crosse regretted his age prevented him from joining but his oldest son had enlisted and his youngest son would soon be of military age. The war was, he said, 'a very grave crisis' but it would be brought to an end more quickly if more men volunteered. He assured potential volunteers that the town would not see a single family in want where a family member was serving.

Robinson said he would call together the thousands of girls he employed and tell them that if they had a young man in their lives who would not enlist, to 'chuck them up'.

The Corn Exchange meeting was addressed by Locker Lampson, who said he wanted to tell Kitchener that the Chesterfield meeting had recruited more men than anywhere else in Derbyshire.

A telegram was also read from Barnet Kenyon, MP for Chesterfield, saying, 'I shall be pleased to hear that our young men have risen to meet the national necessities. Best interests of the nation are at stake. For the sake of our country I hope we shall meet it in the true spirit of patriotism.'

In order to encourage men to join, Lampson promised soldiers leaving Chesterfield would take the admiration, gratitude, love and prayers of every person who was left behind. On their return he would ensure they received the greatest reception Chesterfield had ever seen. He had applied for a commission and although he had yet to receive a response he hoped to meet many Chesterfield men on the Front.

A well attended meeting was held at Chesterfield's Corporation Theatre the following day. Mayor Ernest Shentall (who was mayor for the full duration of the war) presiding, announced that everyone in the town could help but not everyone could fight. He did not believe Chesterfield was full of shirkers but instead full of workers, male and female, prepared to do their duty.

To a 'rousing reception' the Duke of Devonshire addressed the crowd.

Men were anxious, ready and determined to stand shoulder to shoulder and true to their country, he announced, but much more was required. The enemy was not far away, he warned. During the past week the enemy had been closer to London than the distance between Chesterfield and the capital.

He praised the forces and Belgians and urged the men of Chesterfield to take their fair share of the struggle. War would only end when Britain dictated the terms of peace, he said, which may happen quickly or take a long time.

He urged the crowd to show the authorities Derbyshire was not behind other counties in its response to the nation's call.

Violet Markham told the audience that people had still not fully realised the extent of the situation and the ruthlessness of the 'shameless enemy'. She said 'the greatest and most supreme test' had fallen upon the men and women of the country to protect the traditions of Britain and the liberties not only of Britain but the whole world.

Appealing to the women in the audience, she said they must be prepared to come forward in a 'brave, dauntless and self-sacrificing spirit' and plead with their men to 'face the sacrifices with clear eyes and undaunted hearts, for it was the spirit of the women that would carry the standards of their men to victory'.

In agreeing to fight, Markham continued, men should not concern themselves over the finer details of the war, with the final issues resting 'in higher hands'. Instead, the men should 'humbly commend themselves to God' as they went to wage a war in such a way to make future war impossible. Ultimate victory would be as assured and as true as the rising of the sun, she promised.

Archdeacon Crosse told those present that the cause was just, but even if it was not a just cause it was the duty of every man to fight if his country was in need.

At a meeting in Ilkeston in October, concerns, shared across the country, were discussed, about how dependants would be looked after if they went to war and this was holding many men back from joining up. The Mayor of Ilkeston had received a letter from a man attached to the 11th Battalion at Frensham, who told the mayor if they had the assurances their wives and dependants were looked after they would go to the front and fight like hell. The Mayor said he gave that assurance. The Duke of Devonshire added that the country was not immune from invasion, so Territorials were also needed at home.

Not everyone in Derbyshire was so enthusiastic. 'Tradesman' of Hilcote wrote to the *Derbyshire Times* complaining of his village men, none of whom,

A group of men from the 6th Battalion of Sherwood Foresters about to leave Chesterfield in September 1914. *Reproduced courtesy of Michael Briggs*

Soldiers from the 5th Battalion Sherwood Foresters in Derby ready to embark trains to leave for their camps in 1914. *Courtesy of Derby City Council and www.picturethepast.org.uk*

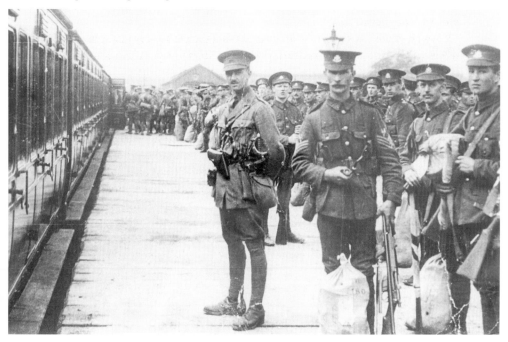

he claimed, had volunteered (with the exception of a few ambulance volunteers): 'Surely they cannot realise what it means to us should we "go under" in this great and terrible conflict. We are in the throes of a struggle, the issue of which no man can foretell. Our heroes at the front are gladly shedding their blood in our defence, but they trust us, at home, for assistance. Shall we betray that trust? God forbid …'

Jas McKay, Vice President of the Liberal Association of North East Derbyshire, wrote to the *Derbyshire Times*, in a letter printed on 8 August, expressing his 'profound dismay' at Britain's involvement in the war: 'After the frightful and heart-sickening loss of life, the making of tens of thousands of widows and orphans, the hundreds of millions of pounds which it will cost, the paralysis of trade, industry and commerce for months to come, resulting in ruin to many and intensifying the poverty and distress of the poor. I ask, after all this, and infinitely more than pen can describe, what have we gone to war for?' He described the government's decision to go to war as 'a crime of colossal magnitude against the highest, noblest and best interests of our country'.

McKay was condemned by the editor who wrote: 'Unfortunately there is a type of Liberal mind, full of its own self-righteousness, quite sure it is animated by the loftiest of motives, which always sees its own country in the wrong. It regards other minds, just as honourable, but which do not see things in the same way, as mean, as wanting war because of the money that is to be made out of it, because of bloodthirstiness, and indeed, most things that are reprehensible. Mr McKay seems to be one of these. We leave Mr McKay to his own conscience and the righteous indignation of every true Englishman.'

Mr H. Stockton Judd of Bolsover showed his indignation: 'I, no doubt with many others, was astonished on reading Mr Jas McKay's letter in which he says "What are we fighting for?" Knowing he poses as an "intelligent" man, one would have thought he knew the meaning of "honour and integrity." If he looks at his dictionary he will find honour means reputation, uprightness, virtue, honesty, soundness. These are what we are fighting for.'

Despite the opposition of McKay and others, and the refusal of some to enlist, the Rolls of Honour regularly printed in the press showed the ever increasing number of men from the county who had agreed to leave their country, often for the first time, with romantic images of battles in their minds as war fever continued to grip the nation.

Those already at war, the *Derbyshire Times* claimed, were 'covering themselves with Glory' and anyone wanting a share of that glory should join up immediately.

Although some of Derbyshire's men joined the Royal Navy, with Derbyshire's inland position there was no naval tradition and so the overwhelming majority of those who enlisted joined the army. Consequently efforts on the home front to support the forces concentrated on providing men, money and comforts for soldiers. However, there were occasional 'navy weeks' held in Derbyshire towards the end of the war to help raise funds for the sailors.

The Royal Flying Corps was established in 1912 and existed until it merged with the Royal Naval Air Service to create the Royal Air Force on 1 April 1918. Until 1915, there were no airfields in Derbyshire and consequently few men joined the Corps. However, on 16 August 1914 people in Derby flocked to the racecourse to see B.C. Hucks, who had joined the Flying Corps, land his plane. It was not until 1915 that Coal Aston Aerodrome opened in the very north of the county but men who were based there were drafted in from other areas and the call for new recruits was later largely answered by men, and later women, from Sheffield. The first recruitment drive for the Flying Corps in Derbyshire took place in 1917 and is referred to in a later chapter.

Even children were encouraged to do their bit, with boys of the Scouts and Boys Brigade being given classes in signalling, sick nursing and other useful skills.

Some boys went much further, however. Although the minimum age for overseas service was eighteen, that did not stop children attempting to join the army. At a time when people did not have identification, and few had birth certificates, if a person looked eighteen the military often accepted their word without question, especially given the desperation to obtain a large body of soldiers.

Vernon Prince of Chesterfield was just fifteen when he enlisted. He was killed on 9 August 1915. William Booth, a foreman joiner on the Midland Railway in Derby, enlisted at the start of the war, aged just fifteen, and joined the Royal Field Artillery. His parents had not known he had enlisted until he passed his medical. Just six months later their son died in Glasgow from cerebrospinal fever. There are many more examples of this in Derbyshire.

CHAPTER 4

Derbyshire's War Workshops

The men who had answered their country's call needed equipment and weapons if they were to have any success on the battlefields, on the seas and in the air.

Prior to the war Derbyshire had many well-established industries and several of them benefited greatly from the conflict, producing weapons, tools and equipment used at home and abroad. Companies were able to expand, providing jobs and increased wages to their employees. It is not possible to include all of the many industries which contributed to the war effort, but the key companies are briefly discussed below.

Rolls-Royce in Derby was concerned at the outbreak of war because many of its orders came from Europe, and at a time of war luxury vehicles were not highly sought after, so there were fears the company would cease to operate. Believing the war would be short lived, it initially did not attempt to obtain government orders. However, by 1915 and with a greater appreciation that war would last longer than initially hoped, it began making aeroplane engines. By the end of the war approximately half of the engines in the aeroplanes of the Allies were produced by Rolls-Royce in Derby and to meet the demand the factory was greatly expanded and hundreds more staff taken on.

During the war the Locomotive Works in Derby quickly turned to the war effort, producing eleven howitzers by the end of 1914. It also produced shells, with 30,000 being made per week at the peak of production, as well as reconditioning shells that had been previously fired.

The Carriage and Wagon Works, also in Derby, produced 200 wagons and ten coaches per week by the end of the war. It also built nine ambulance trains, 890 special wagons, 1,750 army service vehicles, 6,128 railway wagons, 2,600,000 shell fuses, 6,500,000 18-pounder reformed cartridge cases, 180,000 gun parts and gun carriage components and 273,000 component parts for army service vehicles.

The Derby Locomotive Works showing the production of shells. The photograph shows a factory room whose workers were almost entirely female. *Courtesy of Derby City Council and www.picturethepast.org.uk*

Leys Malleable Castings Co. Ltd, set up by Sir Francis Ley, who had unsuccessfully attempted to introduce baseball and American football to England, was another key Derby industry.

British Cellulose and Chemical Manufacturing Co, was formed in 1916 by a Swiss entrepreneur, who was invited by the British Government to set up a factory in Spondon, producing lacquer to coat the fabric covering plane wings and fuselages. The company was later known as British Celanese and at its height during the war it employed thousands of staff; and only ceased to exist in recent years.

Messers Newton Bros of Derby produced aero wireless generators used by the Royal Flying Corps and later the Royal Air Force.

Messrs Robinson and Sons in Chesterfield produced cardboard boxes and surgical dressings, employing approximately 1,600 staff prior to war. As a result of producing dressings used in war hospitals at home and abroad, the company expanded and took on additional staff, especially women.

Plowright Bros Ltd of Chesterfield prospered, producing colliery machinery which was much needed in ensuring an increased output of coal, especially as men left the pits to join the forces resulting in labour shortages.

Markham and Company was a Chesterfield firm of engineers and founders principally involved in iron and steel construction. Prior to war it described itself as being 'probably the most important firm in the building of colliery winding engines in England'. It also produced railway construction equipment. The works covered a large area by the River Rover, and a large electric crane was described in 1914 as being one of the engineering sights of the town. 'Rapid strides' were made as a result of the war, carrying out much structural ironworks for the Ministry of Munitions as well as producing armoured plates for tanks.

Bryan Donkin Co, Ltd, in Chesterfield, manufactured gas exhausters, gas valves and motor parts of use in vehicles and factory machinery. It employed approximately 700 prior to the war, and this figure remained approximately the same at the war's end, although the business expanded.

The Chesterfield Tube Company was almost bankrupt in 1914 but by the end of the war 'rapid progress' was made, with the premises expanding several times to meet government orders. Prior to war the company employed around 300 staff, specialising in the manufacture of weldless steel tubes, but at its height during the hostilities 1,200 men and women were on its books. Alderman Markham argued the Tube Company made more shells, drew more tubes for Royal Navy ships and made more steam pipes for marine engines during the war than any other firm in Britain.

A shot-firing works in Chesterfield created large numbers of bombs and hand grenades.

Potteries across Derbyshire, especially in Derby and Chesterfield, produced bottles and other storage vessels for the forces as well as large pipes for the munitions' factories. In Chesterfield, Pearson's pottery was very successful throughout the war, producing bottles including rum bottles for the Navy.

The Victoria Hall in Matlock opened in 1896, housing a swimming pool, roller skating rink, gymnasium and concert hall. Business was hit by the war and it closed down. However, in 1915 it became a factory producing balaclavas, socks, scarves and other woollen garments for servicemen.

Other key companies in North Derbyshire at the start of the war, which carried out important war work included the Railway Wagon Works in Chesterfield, the Staveley Coal and Iron Company, the Sheepbridge Coal and Iron Company, the Clay Cross Iron Works and the Renishaw Iron Works.

In June 1918, a Sheffield firm expanded into Chesterfield due to lack of space in the steel city and because of better rail connections and proximity to the coal and iron industries. The firm, Robert Hyde and Sons Ltd, were iron and steel founders producing railway wagon components.

A factory was established in Langwith, on Derbyshire's border with Nottinghamshire, where a chemical called ammonium perchlorate was produced. The chemical's properties allowed it to burn very quickly and it proved to be useful in sea mines. The factory covered an area of 27 acres and employed approximately 800 workers.

In addition to those munitions factories within Derbyshire, large numbers of munitions workers, especially women, were required to travel to factories in neighbouring counties, such as those in Sheffield and the Chilwell munitions factory in Nottinghamshire. The Chilwell factory was the most productive shell-filling factory in the country.

Soon after the war began it became apparent that even with expanding factories, new factories and longer working hours there was a tremendous shortage of the means of war being produced, especially munitions. By March 1915, only approximately one quarter of the required amount were being produced. During that month, three days into the battle of Neuve-Chapelle, the forward movement of the troops was halted due to a shortage of ammunition. During the Neuve-Chapelle battle more shells were fired, it was claimed, than in the entirety of the Boer War.

It was estimated in March 1915 that 12,000,000 shells were needed each month and according to Mr O'Conner MP, 'every hour's delay in producing these things is an hour's - perhaps even a month's – prolongation of the war'. Workers were encouraged to strain every effort to produce all they could.

It was what David Lloyd George called, in his war memoirs, 'The Great Shell Scandal.' The Board of Trade, which had the responsibility for labour and munitions, in consultation with the War Office, was clearly failing. In an attempt to massively increase the amount of munitions needed for the war effort, a new government department, the Ministry of Munitions, was created and Lloyd George became its first minister.

The Ministry of Munitions attempted to increase the amount of munitions by:

a) Addressing the skilled labour shortage by checking the enlistment of skilled men and requesting the army release skilled munitions workers from its ranks

b) Ensuring that workers worked their full hours and achieved their maximum levels of performance, also ensuring they remained working in the same factory to maintain continuity of staff and skills

c) Ensuring a more rigid control of establishments selling alcohol in industrial areas

d) Training and employing women to undertake work in the factories

e) Ensuring all available labour was well used in order to meet demands, by transferring all workers to the cities where they could work in established munitions firms or by spreading production across the country.

In June, efforts were made to bring back skilled munitions workers who were in the armed forces, but it was stipulated by Kitchener that only men who were not yet overseas could be released though this was extremely difficult, as Lloyd George remarked it was 'like getting through barbed-wire entanglements without heavy guns'.

The Munitions of War Bill received royal assent on 2 July 1915. The reforms by the Ministry of Munitions helped alleviate many of the problems in producing the vast quantities of munitions needed to win the war by bringing munitions factories under government control and ensuring work was solely to meet government orders; and profits were limited, although as previously shown, many Derbyshire companies did rather well from the war. Over time, especially with the introduction of women workers into the factories, the labour problem was almost eradicated.

In Derby and Chesterfield, bureaus were opened to obtain skilled men for the munitions works. Only those skilled in certain trades were sought. In Derby during the first week, 1,000-1,200 men visited the bureau at the Town Hall, but only 509 were 'suitable'.

Threats of strike and general poor performances at work contributed to the shortages. Mr J.H. Thomas, MP for Derby, pointed out towards the end of March 1915 that victory was dependent on the workers in the factories, workshops and mines just as much as the efforts of the soldiers and sailors. The *Derbyshire Times* added that workers should realise that 'each blow struck in the workshop in this country is immediately echoed on the battlefields of France and Belgium. To a large extent the present war will be won in the factories of this country.'

Threats of strike continued, despite the Ministry of Munitions strenuous efforts to try and prevent industrial unrest. This resulted in much anger from soldiers fighting overseas.

'One of the Holy Boys' wrote to the *Derbyshire Times* in April 1915, expressing his anger towards those who threatened to hinder the war effort: 'When you read of men at home going on strike for a farthing an hour, or a shilling a week, more wages, when England wants to keep up her output of war material, it makes our blood boil. Every "Tommie" is disgusted with such men, who are doing so, for their action may prolong this war and cost old England many valuable lives …' He hoped strikers would be severely punished.

The Ministry of Munitions had a zero tolerance attitude towards strikes. It believed trade union rules regarding pay and conditions were only relevant to peace time and that in the wholly unprecedented circumstances of war the usual work conditions had to be altered if the men on the front line were to receive the weapons and tools they needed. The right to strike was still recognised, except in certain factories undertaking the most important war work, but workers were required to provide their employer and the Board of Trade with twenty-one days' notice so that negotiations could try to avert the strike or arrangements made to reduce the effect on government orders. During the course of the war, wages for munitions factory workers were increased to the point that they had more money than ever before. Complaints about pay and conditions continued nonetheless.

In addition to strikes and threats of strike, alcohol was seen to be a threat to output in Derbyshire's factories, with consumption having drastically increased in the early months of war. In his memoirs, Lloyd George described hearing accounts of workers being drunk and the effect on attendance and productivity: 'Drink is doing more damage in the War than all the German submarines put together', he said in a speech at Bangor in February 1915 and this is why the Ministry of Munitions sought to better control the availability of alcohol. Indeed, a proposal to bring breweries, their public houses and free houses under state control was considered by the government, but was felt to be too expensive.

Although there are few accounts of such behaviour in Derbyshire, alcohol was considered a menace that was hampering the war effort.

The King's decision in April 1915 to abstain from alcohol was quickly followed by Lord Kitchener, and Derbyshire's workers were urged to follow suit.

At the same time it was alleged there was a German plot, with spies working in the munitions factories, stirring trouble among the workers so that they went on strike. The truth of such claims is questionable but threats of strike had certainly been made, and along with stories of workers failing to perform due to drink, there were increased pressures on the working class to do what was expected of them.

T.W. Pratt, MP for Linlithgow, visited Locker's Wagon Works Co. Ltd in Whittington, the Sheepbridge Coal and Iron Co Ltd, and Markham's Works in Chesterfield on 23 September 1915 to encourage workers to 'strain every nerve' to meet the demands of the soldiers and sailors. During the visit to the Markham Works, Pratt said he wanted to thank the men on behalf of the Ministry of Munitions and to ask them to do everything humanly possible. It was not simply a war between the soldiers and sailors of the Allies and Germany, but also a war between the workshops of Germany and of Great Britain. In that war Britain was losing and the difficulties men were facing on the Western and Eastern Fronts were due to the shortage of the means of war. Delays and grievances among workers were lengthening the duration of the war, he added.

He continued: 'To you the call of your comrades comes today telling you not just now to think of your rights, but to fulfil your duties; not just now to quarrel about your interests, but to fulfil your responsibilities; not to calculate how much you can get but rather to determine how much you can give to bring them at the earliest day from their place of peril to re-establish liberties of Europe. ... We boast of our freedom; let every workman of Britain write it on the page of history that we are not only the best fighters on the field of battle, but the best workers on the industrial field as well.'

A similar plea was made by A.H. Marshall MP when he visited Derbyshire munitions factories in November 1915. He appealed for workers to do that 'little bit more' to hasten the end of war.

Although improvements in output were seen, throughout the war the need for even more shells continued. A Derby soldier of the Royal Field Artillery urged munitions workers to work even harder: 'All that we want those at home to do is trust us to do as Englishman have always done in battle and keep those munitions going.'

Munitions courts were held in larger towns where munitions were produced, with employers bringing action against their workers, and vice versa, when rules were breached. The first court sitting in Derby in September 1915 is a typical example of cases presented at such hearings.

One employee claimed a leaving certificate was unreasonably withheld by his employer, Rolls-Royce. His case was dismissed. Although workers were able to apply for a leaving certificate for permission to leave a firm's employment, in practice permission was not usually given because of the great demand for work.

Walter Burgess said he wanted to leave the Hallam Engineering Company in order to join another firm so that he could carry out work more directly relating to the war. His case was also dismissed.

Frederick Hodgkinson, aged fifteen, was fined 15s for being absent between 13 September and 21 September. During another week he had only worked ten and a half hours of an expected fifty-three. William Francis Radcliffe was also fined 7s 6d for being absent from work.

The Munitions of War (Amendment) Act of January 1916 sought to control wages and conditions of the workers. Although factory owners were educated about improving the conditions there was no requirement for them to do so. Often a broken basin and a jug of cold water were the only washing facilities provided. Overalls were not always provided. There were usually no dedicated places to eat, with staff eating their meals whilst stood at their machines.

The factories were noisy, often filled with smoke and noxious fumes, with large numbers of people working in poorly lit, filthy workshops for long hours with few breaks, usually standing up in tremendous heat.

Some provisions were made to improve conditions. In October 1915 a YMCA hut opened at the National Shell Factory in Derby, offering a canteen and rest hut for the workers at Darwin Terrace (an invitation to the opening forms part of the Derbyshire Record Office archive: reference D3772/T38/10/54). It was remarked in the *Derby Mercury* that good food and drink was available to help maintain efficiency. In 1918 a YWCA hut for women and girl workers was opened at the British Cellulose factory in Spondon. However, such facilities were rare.

Unpleasant conditions were detrimental to health but even greater dangers were faced by workers. With the increased strain on machinery and little opportunity for maintenance, with factories in operation day and night, almost every day of the year, and with a relatively less experienced workforce working under unprecedented pressures, accidents occurred all too frequently.

By 8 July 1915 there had been 'several fires' at Robinson and Sons surgical lint and cardboard box factory. The machinery had been in constant use since October 1914, as the company tried to fulfil government orders. However, at around 10pm that night a very serious fire engulfed the works when an object found its way into some machinery causing it to malfunction. A great deal of expensive machinery, used to treat cotton for medical dressings for wounded servicemen, was destroyed as the blaze quickly spread. The fire brigade were telephoned and the building evacuated, with several employees receiving burns as they fled. Thankfully, there were no serious injuries and no lives lost.

A fire at the Langwith munitions factory on 20 November 1917 was one of the many incidents that had a more tragic outcome. The location of the fire was referred to as a 'North Midlands munitions factory' at the time in order to prevent the Germans from gaining information about damage to Britain's war effort.

As the fire raged the manager believed no one was in the building, and this information was corroborated by another member of staff and so priority was given to extinguishing the flames, which it was believed were caused by machinery malfunctioning, and saving as much of the building and equipment as possible. However, once the flames had died down and it was safe to enter the building, the bodies of two men and a woman were found. Each had died of asphyxiation due to the smoke. The woman's body had been burnt so badly she could not be recognised.

At the inquest on 22 November the jury returned a verdict of accidental death and recommended masks be provided for those working in dangerous places. Whilst this may have helped prevent asphyxiation, it would not have prevented the fire from starting.

Any safety measures introduced following the November 1917 fire, evidently did not work because in March 1918 another fire occurred at the factory, killing three women workers.

Although outside Derbyshire, an explosion at the Chilwell munitions factory on 1 July 1918 some of Derbyshire men and women were among the 134 people killed and more than 250 who were left injured.

Other victims of fatal accidents included Walter Cooper, working at the Derby Coal and Iron Company's works, who was crushed between buffers when unloading a vehicle of pig iron, and Joaunes Emilius Carolus D'Hew, a Belgian refugee, who was killed when slag exploded at Derby Iron Works in November 1917.

It was an unfortunate inevitability, and a sad irony, that as more and more weapons of war were produced the means of making those weapons were causing damage, destruction, injury and death.

CHAPTER 5

Down the Pit

Another industry in the north of the county of vital importance in the war effort at home and overseas was coal mining. Coal was needed to power furnaces in the munitions factories, and indeed in every type of industry. It was also needed to produce electricity. It was needed for the trains, which were used increasingly to transport troops and equipment. It was needed to power the engines of naval ships and of course it was needed to keep fires burning in households across the home front.

When the war started many pits in Derbyshire began working 'short time'; a large amount of Derbyshire's coal had previously been exported, especially to Russia, and with the war preventing exports there was, for a time, less demand for coal and so fewer hours were worked. This had a tremendous effect on coal mining villages in the north of the county where due to fewer hours being worked there was less money earned. There was the real fear that whole communities, that had just weeks earlier enjoyed the sight of extravagance in the form of the royal visit, would be devastated. With such hardship, and with the promises of glory at war, miners left the pits for the army in droves and Derbyshire lost many of its most skilled miners.

When it was realised that the war was not going to be as short lived as many had hoped, and believed, by the end of 1914, and more demands were placed on coal to support industries and transportation, and when the numbers of workers down the pits continue to fall, there were increasing demands for miners to work longer hours in order to produce more coal.

The Coal Mines Regulation Act (more commonly known as the Eight Hours Act) of 1908 limited the number of hours a miner could work underground to eight hours per day. However, there were now calls to suspend the Act so that colliery owners could require their employees to work for much longer hours.

Provision was made within the Act to allow its suspension in the event of war or other circumstances where demand for coal exceeded supply. The Act

Ockbrook men working at Dale Abbey Colliery at around the time of the war. The photograph is undated but is believed to have been taken during the 1910s. *Courtesy of Derbyshire Libraries and www.picturethepast.org.uk*

was later, in 1917, amended to include all types of mines, not just coal mines.

In February 1915 the Derbyshire Miners' Association met to discuss the issue and passed a resolution 'strongly protesting' against attempts to suspend the Act. Asking miners to work more than eight hours a day was not justified, it was remarked, when there were collieries in some counties only operating part time.

In his maiden speech in the House of Commons on 28 June 1915, the MP for Chesterfield, Barnet Kenyon, a former miner himself, spoke of the importance of the Eight Hours Act. He showed the House his head and hands which bore the scars of years spent down the pit, where he had been knocked about in the darkness, working far in excess of eight hours per day. The strongest of men were broken up in the prime of their life, he said, as they contended with a 'good deal of danger and a vitiated atmosphere'. He hoped nobody would ask miners to work longer hours in such an atmosphere unless it was absolutely necessary. There were, he added, better alternatives that would allow more coal to be produced. Approximately one third of the collieries in Nottinghamshire did not work on Saturdays, he said, and the same was true of many of the collieries in Derbyshire. If they were to open on Saturdays, he argued, there would be men willing to work.

In addition to calls for increasing the hours worked by miners, there were demands that they should forego their usual extended Easter holidays. Prior to the outbreak of war the holidays had usually lasted almost a week. The War Office instructed collieries, however, that the Easter break for 1915 should be kept to an absolute minimum.

A conference was held in Derby on 22 March between representatives of the Nottinghamshire and Derby Coal Owners' Association and the Nottinghamshire and Derbyshire Miners' Association. It was agreed all pits in the two counties would close for Good Friday and Easter Saturday, and that work would resume on Easter Monday 'in order to support the country in the present crisis'.

The same request was made for the Whitsuntide holidays, which had previously allowed miners in Derbyshire to enjoy four of five days of rest. In May 1915, however, they were permitted, following a meeting of the Council of the Derbyshire Miners' Association, just two days of holiday due to the 'exceptional circumstances' with miners in some of the county's pits only being allowed a single day. The reduction in holiday proved particularly grievous in light of a pay rise being delayed. Early in May, the Prime Minister had agreed a rise in wages for coal miners due to the rise in the cost of living but the promised rise had yet to be implemented.

Requests for shorter holidays and longer hours remained a theme of the war and caused ongoing and increasing resentment and friction, with talk of strike action.

At a recruitment meeting in Tibshelf in March 1915 John Hancock, MP for Mid Derbyshire (who became MP for Belper upon the creation of that constituency in 1918), addressed miners saying that strikes were not justified and that soldiers needed to know the people back home were doing everything they could to support them. Although Easter was an important time for the religious, productivity was lower now, he argued, than prior to the war and this was largely due to industrial unrest and alcohol.

At the end of April 1915 a motion to start a national miners strike due to cost of coal was voted against, but threats of strike continued.

Despite the increasing pressures and the lack of the pay rise which left many miners feeling particularly hard done by, the majority of miners in Derbyshire were keen to perform their patriotic duty. To this end at a meeting of the Derbyshire Miners' Committee, it was decided in June 1915 to combine with miners in Nottinghamshire to fund the purchase, and maintenance costs, of a convoy of fifty ambulances, four touring cars and a repairing lorry costing £35,000, to be sent to France.

Some of Derbyshire's miners were less keen to support the convoy, believing its cost should be met by the union's funds, rather than by deductions from wages. Others did not believe they should contribute at all given that they were already doing too much.

The convoy was, however, funded and proved to be a valuable aid to the Red Cross on the war front. There was great interest in the convoy, with several thousand people having viewed part of it at Chesterfield Market Place in October 1915 prior to its departure for France, and in July 1917 a silver cup was presented to the Derbyshire Miners' Council to commemorate the convoy's work. When further funds were needed in August 1917 for the maintenance of the convoy there was general support.

An issue that affected the output of coal, and was in some way the result of perceived low wages and growing pressures, was that of absenteeism. In many instances there were significant absences. For example, twenty-one men from the Grassmoor Colliery Company were off for a combined total of 215 days during September 1915 alone. The company decided to prosecute the workers because previous efforts to make them realise their responsibility had failed. The company acknowledged there were great pressures on the men given that 493 of their colleagues had enlisted. Four of the men were found to have genuine reasons for their absence, due to medical problems, and a further defendant said he had a child who was seriously ill in hospital with fever. However, one man claimed he was unable to work because he could not get up early in the mornings. With the exception of those who were able to prove they had been ill, the men were fined.

The Grassmoor Colliery Company's prosecution of absentees was not an isolated incident; companies struggled with the problem throughout the mining communities and throughout the duration of the war.

As the war progressed, and conscription was introduced, despite the demands for coal miners were not automatically immune from being called up to the army. The Derbyshire Colliery Recruiting Court considered claims for exemption.

There were many instances where the authorities believed a miner should serve, particularly if the Court believed that he had only become a miner to avoid being called up. For example, on 4 January 1918 the Derbyshire Colliery Recruiting Court decided that two miners should join the army.

The first man had been a colliery worker since the age of twelve, employed at Blackwell and Tibshelf. However, in 1909 he became a professional player for Queens Park Rangers and later Nottingham Forest. In May 1915 he returned to mining and wanted exemption from the military because he was a miner. The second man had been a miner from 1903 to 1909 before embarking on a career in football, which had seen him play for Sheffield United. He too returned to the pit in 1915, working at Morton Colliery.

The claims of both men were refused, with it being pointed out they had only returned to mining because professional football had ceased to be played. It was argued they had only become miners to avoid joining the army. They were not committed to mining because their careers of choice had been football, it was remarked.

By the beginning of February 1918 18,000 men had gone into the Army from Derbyshire mines since war broke out, which had serious implications on the output of coal, but still more men were taken.

A year earlier, on 22 February 1917, a Controller of Coal was appointed to better control the workings of the pits to increase coal output and to better control its distribution but with ever decreasing numbers of miners it was never able to get sufficient grip on the problem, and so once again the debate regarding working hours began to rage.

In response to a letter by a Mr C.F. White in the *Derbyshire Times* arguing for longer hours for miners, a correspondent using the nom-de-plume 'Lux Veritas' wrote in March 1917: 'Mr White admits he knows nothing of mining conditions, but I venture to state he probably knows as much as some of our so-called leaders. Is he aware that under present conditions eight hours men are absent from home sometimes over 12 hours?' He pointed out that in one colliery in North East Derbyshire men were down the mines for ten hours at a time. 'How, in the face of those cases, are you going to get men to work longer hours unless you rob them of sleep altogether', he asked.

Long working hours, and also the introduction of the Daylight Saving Act in May 1917 which saw for the first time clocks changing an hour in the spring, caused difficulties to those approximately one thousand miners employed at the Shirebrook, Creswell, Langwith, Warsop Main and Pleasley Collieries, who all required the train to get to work. Due to the clocks changing the men had to get up at what was described as an 'unearthly hour' because there were no trains that tied in with their work shifts. Men from Kirkby and Sutton had to get up at 3am in order to get to work for 6am. Presumably the mines were working to the revised times whereas the trains were not.

At a meeting of the Derbyshire Miners' Council on 19 July 1917 it was decided to recommend the 30,000 members take only one day of holiday in August instead of the usual three or four, due to what was believed to be a serious shortage of coal. Whilst the Council was willing to cooperate with the government regarding extra work to meet the coal needs of the nation, there was growing anger at what were believed to be inadequate wages. Mass meetings were held to protest against the high cost of living, especially the 'scandalously high prices' of food.

Industrial unrest quickly developed and lead miners at the Mill Close mine in Darley Dale went on strike, although the strike ended in August 1917 pending a settlement by arbitration or mutual agreement. In January 1918 they went on a brief strike following the laying off of seven men.

Unrest continued for the remainder of the war, despite a pay rise being granted to miners during the summer of 1918. At Creswell Colliery arguments about the pay rise promised a year earlier for surfacemen led to 1,500 men and boys going on strike. It was, however, short lived, commencing on Wednesday 14 August and a settlement was reached the following day following a conference with the Coal Controller in London. Work was resumed on Friday morning.

Similarly disputes at the collieries in Markham and Morton at this time were settled and work recommenced.

Back at the Mill Close mine, after a period of peaceful work, the situation was more serious. It had been decided, following arbitration, to grant the 180 miners a pay award. However, the trustees of the mine refused to implement the award, resulting in the men going on strike during the summer of 1918. By 14 September the men had been on strike for seven weeks and it was considered, by the Derbyshire Miners' Council, that a settlement was unlikely because the trustees had threatened to close down the mine altogether, by lifting the pumps so that the mine filled with water. It was, the trustees had argued, uneconomical to run the mine if the workers were better paid. The Derbyshire Miners' Council concluded that 'determined action' was needed to address the situation and passed a resolution stating that it was the council's duty to protect the men from victimisation. The General Secretary, Frank Hall, wrote to the Coal Controller informing him that unless a settlement was made at an early date, the miners in Derbyshire would take a ballot with a view to enforcing a settlement by stopping all the coal mines in the county. The resolution ended with the words, 'Desperate and extreme as this policy may appear at this critical time, we believe it is preferable to the slow and agonising process by drowning the mine out and in starving the men, women and children.' A settlement was reached during the autumn.

In Bakewell, twenty-eight men at the Holme Bank Chert Mine went on strike in August 1918 over pay. The owners refused to increase their pay because the price of chert, which was commonly used to grind flint, had not increased and therefore there was no extra money to pay additional wages. Rather than increase wages their preferred course of action was to shut down the mine for the duration of the war.

The disputes over pay, particularly by coal miners, came at a particularly difficult time because, as the Coal Controller described it, coal was the key to winning the war. Speaking at a meeting in Southport, which was reported on in the *Derbyshire Times*, he told the Miners' Federation on 20 August 1918 that the coal situation was desperate and precarious. There was, he announced, a shortage of 36,000,000 tons. Although coal rationing would save between eight and nine million tons, this still left a deficit of 27,000,000 tons. Further rationing of coal for industries which were not directly producing the weapons and tools of war had to be considered. Alternatively or additionally the coal output would have to be increased, he said. The country had not met its obligations to the Army and navy during July. Indeed the output of coal in July 1918 was the worst since the war started. The Coal Controller acknowledged a key problem was that many experienced miners had left the pits to join the army and that although some men were being brought back from the forces to work in the mines, these less experienced men obtained no more than three-fifths of the amount of a 'first class coal getter' who produced on average 300 tons of coal per year.

Industrial disputes were, during war, generally of a small nature with strikes being limited and usually quickly resolved, in part because colliery owners were keen to ensure their profits did not suffer and because there was a feeling of patriotic duty amongst the miners. However, following the cessation of hostilities when thousands of miners returned from war intending to return to their old jobs, with the resulting pressure on the labour market, and the cost of living continued to rise, industrial disputes became more frequent and this particularly angered people with loved ones who had still not been demobbed. Indeed as Derbyshire celebrated peace in July 1919, 20,000 miners were on strike in Derbyshire and pumps were removed to flood the mines, which also filled with foul gases. This resulted in a shortage of coal requiring economy in the home, curtailed tram services, reduced train services and reduced gas and electricity supplies. It was, as the *Derby Mercury* reported, 'a sad ending to a week which began with joy days of peace to end in tragic times of industrial war'.

CHAPTER 6

War Hospitals

Within weeks of the commencement of war, wounded soldiers (British and Belgian) were shipped back to Britain and from the southern ports were transported by train across the country; and a steady flow of wounded servicemen continued throughout the war. Derbyshire took on the role of treating some of these men and aiding their recuperation.

The established hospitals, such as Derby Royal Infirmary and the Chesterfield and North Derbyshire Hospital accommodated the most seriously wounded, treating them alongside civilian patients. The No. 4 Military Hospital at Derby Barracks was a key institution for this purpose. However, it was quickly determined that the number of men in need of care far exceeded that available in pre-existing hospitals and so additional make shift hospitals were established, with large houses, public buildings and schools taking on this new function.

The Red Cross and St John's Ambulance created Voluntary Aid Detachment (VAD) hospitals across the county in order to try and cope with the demand. They were largely staffed by nurses who had no previous medical knowledge, having quickly been trained following the outbreak of war, and were generally used for the treatment and recuperation of those who had suffered injuries which were not life threatening.

There were VAD hospitals in Derbyshire prior to war at Belper, Derby, Long Eaton, Ockbrook and Spondon, but more were needed.

In total there were forty-one detachment hospitals in Derbyshire during the war, including those at Alfreton (the Blackwell Auxiliary Hospital), Ashbourne, Bakewell, Belper (located in Green Hall), Buxton (the Devonshire Hospital), Chesterfield, Derby, Aston Hall (just outside Derby), Darley Dale (the Whitworth Institute), Matlock (the Matlock Auxiliary Hospital), Cromford, South Wingfield (situated in Mill House), Long Eaton, Smalley, Chapel-en-le-Frith, Elmton, Aston-on-Trent, Hathersage, New Mills, Duffield, Creswell, Ilkeston and Dore (Dore being a part of Derbyshire at this time).

Wounded soldiers and nurses at the Derby Infirmary during the First World War.
Courtesy of Derbyshire Record Office - Archives and www.picturethepast.org.uk

The Willersley Red Cross Hospital in Cromford was located at Willersley Castle, which was offered to the Red Cross for the duration of the war. Its owner, Mr F.C. Arkwright and his family lived in just two rooms, with the remainder being freely available for war work.

This building was used as a Voluntary Aid Detachment Hospital in Dore -
formerly part of Derbyshire. *The Author*
(Inset) A mural on the former Dore VAD hospital. *The Author*

Wounded soldiers at Ilkeston War hospital. *Courtesy of Derbyshire Libraries and
www.picturethepast.org.uk*

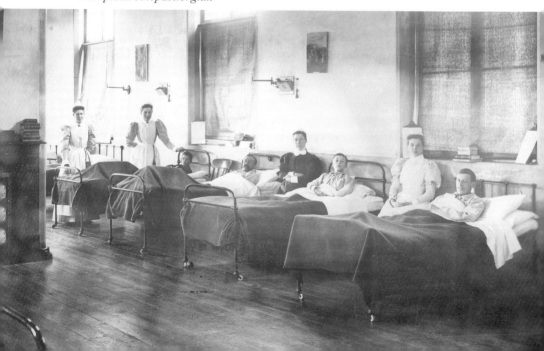

The church hall in Duffield, used as a hospital. *Courtesy of Bromby Collection and www.picturethepast.org.uk*

In March 1915 the County Council, despite opposition, decided to close its asylum in Belper to make room for more wounded soldiers.

Additionally, there were special hospitals for Canadian servicemen at the Peak Hydro in Buxton and at the Royal Hotel in Matlock Bath.

The Chatsworth Royal Naval Convalescent Hospital was established in Edensor and opened in September 1915. Among its facilities were a room for massage and 'electrical treatment'. Four revolving shelters were provided for patients requiring open air treatment. Originally accommodating thirty wounded sailors, extensions provided a further fifty beds.

Still more hospitals were needed and towards the end of hostilities, in August 1918, the Rockside Hydro in Matlock was commandeered by the recently formed Royal Air Force for use as a convalescent hospital, displacing some residents who had made it their home for twenty years.

The existing hospitals had additional pavilions and 'open air shelters' constructed to provide extra beds for wounded soldiers and sailors. Furthermore, where buildings were unavailable huts were constructed on vacant land such as at Netley where two huts provided forty beds. The Derby Royal Infirmary had temporary huts and in April 1917 extensions allowed it to accommodate up to 170 servicemen.

The above mention of 'open air' treatment relates largely to those who had infectious diseases. In the early part of 1915, infectious diseases among

British soldiers became a serious problem and one that the Home Front in Derbyshire was expected to assist with. The War Office requested the erection of huts on all available land at civilian hospitals. It was agreed that land would be available at hospitals including Morton, Langwith, Dronfield and Mastin Moor. Penmore Isolation hospital was also extended, and the newly-built sanatorium in Chesterfield was taken over by the military, providing 300 beds, with civilian sufferers of tuberculosis required to remain at home.

Whilst in hospital, military patients wore 'hospital blues'; a uniform consisting of a blue top and blue trousers, as opposed to their usual khaki uniforms, so that they could still be easily identified as members of the military but that it was instantly known they were convalescing if they were out in public.

Wounded patients had reasonably free movements. Health permitting, they were able to go on trips to entertainment venues, or YMCA rooms for reading, games or other recreation, if such venues were in close proximity. Often members of the local community invited them to their homes for tea. They also spent much of their time exploring the Derbyshire countryside and fraternising with locals, sometimes forming relationships with some of the county's women.

Schoolchildren occasionally visited some of the hospitals to provide entertainment and, from time to time, the servicemen visited the schools for an afternoon of entertainment and tea.

Concerts were performed, especially at Christmas, and for those on the road to recovery they were able to engage in sports such as football, cricket and bowls.

The local communities also provided comforts in the form of clothes, magazines, newspapers, books, games, musical instruments, gramophones, cigarettes, tobacco and some food. Although the hospitals received government grants they only covered some of the costs of running the hospitals and so the public's help was greatly needed.

There were restrictions on the patients, however, which was one reason why they were required to wear 'hospital blues'. They were not allowed to drink alcohol, and it was an offence to sell alcohol to a military patient or to anyone buying alcohol on behalf of patients. It was equally an offence to buy alcohol on behalf of a military patient.

Despite frequent and successful fund-raising events the treatment of wounded and infected soldiers placed huge financial pressure on the county's hospitals. The Chesterfield and North Derbyshire Hospital was plunged further into debt and plans to extend some of the county's hospitals to meet the War Office's needs generated tremendous controversy when discussed in May 1915. A scheme of extensions, and an open-air hospital station at Morton, costing £16,750 to provide an extra fifty-six beds for the county, was criticised by the Chesterfield Rural District Council, with a request to defer the work until after the war. It was remarked that hospitals had been overcrowded for considerable time but the cost was prohibitively high. Instead, it was agreed the government should erect temporary cabins on hospital grounds at its own cost. The County Council had by this time placed a ban on funding hospital extensions. J.W. Turner argued there was little point in having hospitals for the treatment of infectious diseases because despite their establishment and their high cost, fever rates were still high. C.W. Kendall also believed hospitals were not working, with beds taken up by children who could be treated just as well at home.

By November 1918, there were twenty-four VAD hospitals in Derbyshire for the war wounded, with the remainder having been closed because the War Office had ordered the closure of those providing ten or fewer beds. Although accurate figures for the number of treated in Derbyshire for the full duration of the war could not be found, figures show that 36,601 servicemen received treatment in the county during a twelve-month period towards the end of the war.

By the end of war in June 1919, most of the war hospitals had all ceased their work and those patients with long-term health problems and disabilities became the responsibility of charities set up specifically to provide welfare, treatment and, where possible, job opportunities, such as the Royal British Legion and the National Federation of Demobilised and Discharged Soldiers.

CHAPTER 7

German 'Aliens' and Anti-German Feeling

At the outbreak of war, there was a small population of Germans in the county, mainly in the larger towns such as Derby where, according to the 1911 census, there were thirty-three German residents.

On the eve of war being declared, a German waiter was thrown over a wall in Buxton and hostility against Germans across the county began.

Under the Aliens Restriction Act of 5 August 1914, it was a requirement that people of German or Austrian birth should present themselves to the Registration Officer, who recorded them as 'enemy aliens' and assessed their risk. Those considered to pose a risk to security were detained, but in most cases where there was no evidence of any national security risk they were released although restrictions were imposed on their movements and activities. They were required to present themselves to the authorities each day and had telephones removed from their homes so that they could not communicate overseas.

A man of German birth, who had lived in Matlock for twenty years, failed to register. There was no evidence that William Stewe's failure to register was due to any criminal or war-related intent and so he was given some leniency, with a prison sentence of three months with hard labour (rather than the maximum sentence of a year's imprisonment).

Men of German or Austrian birth in the county, who were of military age, were requested to report to the local police station in October 1914 where they were arrested and held in custody. Most surrendered themselves but those who did not found themselves being hunted by the police. They were then taken by train to York where they were kept in the city's Exhibition buildings before being transported to other internment camps across the country where they remained until 1919 when they were repatriated. The Isle of Man was the largest of these camps, with 25,000 German and Austrian detainees.

GERMAN 'ALIENS' AND ANTI-GERMAN FEELING

The detention of men of military age appeased most concerns that the presence of Germans within Britain was a threat. By early May 1915, there were 19,000 enemy aliens interned in Britain but there were 40,000 who remained free within society.

However, this sizeable number of Germans was considered to be a threat as German attacks on British civilians began, firstly with the East coast attacks of December 1914, then with later Zeppelin raids and, more so, when a German U-boat torpedoed the *Lusitania* on 7 May 1915, killing 1,198 of the 1,959 people on board in an act that was described by the *Derbyshire Times* as 'murder most foul'. The sinking of the ship was quickly followed by a German air raid of the Essex coast and came at a time of well-told stories of wounded British soldiers being deliberately shot and burned to death by Germans.

'The first and foremost consideration of every one of us, men and women alike, must be "what can I do to avenge the innocent and punish the greatest criminals the world has ever seen?", *The Derbyshire Times* asked.

News of the huge loss of civilian life just miles off the Irish coast led to 'considerable disturbances', with German civilians in British towns and cities being targeted by an angry British public who decided that they would avenge the innocent at home whilst the army was avenging them abroad. Major riots in Liverpool, which was the intended destination of the *Lusitania*, were followed by attacks on the property of Germans, across the country. A native of Derbyshire was arrested in connection with a shooting in Goldthorpe, between Barnsley and Doncaster.

In Derbyshire there were attacks on the shops and other businesses owned by Germans.

On 15 May 1915, German-born Frederick Stunder's pork butcher's shop on Whittington Moor was targeted by a large mob. Indeed, at a hearing at the Chesterfield County Police Court on 22 May it was claimed that a 'very ugly crowd' of up to 2,000 people had been present between 9pm on the Saturday night, until 1am the following day when they were finally dispersed by the police. John Lee urged the crowd to join him in smashing the shop and dragging Stunder out into the street. The shop window was smashed and stones, bottles and other missiles were thrown. When challenged by the police for throwing missiles, Sarah Chappell accused the police of being worse than the Germans for 'sticking up' for Stunder. 'What pity would the Germans have for the likes of us women and children?', she asked. Fining Lee and Chappell, C.P. Markham remarked, 'Talk about the Germans behaving badly – Whittington people can also behave badly, apparently. You had no business to break this man's window although he was an alien.'

As a result of the huge hostility that Germans civilians now faced in Britain, it was announced by the Prime Minister on 13 May 1915 that further arrests of adult 'enemy alien males', would be made and that, 'for their own safety and safety of this country', they were segregated and interned. All of those who were older than military age were repatriated. Women and children were also repatriated, although some remained in the country. An advisory body was established to consider any applications for exemption from internment, although all men of military age were interned. The Advisory Committee also had power to intern aliens who had gained British citizenship if they were considered to pose a risk to national security.

In the aftermath of the *Lusitania* sinking Germans living in Derbyshire tried to show their loyalty. A. Behren, who had lived in England for twenty-five years and was a British citizen, wrote to the *Derby Mercury*, saying, 'I have viewed with abhorrence and detestation the cruel and inhuman acts committed by the order of the German authorities and my sincere wish is that British arms may prove successful.'

W.R. Brass, who had lived in England for nearly thirty years and had also become a citizen, wrote in the same paper of his 'Indignation and horror of the barbarous procedures of the Germans in this terrible war.'

The internment of men of military age whose only crime was to be born in a country with which Britain was at war, yet who had lived peacefully in their new country, irrespective of their circumstances, had implications for their families.

Although dependants of those Germans who were interned were given some financial support, this was often much less than what the families might otherwise have received, and this support, little as it was, was means tested.

In August 1917, the English wife of a German who had been interned appealed to the Chesterfield Board of Guardians with regards to financial assistance, claiming that she was suffering as a result of her husband, who was described as a pork butcher of Whittington Moor, being interned on the Isle of Man. Although not named, the German concerned must have been Frederick Stunder, whose shop had been targeted two years earlier.

It transpired that the woman had been receiving relief money in her husband's absence, but the payments had been discontinued because her husband had a savings account containing between £500 and £600 and it was decided she should use his savings to keep herself and their three children rather than be kept by the ratepayers. A lengthy debate followed during which the woman argued that the savings, of which she had not previously been aware, should not prevent her from receiving the weekly payment from the

Board of Guardians. 'I don't think it is fair to spend his money while he is away. What is he going to do when he comes back and how shall we live then?', she asked. Upon being told by the chairman that her husband should keep her, she remarked, 'They should have let him stay here then to keep me, and not interned him as they have done.' Upon being told that she should write to her husband to authorise the bank to give her access to his money she added, 'I would rather starve first. He has worked hard to save this money, and it isn't right that I should spend it. I'll starve first.'

The air raid in Derbyshire on the night of 31 January and early hours of 1 February 1916, which led to seven deaths in the county, as well as causing damage and fear, fuelled tremendous anger towards the German race and determination to crush the enemy. The editor of the *Derbyshire Times* summed up the feelings of Derbyshire folk when he wrote, 'Every fresh example of German frightfulness, every innocent life sacrificed to the bloodthirsty lust of the Hun for slaughter when he can effect it without risk to his own skin, shall be paid for a thousandfold. The day of reckoning is not yet, but it is drawing near.'

Reverend J. Ducker, vicar of Christ Church, Chesterfield, evoked his feelings much more strongly. The Kaiser was one of the Devil's satellites, he said, and the only language he could understand was force. For every murderous visit by the enemy it was our duty to reply with force. Blockades to starve the Germans were cruel because they would lead to children having a long and suffering death with an increased chance of disease, he believed. It was, he felt, much more humane to bomb them.

Some of the Germans who were captured on the Western Front and on the seas were held as prisoners of war in camps within Derbyshire, which included those at Ambergate, Ashbourne, Duffield, Ilkeston, Sudbury, Shardlow, Bretby Hall Stables, Burbage, Buxton, Chapel-en-le-Frith, Denby, Etwell, Crich, Normanton, Bolsover Castle Stables, Hasland Hall and Willington. Some records state there was a prisoner of war camp in Castle Donington in Derbyshire. However, the camp was based at Donington Hall, just inside Leicestershire.

Other German prisoners made brief visits to the county, in the form of escapees, and all but one of the men were recaptured in Chesterfield.

There was 'great excitement' in the village of Brimington in Chesterfield on 30 September 1917 when four German officers were captured, having escaped from Sutton Bonington camp, Nottinghamshire, on the previous Monday.

On that Sunday afternoon, William Darkin and George Fretwell were walking in Blue Bank Woods when they saw a group of men carrying lots of luggage, who appeared to be trying to conceal themselves. Darkin's suspicions were confirmed when he greeted the men and they responded with foreign accents.

Darkin headed towards the village, unsuccessfully trying to find a policeman. Instead he came across Albine Stott, who held the shooting rights for the Blue Bank Woods. Darkin tried to persuade Stott that there were four Germans in the woods but Stott was sceptical. It took half an hour, and all of Darkin's power of persuasion for Stott to return with him to the woods, and even at that time Stott was sceptical.

However, Stott's attitude changed upon catching sight of the four men and he later claimed he immediately knew they were escaped prisoners of war and this was confirmed when he too bade them a 'good morning', and received responses in a foreign accent. At this point he asked Darkin to go and find Police Sergeant Parnham whilst he kept them under observation and briefly conversed with them. One of the Germans, later identified as Lieutenant Karl Koch, said they were doing no harm. He claimed one of the men was 'a little Frenchman we picked up last night called Jackie', but he could not fool Stott. The same German was very interested in the railway and the works that he could see in the distance. The Germans then continued walking and Stott watched them as they walked along the canal.

Darkin subsequently returned with PC Outram and Mr H. Levers of the Red Lion. When Parnham arrived the Germans had not been seen for ten minutes but it was known they must be hiding nearby. Their luggage was quickly located, covered with bracken and undergrowth showing they had left it in order to make good their escape, intending to return later to collect it. Stott was able to inform the policemen in which direction they had travelled.

The men were found near Dixon's Wharf in Brimington and surrendered when the Sergeant arrived. 'The game is up' said Koch who quickly admitted they were escaped German prisoners. The men were searched and found to be unarmed. They offered no resistance, largely due to exhaustion, and it was not felt necessary to handcuff them. They were led to Brimington village and from there taken by car to Chesterfield police station. News of the capture had spread like 'wildfire' and there was a large crowd to see the vehicle leave Brimington. A group of women and girls threw missiles at the prisoners but no one was hurt.

The men, Lieutenant Karl Koch, Lieutenant Frederic Sieberger, Lieutenant Joseph Wailmann and Dr Hans Rautenburg were among twenty-two Germans who had taken part in a well-planned escape, with a tunnel excavated over a course of three months. The tunnel led from the hut holding the lower ranking prisoners, under a private road, coming out in a turnip field. All the escapees were captured within a week, the four men in Brimington being the last to be caught.

The four men had spent Saturday in Ashover and came to Chesterfield in the dark in order to catch a train, but they missed it by three minutes. It was later established they had enough food to last a fortnight.

On Monday morning, a military escort arrived and the prisoners were marched to the Midland Station. A large crowd, mainly of women, gave the men what was described politely as a 'loud' send off. They were conveyed by train back to Nottinghamshire.

A few weeks later, the men were court-martialled and sentenced to short terms of imprisonment in prisons, along with criminals. Once their sentences were served they were returned to prisoner of war camps.

Three weeks after the 'excitement' in Brimington, on 20 October, two more German prisoners of war, who this time had escaped from the camp at Burbage near Buxton, were captured in Chesterfield. The men, Karl Hauffler and Otto Bernhadt, were seen in Beeley walking in the direction of Chesterfield and the Chesterfield Borough Police were alerted.

As with the Brimington capture, it was the suspicions and vigilance of civilians which led to the men being caught. As the two Germans walked through Brampton, walking apart from one another to prevent suspicion, a Mr Lowe, who was walking with his wife, caught sight of the first man and became curious. Although he had no knowledge that there were escaped prisoners on the run, he found the man's behaviour unusual and the fact he was carrying a large bag added to his suspicions. Lowe greeted the man with a 'good night.' The man responded with a 'distinct Teuton accent' and immediately Lowe knew the man was a foreigner, but let him carry on walking towards the town centre. Lowe soon saw the second man approaching and, as he drew close, asked him for a match. The second man's accent was also distinctly foreign and Lowe became convinced both men were Germans. He went immediately to the home of Mr C. J. Howann, a Justice of the Peace and from there a telephone call was made to the police.

The police had already left the station, and had decided to wait at the tramway terminus on Chatsworth Road. In order to confirm their German nationality, as the first man approached Sergeant Hogg challenged him, speaking in German. Off his guard, he replied in German. As the second man approached he too was challenged and apprehended. Immediately both men admitted their identities and offered no resistance. They were held in the cells of Chesterfield police station for the remainder of the weekend before being taken by military escort back to Burbage. Following their arrest it transpired they were heading to Chesterfield in order to obtain food so that they had enough supplies to reach the coast, where they hoped to return to Germany. Although they had food in their baggage much of it had been spoilt by heavy rain.

It was not the last time that escaped Germans were captured in the town of the Crooked Spire, and once again it was a civilian who was instrumental in the capture of two Germans, on 21 January 1918.

A Brampton butcher named Mr H. Lenthall was driving his milk float when he was stopped by two 'thick-set men'. One of the men asked him, 'Can you tell us the road to Brimington?' His foreign accent raised suspicions. Lenthall duly obliged but then drove as quickly as he could to the home of Detective Inspector Parkin on Old Road, Brampton. The detective was at home and immediately the two men went in pursuit of the Germans.

The fugitives were observed walking on opposite sides of Goldwell Hill. Getting the two men together, Parkin questioned them. The men at first claimed to be Swedish but could not present their alien registration papers. They were arrested and taken to the police station. During the journey they tried to persuade Parkin that they were in fact sailors who had come from New York six weeks earlier, and they had been staying in Newcastle. However, when they arrived at the police station one of them announced, 'It is no use telling you lies. We are Germans' and gave their names as Hans Boettcher and Wilheim Kierry. However, the men were not prisoners of war, but civilians who had been interned due to their German nationality. They had escaped from a civilian internment camp at Sealand, Flintshire, on 10 January and were heading for Grimsby from which they hoped to travel to Germany. Both men had a large quantity of food, money and cigarettes. They spent the night in Chesterfield police station and were later escorted back to Sealand camp.

The reason why Brimington was sought by escaped Germans was that until 1956 there was a railway station located close to he village. It was probably safer to travel from that particular station than the Midland Station in the town where there was a greater chance of being identified as being German.

One German prisoner of war succeeded in returning to Germany, having briefly been present in Derbyshire. Gunter Pluschow was one of two men who escaped from the Castle Donington camp. He cycled to Derby where he caught a train to London and from there travelled to the coast where he sailed to the continent. His fellow escapee was quickly recaptured. In his book, *My Escape from Donington Hall,* Pluschow described very comfortable conditions and claimed prisoners were able to enjoy sports including polo. He later revealed the claims were untrue.

Whilst a small number of Germans caused difficulties for the authorities by attempting to regain their liberty, large numbers of the detainees performed useful duties to Derbyshire's home front, largely in agriculture.

There were naturally great concerns and anger from farmers at the prospect of enemies working in Derbyshire, working alongside civilians and in and around their homes, their wives and their children. These men had been involved in battles where British soldiers had been killed and were the same enemy that had dropped bombs on Derbyshire and were causing hardship by perpetuating the war. It came as no surprise, therefore, when at a meeting of the Chesterfield War Agricultural Committee in September 1917, on it being announced that German prisoners of war would be able to assist in corn threshing and other work that farmers desperately needed help with, there were loud cries of 'We don't want them.'

Nonetheless, German prisoners of war were compelled to work on some farms in the county and were found to be good workers, with some farmers preferring them to women. Farmers were encouraged to view the matter from a business point a view; they needed help and Germans were available. Furthermore, it was argued that Germans ought to work for their keep in the same way as British prisoners of war in Germany had to. By March 1918, there were thirty-five German prisoners in Ashbourne where it was said they had done 'satisfactory work' in hedging and ditching. More German prisoners followed and during the summer of 1918, fifty prisoners assisted in the nurseries in Darley Dale, saving young trees.

German prisoners in Derbyshire also worked in quarries, such as those in Crich.

Prisoners were supervised and were said, by Captain Boyd of the Board of Agriculture, to be 'most amenable to discipline' and a useful source of labour.

However, at a time when there was insufficient food to feed British civilians there was resentment that foreign enemies were being fed and accommodated in what were thought to be all too comfortable conditions. Stories of 'kid-gloved treatment' only served to increase such feelings, especially when accounts of brutality suffered by British prisoners of war in Germany were so frequently revealed in the press.

For example, one British soldier, released in July 1915 as part of a prisoner exchange, recounted how he was often spat at, and forced to sleep outdoors in torrential rain, before eventually being given a tent which was shared by large numbers of men who became filthy and verminous. Food was often described as being almost inedible and in very short supply.

Whilst most people did not want the Germans to be treated in such a manner, it was argued by the *Derbyshire Times*, during July 1918, that the Germans should at least suffer the same hardship that British civilians were experiencing.

CHAPTER 8

Belgian Refugees

At the start of the war, and to a lesser degree in the following years, Derbyshire became home to some of the 250,000 Belgians who were forced to flee their country when the Germans invaded.

On 24 September, Derbyshire's first Belgian refugees arrived at Chatsworth, with fourteen arriving in Chesterfield six days later, residing at The Terrace, Saltergate. Thirteen more Belgians, some of them wounded soldiers, arrived in Chesterfield in October and stayed at Fairfield Road.

In early October, a committee was formed by Derbyshire County Council for Belgian refugees after it was announced the county might be required to accommodate 1,000 refugees. Appeals were made for anyone willing to help house the Belgians.

On 10 October, twenty-four Belgians arrived at Long Eaton, carrying small bundles containing all their worldly goods. Their appearance touched the hearts of Ilkeston folk as they got off trains, with kisses and money being given to the children. One woman who was carrying a seven-and-a-half-month-old baby had rushed out of her house when she heard shells exploding nearby. She had not seen her husband since.

A newspaper, titled *Le Courrier Belge*, was printed in Derby for the benefit of Belgian refugees and intended to help unite families who had been separated. It was distributed across the country.

In October 1914 the Derby Borough Refugees' Committee was formed and was asked to arrange accommodation for twelve Belgians. Premises were found at Wilson Street and at Hargrave House on Burton Road, with the first contingent of eleven arriving on 13 October. They were temporarily housed whilst arrangements for Hargrave House were completed. As more Belgians arrived approximately eighty or ninety Belgians were accommodated for several weeks in the spare rooms of willing volunteers who no doubt were fascinated by the different culture, with few if any likely to have visited Belgium, and to hear stories of invasion, until more suitable accommodation could be obtained, such as the Isolation Block of the Mental Hospital,

A group of Belgian refugees in Ripley. *Courtesy of Wood Collection and www.picturethepast.org.uk*

Brunswick House at 253 Normanton Road, a house at Old Normanton, four houses in Hartington Street, White Cottage in Alvaston, a house in Clover Street and a house in Vernon Street.

On 1 November 1914, twelve Belgians arrived in Derby and were taken to Ashbourne, where they found a new home on Wirksworth Road. They included a wounded soldier and an 84-year-old man.

Belgians continued to arrive in Derbyshire in all towns, and some villages. By 13 January 1915 there were 750 refugees housed in sixty-one parishes who were given assistance under the Derbyshire County Council's Belgian Refugees Relief Scheme. The actual number of refugees in the county was not known because there were others supported by private individuals and other organisations. In Derby alone there were approximately 400 by the end of the first year of war.

Although generous property owners leased their houses at greatly reduced prices, and some allowed their property to be used free of charge, accommodating the refugees and providing food, clothing, fuel, entertainment and other costs were large and so there were frequent appeals for money and comforts.

Comforts were sought because often the refugees had few or no possessions when they arrived in England, having quickly fled their homes.

Shilling funds were opened, whereby people subscribed a shilling a week towards refugee funds.

In Matlock the Catholic priest, Father Le Roy, was instrumental in raising much needed money for the refugees in that town. He visited many a home to appeal to householders. By December 1914 there were twenty-four Belgian refugee families in the Matlock district with more arriving early in 1915.

Tramcar collection boxes in Derby were 'a lamentable failure', with little more than £20 raised over the course of four Saturdays on all routes. In Derby the finances of the refugees committee were so poor that help had to be provided from the London General Committee who paid half its costs, which were on average £30 per week.

By the autumn of 1915 most Belgians in Derbyshire were working and so were able to support themselves and their family. They were also able to contribute towards the Belgian refugee fund in Derbyshire as well as contribute towards the relief of Belgians back in their own country, although in Derby there was disappointment that the men did not contribute their fair share towards the costs of their accommodation.

There were also efforts to enlist the Belgians of military age into the Belgian army and so there was scarcely a young man left who was in good physical health and those who were, often worked in heavy industry contributing to Britain's war effort.

When the Belgians left Derbyshire, to work elsewhere in the country or to join the armed forces, they often wrote to the committees that had helped them whilst in Derbyshire. The Vergauwen family lived, for almost a year, in Belper. Upon leaving for London, where the head of the family began training to work in the munitions factory, a letter (Derbyshire Record Office reference D3772/T38/10/65) was sent to the Belper committee expressing the family's thanks. Part of the letter read, 'We may say that it is due to the kind attentions you have always had for us, that we have been able to forget the past, and to look with a brighter view into the future.'

Entertainment was provided for the Belgians to make them feel more at home. On St Nicholas Day (a public holiday in Belgium) 1914, approximately 100 wounded refugees and Belgian soldiers were treated to a 'sumptuous tea' at Chesterfield hospital. They were welcomed to the town by the Mayor and gifts were given to each of them before music, singing, dancing and games were enjoyed. Entertainments were held in every town where refugees were homed and people were encouraged to show hospitality by inviting them to their own homes.

The Belgians were a source of intrigue on account of their differing culture and their experiences. Those being treated at Derby Royal Infirmary aroused considerable interest, so much so that the hospital board limited the number of visitors because patients' recovery was being affected.

There was also great interest when Jane Heps and Gerard Browers, both of Antwerp, got married at the Annunciation Church in Chesterfield in November 1914.

There was great sympathy towards the Belgians for the suffering they had experienced due to the German invasion which had forced them to flee their homes and their country. People listened to their stories and used their experiences to encourage men to join the British forces so that Britain would not suffer a similar fate. A story of Belgians in Matlock was used as an example of the fear they possessed. Whilst eating breakfast one morning a blast was heard from a nearby quarry and the Belgians quickly hid under the table, just as they had become accustomed to doing so in their homeland.

Not everyone was so welcoming or sympathetic. In Derby, particularly in the poorer areas, there was disquiet that Belgian refugees had free tram passes when some of the refugees worked and were in a better position financially than many of the locals. There was a debate about the issue in January 1915 with some councillors arguing for the passes to be withdrawn. Mr Dean successfully argued the system should not be interfered with because the Belgians had suffered greatly and that a 'few coppers' given by way of concession was not a great cost to the town. However, the passes were withdrawn later in the year.

There was also some disquiet about Belgians taking jobs. One unnamed Belgian was the subject of an attack by 'British Bulldog' in a letter to the *Derbyshire Times* in June 1917. The Belgian, a manager at a 'product plant' was allegedly terrible to work for, leading the correspondent to write, 'Personally, I contend that all such men should be deported to their own countries. There are, I feel assured, plenty of competent Englishmen to fill these positions. I have spent a considerable period in Belgium at the outset of hostilities, and have been discharged from the Army, broken in health. Does it seem feasible and proper that I am to come back to be thus treated by a man whose skin and country I have been out to help to preserve? The presence of such men in these positions is very pernicious and does not sugar well for the achievement of future industrial peace. If we are going to be British after the war, let us be British now and have all aliens irrespective of nationality removed.'

CHAPTER 9

Life Goes On

With so little attention paid to events in Europe by most people living in Derbyshire, the outbreak of war appeared to be a sudden development and so people were unprepared; and there was 'pandemonium', as Vera Brittain described it, in Buxton; and this term can similarly be applied to most parts of the county.

A government appeal told people to 'Keep your heads. Be calm. Go about your ordinary business quietly and soberly. Do not engage in excitement or foolish demonstrations. Secondly, think of others more than you are wont to do. Think of your duty to your neighbour. Think of the common weal.' They were advised not to hoard gold and to pay any bills they owed, especially to washwomen and charwomen. Clearly the government predicted hardship for women in the absence of their men folk. Finally, the appeal asked people to 'do what you can to cheer and encourage our soldiers. Gladly help any organisation for their comfort and welfare'.

The war news was fairly positive in the early days, although it was mixed with rumours of naval battles in the North Sea and off the Thames estuary, with reports of a German mine layer being sunk and many German merchant ships seized.

At the outbreak of war the official advice was that British citizens overseas should remain where they were, even if in Germany and this affected several Derbyshire folk.

Steve Bloomer, who had retired from Derby County FC at the end of the 1913/14 season, had moved to Germany to become the coach of Berlin Britannia FC. He arrived on 14 July 1914 and when war broke out was arrested and imprisoned at the Reuhleben Civilian Internment Camp just outside Berlin. There he helped run football matches to keep up the morale of other civilian prisoners. He was eventually released, owing to ill health, in March 1918 and returned to Derby.

Sir Alfred Haslam was in Germany at the outset of war. Although he was detained briefly he managed to return to Derbyshire.

Miss Phillips of Derby was detained in Hamburg at the start of the war, but managed to return to the county towards the end of September.

Miss Smith of Belper was in Germany, near Kiel, when mobilisation of the German troops began. She did not believe war would break out and so she continued her travels and when war did commence she had immense difficulty returning to England.

Mr and Mrs H.H. Cox of Hasland, were also in Germany on holiday. Their escape from the country followed a period during which they were kept captive on account of Mr Cox being in possession of a marked map of the Elbe showing the positions of German warships. Somehow they managed to escape, having feared Mr Cox would be shot for espionage. Their return to England took almost nine days.

Meanwhile, some of the more wealthy members of Chesterfield society attempted to travel to Germany but were prevented from doing so. A party including Alderman C.P. Markham should have been on a cruise around Hamburg and Norway, but they were advised to cancel the trip. Mr A.C. Seals of the Portland and Angel Hotels, A. Nuttall and D. Stephenson, schoolmaster, had planned a European tour but they only managed to travel as far as London.

For the majority, there were more pressing concerns than the restrictions on travel to Europe, such as a fear of invasion, with Territorials including men from Derbyshire positioned on the Yorkshire coast to prevent attack. Reports of naval battles in the North Sea inevitably led to panic and fear.

Fears would have been heightened somewhat when there were reports of a possible spy in Clay Cross. On 15 August 1914, it was reported in the *Derbyshire Times* that a man had been spotted taking photographs of the mouth of the Clay Cross tunnel and its immediate surroundings. He had been at his pursuit for more than an hour, which was considered highly unusual by those who observed him. When the man realised he had been seen he quickly fled the area on his bicycle. He was not captured.

In late August, fears of an invasion resulted in a devastating tragedy in one Derbyshire community. After reading of the war news, in particular the treatment of Belgians following the German invasion, 10-year-old Joseph Elliott of Kniveton asked his mother if English women and children would ever be captured. His mother replied that she hoped the Germans would not invade. The response failed to console him and later that day he took his father's gun and shot himself dead.

There were worries that the price of coal would rise to an unaffordable level and that collieries would be forced to operate for shorter numbers of hours which would mean less work for the miners, because most of the coal they produced was exported to Europe.

There were fears about food prices and food availability, with some beginning to worry the country would starve in the event of invasion, leading to panic buying and food hoarding, resulting in shortages and large queues outside shops. In Buxton, Vera Brittain described how, 'habitually quiet and respectable citizens struggled like wolves for the provisions in the food shops, and ventured upon the distracted assistants their dismay at learning that all prices had suddenly gone up'.

'Excessive purchases are being made by needlessly alarmed customers, whose unreasonable conduct cannot be too strongly deprecated', the *Derby Mercury* wrote, to discourage such behaviour.

In early August 1914 there was an abundance of cheap potatoes. However, a number of foodstuffs including corn and sugar had their prices significantly increased. The *Derbyshire Times* wrote, 'There is abundance of food in the country and supplies will continue to come in. Small shopkeepers should not pay any increased prices demanded by the middleman and they should not put up prices to their poor customers. Every halfpenny charged additional for food now is robbery and the public must see to it that they are not robbed.'

Readers were advised that they could report shopkeepers who did overcharge for their produce to the Board of Trade.

However, such efforts did not stop what was believed to profiteering. One person, calling himself 'A Victim', expressed his anger and frustration, which was shared throughout the county: 'Will you allow me to trespass on your space to enter my protest against the manner in which some of the shopkeepers of Chesterfield showed their "loyalty" to their country and their poorer countrymen by rushing the prices of the foodstuffs to the height they did do the last week. Their avaricious, grabbing, business methods are most barbarous – they thought only of self in the crisis … Trusting that the Government will deal with them as they deserve and that the public will get an opportunity of getting its own back.'

Despite the claims of an 'abundance' of food it was stated on 15 August that there were sufficient ingredients to make bread to last the country five months, and only six weeks-worth of meat. However, in those early days and weeks of war it was commonly believed the conflict would be short lived.

There were appeals for the public's help. Mary Augusta C. Salmond, the Honorary Secretary of the Derbyshire branch of the Soldiers and Sailors Help Society wrote to the *Derbyshire Times* asking for donations because men would be wounded during the war and that they would need help potentially for the rest of their lives.

Donations of money and old clothes were also sought, by the Red Cross. Any clothes that women wished to make for the forces were made to patterns supplied by the military. An appeal was also made for clothes for those facing hardship due to husbands fighting overseas.

A Derbyshire War Relief Fund was quickly established for the relief of distress. It was anticipated that financial hardship would be faced by people across the county, and across the country, due to breadwinners joining the armed forces thereby not contributing to the family living costs. Whilst many employers continued to pay part of the wages of men who volunteered to fight, and the Government provided some benefits, there was a shortfall in income in large numbers of households.

The Prince of Wales National Relief Fund was also set up. In Derby the Mayor sent circulars to the large firms asking men to subscribe and in places of work across Derbyshire meetings were held among the workers who often agreed to contribute. The same generous gesture was, from time to time, made for the benefit of other causes associated with the war. Mayors and other officials of all towns in the county appealed at every opportunity for donations to the relief funds. Throughout the war charity events were held to raise much needed funds.

The Derbyshire councils also created Distress Committees in an attempt to find, or create, work for those who had lost their jobs as a result of the war.

Domestic servants were hit particularly hard by the outbreak of war, with considerable numbers losing their jobs. In the early months of war the government in New South Wales, Australia, and the New Zealand Government offered jobs to servants. To encourage workers to emigrate to Australia, only £1 had to paid up front for the cost of travel in 'comfortable steamers', which cost between £3 and £6. Good wages, pleasant living and working conditions and good health care were also offered to induce servants to the 'attractive country'.

The loss of so many servants' jobs was not justified according to E. Martin Massey, proprietor of Mrs Masseys agency for servants, Derby and London, but still more women were thrown out of work.

Efforts were made to help women facing this situation and in October a fund was set up in Derby for women who had lost their jobs. It was run by the Mayoress, as part of Queen Mary's national appeal.

A day of national prayer was held on 21 August to give the nation strength and to appeal for divine intervention. Churches announced they would offer spiritual comfort and guidance during the difficult times ahead for the benefit of the soldiers and those who remained at home.

Some elements of life continued almost as normal. The main two football teams in Derbyshire, Derby County FC and Chesterfield FC, continued to play games as the football season began in August, despite criticisms from those who felt players had a more important match to play, against the Germans, and should be joining the army or carrying out other war work, and that spectators should be more interested in fighting than football. There were even debates in parliament regarding whether football fans should be taxed if they were not wearing khaki. However, both teams made donations from the proceeds of all matches to the Prince of Wales Relief Fund.

The chairman of Derby County said they were contractually obliged to play matches, adding there was no desire to attract men who should be fighting.

By November 1914 injuries and military recruitment had depleted Chesterfield FC's team. In one week around Christmas 1914 several enlisted, although some continued to occasionally play if stationed locally. The match attendances fell as men enlisted, with numbers at home games below 2,000 leading to a financial crisis, but the club continued to play.

The entertainment venues across the county also continued to provide amusements and in doing so often helped raise money for the Relief Funds.

Whilst sport and theatre provided brief distractions from the serious situation that the country was in, the war was ever prevalent in the minds of all. There was a gloomy feeling a month after the war had begun when people in Derbyshire learnt of German advances. It was revealed the Germans were within thirty miles of Paris and the French Government had moved to Bordeaux. In her diary, Maria Gyte of Sheldon recorded, 'A many in the house tonight but they were quiet and subdued.'

The war news continued to look bleak when on 26 September the 2nd Derbyshire (Howitzer) Battery were cut up in France and only fifteen men were left standing. A month later the 1st Derbyshire Battery had a similar fate in Belgium.

The horrors of war had begun to make themselves evident with news of injuries and deaths. Derbyshire saw its first victims in late September when a train full of wounded soldiers made a brief stop at Derby station on its way to Sheffield. A correspondent of the *Derby Mercury* spoke with some of the men, one of whom had had his nose shot off.

CHAPTER 10

Over by Christmas

Despite having been at war for four months as Advent commenced, efforts were made to make Christmas pleasurable.

Shops in Derbyshire, with the rallying cry of 'business as usual', attempted to draw in customers with offers of 'gifts galore'. To appeal to the patriotic, items with names associated with war were promoted. A 'Victory' suite (comprising a wardrobe, dressing chest and washstand) was on offer at Eyre & Sons in Chesterfield, and a 'popular Victory model piano' and 'Triumph' model organ were on offer at White & Sons Ltd, also in Chesterfield.

For Derbyshire's soldiers and sailors overseas, and in training closer to home, there were appeals for gifts to ensure each man was remembered. The *Derbyshire Times* had set up its tobacco scheme prior to Advent, but as Christmas approached there was a greater appeal for gifts of tobacco and cigarettes, for the Sherwood Foresters.

Warm garments were also popular presents that were produced each winter, and especially at Christmas for the troops.

In Derby the Mayor and Mayoress visited wounded soldiers at Normanton barracks, noting they were bright and cheerful in spite of their wounds. However, days later, one man at the barracks, who was not a patient, expressed very different emotions. Private William Sherrard committed suicide by slashing his throat. He had served in India and was nervous about rejoining his regiment and going to war in Europe.

The members of the 2nd/6th Battalion of the Sherwood Foresters, at their training camp in Buxton, which had the Empire Hotel as its Headquarters, received an early Christmas present when they were presented with a rough-haired Airedale terrier named Jack.

There was plenty of entertainment on offer for theatregoers. At Derby's Grande Theatre the Aladdin pantomime caused 'constant ripples of merriment' and at the Hippodrome there was *Jack and Jill*, a play based upon the nursery rhyme.

EMPIRE HOTEL-BUXTON.
HEADQUARTERS FOR SHERWOOD FORESTERS, NOTTS' & DERBYS.   100.

The Empire Hotel in Buxton, which formed the headquarters of the 2nd/6th Battalion Sherwood Foresters. *Reproduced courtesy of Michael Briggs*

In Chesterfield, The Corporation Theatre had a performance of *Loon and Mack's Xmas pantomime* and also showed *Babes in the Wood*. At the Hippodrome a musical montage was provided by Daisy Squelch and Co. Other treats at the Hippodrome included The Foss (playing music with xylophone and piano), Kate and Harry Spiers (the Black and White Comedy Duo), The M/C Quartette, star comedian Fred Curran, Harry Drew (a Welsh Basso), nine Empire Opera singers, Little Miss Carpenter ('England's Little Novelty'), Frank Le Dent ('world renowned juggler') and Prince Kuroki (a Japanese magician). *Casey's at Home* (a 'Charismatic Homely Irish humour in two scenes') and various motion pictures were also shown. At the Victoria Picture House pictures included *The Death Call*, *Home Sweet Home*, *Bravo Kilties*, *Our Father* and *It's a Long Way to Tipperary*. Whilst at the Cinema House patrons were able to watch *A Spellbound Multitude*.

In aid of the war fund and local charities, Chesterfield Literary and Social

Union presented a 'popular astronomical lecture' by Professor H.H.Turner entitled 'A Voyage into Space.'

A feeling of festive cheer was aided by some optimistic news in the weeks preceding Christmas. For example, it was reported in the *Derbyshire Times* that the German army on the Eastern Front was beginning to 'feel the pinch' from the Russians. Derbyshire men were also being hailed as heroes, such as Private Siddons of Tideswell. He was awarded the Distinguished Service Medal for getting ammunition whilst under heavy fire. Progress appeared to be being made, although those who had predicted an end to the war by Christmas were shown to have misplaced optimism.

That changed on 16 December, when a fleet of German ships bombarded the eastern coast, causing destruction to Scarborough, Whitby and Hartlepool, the latter suffering a particularly high loss of life. By the end of the year the death toll in Hartlepool stood at 108, and buildings lay in ruins in that town; and also in Scarborough and Whitby, where part of the iconic abbey had been hit.

People fled in packed trains from Scarborough to Hull and from there to other parts of the country. Two boys were amongst the first to head to Chesterfield where they stayed for some time. The boys, Geoffrey 'Dick' Pawson and Wilfred 'Sam' Pawson, were the sons of Reverend Arnold Pawson, formerly of Chesterfield.

Derbyshire folk realised that the war was not only something experienced across the English Channel, but that enemy fire was capable of causing devastation at home. Even residents of inland counties such as Derbyshire felt fear that a coastal attack would be followed by an invasion. Such a fear was compounded when, on Christmas Eve, the first attack by air was made. A plane flew over Dover and a bomb was dropped, but caused only minor damage to a church rectory.

Fears of air raids were already widespread. In Chesterfield a week before Christmas a correspondent calling themselves 'cautious' wrote to the *Derbyshire Times* urging that the Workhouse Infirmary reduce what was described as 'a blaze of light', so that Zeppelin crews would not be aided by the lights. Details of air raid precautions can be found in another chapter.

Accounts of the conditions in the trenches, with tales of soldiers having limbs amputated due to frostbite, and the increasing number of injuries and deaths also cast a gloom over the festive period.

Almost ninety wounded soldiers arrived at Derby Royal Infirmary on 17 December. Frostbite was a particularly common affliction. One man of the Sherwood Foresters, who hailed from Chesterfield, said he and a friend were suffering from frostbite made worse having recently returned from India. Soldiers reported that it was so cold that their weapons had frozen.

Corporal J Potter of the 1st Battalion Sherwood Foresters wrote to his mother, Mrs Colley of Carr Vale, from his hospital bed in Glasgow. In his letter, which was printed in the *Derbyshire Times* on 12 December, he described four men being killed in a period of, he believed, six seconds:

'I got frostbite during the severe winter we experienced in the trenches and as I was also suffering a great deal from exhaustion the doctors sent me out of it. Some of our fellows have lost limbs through frost bite but I have nothing like that to fear and I shall be as well as ever. We were holding a position near Lille, and I can tell you we were in a pretty warm corner. One part of our trench was named Port Arthur on account of the large number of men who were killed and wounded there. One day I and another man named Waldron were the only two left out of six in as many seconds. Waldron deserves to get a distinction for what he did that day. After it was all over we both cried like children, more from temper than anything else, because we were unable to get at the snipers who shot the other poor beggars.'

The human cost of warfare was all too familiar to Mrs Colley, whose other son had died early in the war, on 20 September, just days after arriving in France.

Welcome relief was provided to many families when some soldiers and sailors returned home on leave over the Christmas period. As trains pulled into main stations the servicemen on board found enthusiastic crowds welcoming them home. However, there was annoyance that soldiers were given little financial help to return home for Christmas from their camps. Train fares were said to be excessive, especially considering they were paid so little. The leave of the Territorials who were still in England was later postponed.

Despite the efforts of the theatres and other entertainment venues, and Christmas parties that tried to lift the public spirit, it was not a good Christmas for many Derbyshire families. During December families across the county learnt of the deaths of loved ones in the battlefields.

The parents of Lance Corporal Ernest Wood, of Clowne, were told that their son had been killed on 11 November. In Bolsover, the family of Private J.W. Warner were told he had died on 17 November, having been severely wounded weeks earlier. George H. Symonds, formerly a police constable in

Brimington, became the first victim of that village when he was killed in action. The family of Lance Corporal William Henry Forster of Chesterfield had heard rumours that he had been killed, after a comrade who had been wounded wrote to friends in Brampton. It was weeks later, in the run up to Christmas, that the rumours were confirmed. There had, at one time, been hope in the hearts of the family of Private Albert W. Allen of Snitterton, who had been wounded at Ypres in October. However, just two weeks before Christmas he died from his wounds.

Although their families would not find out until early into the New Year, 119 Derbyshire men from the 2nd Battalion Derbyshire Regiment were being held in a prisoner of war camp in Hanover. Many of their loved ones, having not heard from them over the Christmas period, had feared the worst.

The uncertainty of the welfare of loved ones overseas was prevalent throughout the war's duration but was particularly felt at Christmas time. Many families who had not recently heard from a loved one would be unsure of their well being, hoping for the best but fearing the worst.

The editor of the *Derby Mercury* remarked it was an 'unusual Christmas' and not a 'Christ Mass but a Devil's Mass'. However, there was gratitude that, apart from the east coast attack, the country had not suffered like that of the Belgians.

Christmas on the Home Front was enjoyed as best as possible in most homes. 'That first wartime Christmas seemed a strange and chilling experience to us who had always been accustomed to the exuberant house-decorating and present-giving of the prosperous pre-war years', Vera Brittain recalled. In her diary at the time she recorded, 'A good many people have decided that they are both too poor and too miserable to remember their friends, particularly the rich people who have no one at all in any danger.' However, she added, 'The poorer ones, and those who are in anxiety about something or other, have all made an effort to do the same as usual.'

It was a frosty and icy Christmas, with some revelry and people going into the towns as usual. In Derby, it was remarked that the most popular 'carol' was *Tipperary*. It was also claimed that the Christmas of 1914, in Derby at least, was little different to previous years despite the absence of a larger number of men and concerns about the war. 'On the whole we have not deviated very much from our Christmas customs', the editor of the *Derby Mercury* wrote, adding that shopkeepers had done well from Christmas purchasers as a result of people's wages having improved. 'We are having quite as good a khaki Christmas as we have any right to expect', he ended.

At the county's hospitals, efforts were made for the benefit of wounded servicemen and civilian patients with decorations, Christmas dinners and entertainment. Each convalescing soldier, sailor and airman received a card from the King and Queen. At the Derby Royal Infirmary the decorations were not as elaborate as in previous years but they gave a pretty appearance to the wards. An 'artistic and gigantic' cake weighing 120lbs was the centre of attention. Choirs and concerts helped give festive cheer to the soldiers, and in the children's ward Father Christmas paid a visit, bringing toys.

Patients at the Chesterfield Hospital had a 'happy time', with the hospital having 'bright and tasteful' decorations throughout. A 'delightful entertainment' was provided following dinner, with nurses performing sketches and singing and reciting poetry. On Saturday the focus was on entertaining the children who were described as having a 'rollicking time'. A heavily-laden Christmas tree gave much delight, as did Dr Keating dressed as Father Christmas. Concerts and other entertainments were held in the following days.

Pupils at the Shirebrook Model Village School enjoying Christmas in 1917. *Courtesy of Derbyshire Libraries and www.picturethepast.org.uk*

A special effort was made for the children. On Christmas morning, 966 children attending the elementary schools in the North Ward of Chesterfield were given a 'merry time' with a formidable feast being enjoyed and each child given an orange and a packet of sweets as a gift to take home and similar scenes were witnessed in schools and other public buildings across the county.

An appeal was also made for generosity for the children of serving soldiers and sailors of Chesterfield. A party was to be held for those children early in the New Year.

In the trenches, Derbyshire's soldiers tried to make the best of their Christmas, and their accounts sent in letters to friends and loved ones made interesting reading back home. Much has been written about the Christmas Day truce of 1914, when agreements were made not to fight. Whilst tales of many large, organised football matches may be exaggerated, with much of the day spent collecting dead bodies from the field of battle, certainly in some instances the festive spirit was shared between enemies.

Clay Cross Bombardier J. Birkin of 24th Brigade RFA, wrote to G.E. Allen, in a letter printed in the *Derbyshire Times*, to tell him of his Christmas in the trenches. He had heard news of the east coast attacks and regarded the Germans as 'dirty dogs' who had done 'awful things'. 'Christmas is all over', he continued, 'What we saw of it was not much, but we knew it was Christmas because there was no fighting. We had made arrangements with the Germans not to do any that day, so we all had a good rest. We came out of the trenches and went over to the German trenches and shook hands with some of them and gave them cigarettes, while they gave us other things.'

CHAPTER 11

On the Farm

The war severely affected agriculture as farm workers left the land to join the armed forces and a reduction in the amount of food imported from overseas led to an increased need for food to be produced at home. In order to feed the nation the farming communities of Derbyshire had to work harder than ever before.

In an age where motorised farm equipment was not in the possession of the majority of Derbyshire farmers, and was somewhat feared by those who preferred traditional farming methods, horses played a key role in agriculture in transporting equipment and harvested crops, as well as pulling the plough. In the days and weeks following the outbreak of war farmers lost the strongest and healthiest of these essential animals as they were commandeered by the War Office. Some farmers were doubly unfortunate in losing their horses and some of their farm hands.

Food shortages were not a serious issue until 1917, despite initial food queues and hoarding. However, there were concerns about the 1914 harvest and whether there would be enough manpower to harvest the crops. Appeals were made to assist the farmers with this task.

C.S. Cockburn of Chesterfield wrote in the *Derbyshire Times* in August 1914 promising that '... each man who comes to their assistance will have the satisfaction of knowing that every sheaf of corn, and every haycock he helps to get into the back yard, means so much more bread for our families, and as much milk for the little ones during the anxious months ahead of us'.

Despite difficulties, the 1914 harvest was largely successful. Farmers faced increasingly difficult situations as those 'anxious months ahead' turned into the years of the war's duration, and continued into peacetime.

The real difficulties began in 1915. At the annual meeting of the Alfreton branch of the Derbyshire Farmers' Union in February, the President of the Union, Mr W. J. Cutts, spoke of the need for more food in the 1915 harvest and the problems that were to be faced by farmers. He was impressed with the farming techniques that he saw in Derbyshire, which he thought could not be bettered, but he hoped farmers would use artificial manures to increase the size of crops of hay and wheat. Hay was needed in large quantities by the War Office to provide fodder for the horses and the War Office needed the support of farmers in the county and he encouraged them to cooperate.

The major problem, Cutts explained, was that young men were 'being allured away' in increasing numbers to go and fight. This meant there were fewer people to work on farms and so labour would have to be sought from elsewhere. Men also left to work in factories and mines.

The labour issue was a matter of concern throughout the war. Early efforts were made to replace men with boys aged twelve and over. Cutts believed that if boys could leave school earlier in order to work on the farms it would be a service not only to farmers but the whole country.

At the monthly meeting of the Derbyshire Education Committee in Derby, in January 1915, consideration was given to whether boys over the age of twelve could leave school to work on farms. It was agreed that although farm labour was a problem, children should not leave school until the age of fourteen. The Committee asked the Board of Education whether some amendment to the current rules was possible, but it was pointed out that people could already apply for a twelve or thirteen-year-old to be released.

The Board of Education refused to allow children to leave school earlier. Instead, a scheme was suggested to encourage teachers to work on farms during the summer holidays.

There was some support from teachers who recognised the difficulties faced by farmers. In February 1915, during a meeting of the East Derbyshire Teachers' Association, a teacher named Mr E. J. Roberts argued that it would not matter if a school shut for twelve months in order for students and teachers to help the farmers, because the country needed everyone to work towards bringing a swifter end to the war.

A Matlock farmer named W.H. Lowe argued, in a letter to the *Derbyshire Times* in February 1915, those against the use of children on farms were often those who did not understand farming. It was his belief that if the labour situation was not substantially improved, 'the land must become derelict' because 'the countryside is depleted of all her useful and handy men'. He dismissed the notion that farmers wanted children in order to exploit them with low wages. 'No farmer wants a boy of twelve if he could get a lad of fifteen or sixteen or more years that would be willing to work six full days in the week, and often a good half-day on the seventh', he said. Rather than being exploited they would receive food and accommodation, taking away the burden from the child's family.

Whilst arguments for school boy labour were taking place, there was a small gesture of assistance from the Government. At the annual meeting of the Derbyshire Farmers' Union held in Chesterfield in February 1915 Cutts announced that the Board of Agriculture and the Labour Exchange were willing to assist in providing labour. Although they could not create labour where it did not exist, Cutts believed it meant the Government was trying to help.

At a meeting of Derbyshire County Council in June 1915 the issue of child labour was again discussed. Mr A. L. Jenkyn Brown, Director of Education, agreed the need was urgent and that farmers were experiencing difficulty in finding adults willing to work for reasonable pay. It was agreed children should be allowed to work on farms upon a successful application for exemption being received. However, the period of exemption from school was limited to three months and during that time the children were to be regularly visited to see that they were employed satisfactorily.

Despite rules allowing farmers to apply for a child, in practice it was too difficult in most instances to obtain a single child let alone the numbers needed. At a well attended meeting of the Chesterfield War Agricultural Committee in January 1916 it was said that despite the House of Lords wanting boys to help farmers, bureaucracy stood in the way.

Whilst there was some support amongst teachers for boys to work on farms, one Derbyshire teacher suggested farmers should give work to the 'feeble minded' from institutions and sanatorium patients with tuberculosis. Her suggestion was referred to at the February 1916 meeting of the Derbyshire Farmers' Union, where there was much 'derisive laughter'.

Pensioners were also sought to work on farms. However, there was greater reluctance for them to do so when, in May 1916, a man who regularly carried out some work on a farm had his pension stopped.

During June 1915 there were severe frosts causing damage to crops in and around Derby, threatening the success of the harvests in parts of the county.

As more and more men left the land to fight overseas, a system was put into place in July 1915 to allow farmers to appeal against their workers being taken if they had joined the Colours. The farmer was able to apply to the recruiting officer for the man to be withheld from service. If the application was unsuccessful the farmer could apply to the magistrates who would appoint an arbitrator.

One farmer who applied was George Wood of Callow Carr, whose farmhand had been under contract to work until Christmas but left in August, leaving him 'fairly stranded'.

As conscription began in 1916 there were concerns that the needs of the agricultural community were not being considered, with men being taken for the armed forces when they were desperately needed on farms.

Mr S. Taylor, who owned 140 acres, including twenty acres of arable land, with thirty horned cattle, eight horses and two breeding cows, unsuccessfully appealed against the enlisting of his two labourers. He told a meeting of the Derbyshire Farmers' Union that the members of the tribunal had not understood his case. This was understandable, he said, considering they consisted of two colliery owners, a mineral water manufacturer, a retired grocer and two property owners; in short no one who understood the needs of farmers.

Francis Acland MP, who attended the meeting, said he was surprised by complaints that tribunals were too severe, because he had heard that the Tribunals were too lenient to farm workers. Military authorities, he said, considered agriculture was being unfairly favoured.

Acland urged farmers to stand for parliament to get their views voiced, but it was a suggestion of little help, with no general election until after the armistice. He added that farmers should not expect changes to laws governing the school leaving age. However, every effort was being made to encourage women to work on the land, with inducements such as armlets and certificates. Acland confirmed that the government's policy was to maintain the minimum and necessary amount of skilled labour on farms and supplement that basic level of labour with women. Only when women were unavailable would children be considered. Soldier labour had been of some help, with men being retained from active service on a temporary basis to assist with harvests, although there were far from enough soldiers to meet the demand. In the future, Acland warned, soldiers would only be allowed to work on farms for a maximum of four weeks. After all, soldiers were needed to fight, not farm.

Around 500 soldiers were available in Derbyshire in July 1916 but there was some disappointment that farmers whose sons had been called up would not be released.

By September 1916 it was estimated approximately one third of men who had worked on farms prior to war had been taken by the army.

If Derbyshire's farmers thought things could not be more difficult in 1915 and in particular in 1916 as conscription took men away, they were mistaken. In 1917, as food shortages began to bite, there were increased demands not only to farm the amount of land they had farmed for years, but in spite of a reduced workforce they were to farm even greater amounts of land and produce much more food than had been thought possible even before the war. In large areas of Derbyshire little farming could take place between February and April 1917 due to heavy frosts and snow.

In January 1917 it was announced that following instructions from the Board of Agriculture, the Derbyshire War Agricultural committee had organised the 'systematic survey' of all the farmland in the county to determine how much land was available to plough for the 1918 harvest. Details of the labour available to the farmer were compiled so that it could be determined if the recommendations were viable. According to the Board of Agriculture, 'an addition to the land under the plough is urgently needed'. Thirty thousand acres of additional cultivated land was required for Derbyshire, with grassland having to be broken up to meet this quota.

The scheme, as outlined in the January announcement, did not sound too daunting. It implied that the farmer's circumstances and ability would be given due consideration in forming recommendations. It will be shown that in practice this was not the case.

In order to encourage the farmers to cooperate, efforts were made to make them realise just how precarious the food situation would be if the farmers did not do all that they could.

At a meeting in Derby on 2 February 1917 almost 400 farmers were addressed by the Controller of Cultivated Areas, Mr Eve, who explained that because of the growing menace of German submarines more food would have to be produced at home. He urged farmers to forget all the neglect they had suffered from the government in the past and to do what they could to help the nation. He added that women would be able to help contribute to agricultural work and that as a rule there had not been the welcome to women on farms that there ought to have been.

Female labour on farms, whilst reluctantly accepted and not always gratefully received, became increasingly helpful in resolving the labour issue. The same is true of German prisoners of war, who were quite naturally not wanted by most farmers until the lack of labour made some change their attitudes. Some of the conscientious objectors were also compelled to work on farms to do their bit for the country as a condition of exemption from the army. The work of women and German prisoners of war, is discussed in detail in other chapters.

In March 1917, Wirksworth Urban District Council agreed all council staff accustomed to farming should work on farms during March and April.

Such short-term measures provided a little help, but the farmers were soon scandalised to learn the Government intended to take a further 30,000 farm workers for the army. At the February meeting of the Chesterfield War Agricultural Committee, it was said to take more men would be disastrous for agriculture. It was feared that only men considered entirely unsuitable for active service, and only capable of clerical work and other sedentary roles, would be available for farm work and if this was the case the land could not be kept up.

In April 1917, farmers learnt even more men were to be taken for active service and replaced with lower-skilled men. At the April meeting of the Chesterfield War Agricultural Committee, it was remarked this would lead to crops being reduced so much that British farmers could no longer be relied upon to any appreciable extent to feed the nation.

Meanwhile, the survey of farms identified several in Derbyshire that were neglected. This was largely due to the lack of labour and poor prices being paid for farmers' produce. However, it was acknowledged that if land was not being properly tilled then the farmers would be reported to the County Authority and if farmers continued to neglect their farms then others would take their place. It was also recognised that in addition to the shortage of labour was the shortage of seed. The government had demanded that more crops be produced but without seed this was not possible.

On 19 May 1917 the increased amount of land to cultivate, along with falling numbers of workers, led Cutts to make a desperate plea that farmers should be heard. At a Derbyshire Farmers' Union meeting he spoke of how there were not enough men available to get in the harvest for that year and that it was the government's fault. He added, 'We have been like voices crying in the wilderness since the war began, and it now looks as though retribution is going to come. We don't wish to cast any reflection on the Government, but it is unforgettable that the farmer has been starved, the land has been starved, and it is just possible that in its wake, the people will be starved. And if it were not for the disaster it will bring, it will serve the authorities right.'

More land was wanted for the growing of wheat. At a meeting of the Derbyshire War Agricultural Committee in May 1917, Captain FitzHerbert Wright MP, a native of Derbyshire who lived at Yeldersley Hall, but was MP for Leominster, had become responsible for increasing the acreage under wheat in 1918. He hoped that between 40,000 and 50,000 acres of additional land would be found for wheat. The scheme would, he added, only go ahead if the necessary labour was forthcoming. The Committee agreed to carry out the new scheme if the government promised that more labour would be made available. It was reported that soldier labour had been of some assistance. There had been 674 applications for soldier labour in Derbyshire, but unfortunately 400 soldiers had to return for military service on 10 May, although the remainder were permitted to remain on the farms until 25 July. The Committee was also pleased to report that skilled shepherds were to be released from the army during the sheep-shearing season.

In June 1917, farmers in the Peak District faced a new problem when an 'army' of caterpillars (although the *Derby Mercury* referred to an invasion of locusts) said to be in their millions destroyed crops. The 'plague' blighted farmland across the county and one farmer near Chapel-en-le-Frith lost an entire field as a result of the pests. Five spraying machines were sent to eradicate the pests but a more natural form of extermination arrived approximately a week after the caterpillars. Thousands of rooks flew into the county, from Castleton to Chapel-en-le-Frith, and fed upon the caterpillars. Before long the 'army' had significantly diminished.

That same month, Colonel Chandos-Pole-Gell promised that no farmer or tenant would suffer a loss as a result of the new demands on breaking up grassland. He added that the government would help with labour and provide compensation for the grass land. The farmers present said they would continue the scheme of turning grass land into arable land provided the government guaranteed labour, horses and machinery and compensation.

Cutts informed farmers that there were some men being brought out of the mines to work on the land, although this exacerbated problems with the output of coal.

The government finally appeared to realise the urgent need for help on the land and hopes that the situation would be somewhat eased were raised at the end of June 1917 when it was announced in the House of Lords that between 70,000 and 80,000 soldiers, many with agricultural experience, were to be made available on farms across the country between July and September and they were not to be recalled unless suitable replacements could be found for them. An absolute order was issued to cease the enlistment of men working on farms except in cases where the agricultural committee gave its consent. Men in the army who had been recalled to the colours on 25 July were to continue their agricultural work unless they could be replaced by men of the same standard, it was added.

The statement that the enlistment of men from farms would cease was not fully heard by the tribunals. Between 14 June and 11 September 1917 there were 803 applications made for exemption from the armed forces on behalf of farm workers in Derbyshire, with seventy-five applications refused.

There was also some help from children when, in June 1917, a temporary release of schoolchildren to work on the land was approved by the Derbyshire Education Committee.

Ten cases of badly cultivated farms were dealt with by the Derbyshire War Agricultural Committee in August 1917. In some cases uncooperative farmers were issued with an order compelling them to break up the land, although these orders were not at this time properly enforced. In other cases the farmer or landowner was sent a letter advising him of his responsibilities.

One farm in Alton was in such a poor condition that it was recommended the land be taken from the farmer's possession. His neighbours argued the land was too difficult to cultivate, especially with inadequate labour. It was, they said, dry, sharp, hilly, full of stones and far from the farmer's home. They would assist the farmer, they added, if the order was withdrawn. However, it was decided that the 'shockingly farmed' land ought to be given to someone more capable.

A farmer from Swanwick had joined the Derbyshire Yeomanry on the outbreak of war. However, since then the men who worked for him had been called up and his wife was now seriously ill and by September 1917 his land had been badly neglected. A meeting between Cutts and the authorities resulted in the man being transferred to a unit that would only be called upon if the country was invaded.

By September 1917 the surveys of farmland in the county had been completed for 3,900 of the 5,300 farms, the Derbyshire War Agricultural Executive Committee heard at its monthly meeting in Derby. At the farms visited there had been promises to break up a total of 12,000 acres of land for new cultivation. Farmers in Bakewell and Ashbourne districts had been the most supportive but even in those districts not enough land had been promised to meet the quota expected of them. It was also remarked that the condition of many farms was unsatisfactory and warning letters had been issued. In addition to the lack of labour, there was a lack of threshing machines.

The training of the available labour was also a serious matter. In the autumn of 1917 it was announced that training was to be provided to ensure men were better skilled in ploughing. A scheme was set up by the Board of Agriculture to allow men to be sent to any farmer who was willing to train them. The farmer would pay their wages and board for two or three weeks until they became sufficiently skilled to the satisfaction of the committee's representative. It was, however, the belief of the Committee that two or three weeks was insufficient time.

Still, as September turned to October there was a shortage of threshing machines and seed. Derbyshire farmers urged the Board of Agriculture to release the threshing machines and, crucially, train men in how to use them.

These shortages of labour, equipment and seed did not prevent the authorities taking action against farmers who were struggling and whom they considered to be negligent. The Derbyshire War Agricultural Committee 'regretfully' issued many compulsory orders to the 'negligent and the indifferent' to plough the amount of land expected of them. In Bakewell and Ashbourne the response had been admirable, but elsewhere the voluntary scheme had been a failure. Of the required 30,000 acres only 13,671 acres had been pledged.

British farmers had recently been publicly thanked by the Prime Minister for their efforts. Lloyd George had also expressed his sympathy for all the difficulties they faced and, in response to popular claims that farmers were trying to profit from the war by charging more money for their produce than was necessary, he said such claims were completely false. Further, he had pledged that a quarter of a million men were going to be returned to the land due to the shortage of labour.

At the October meeting of the Derbyshire Farmer's Union Lloyd George's speech was welcomed. He had acknowledged the great responsibility that rested with the farmers and how dependent the country was on 'the strong men of Britain'. The farmers could certainly provide all of the country's needs and prevent famine, it was said, but only if they had the right support and conditions. Members of the Union took pleasure in the knowledge they were right all along when they had argued that too many men were being taken from the land. The fact the Prime Minister had said that so many men were to be returned had shown that the government's policy had been wrong and that the tribunals had been unduly harsh. The tribunals still opposed the retention of men on the land but the best answer farmers could give to the tribunals' complaints was to have those men do their best with and to make more land available for ploughing.

It was not just a case of the military taking men from farms. Some farmhands left their positions as they pleased in order to join the army. In October 1917, there were calls from the county's farmers for a requirement that farm workers apply for a leaving certificate from the Agricultural Committee, essentially apply for permission to leave their job in the same way that munitions factory workers were required to.

Although some steps had been taken to increase the number of horses, machinery, fertilisers and seeds, which helped a minority of Derbyshire's farmers, the county was warned that little more could be done, despite the Prime Minister's sympathies. The labour issue could not be eased to the farmers' satisfaction, they were told, because it was not possible to provide fully skilled men when there were none available. Instead, they were told to make full use of any available labour in the form of soldiers and women and train them to be proficient.

Increasing bureaucracy during the course of the war made an already difficult job all the more so. A 13-page document regarding the need for permits to sell potatoes, caused Derbyshire farmers much confusion in October 1917. It was said that if any farmer could understand the confusing document, he would be able to very quickly find another, more lucrative profession.

The bureaucracy was not the only problem when it came to the growing of potatoes. In 1917 the harvest was relatively poor, with Derbyshire having a deficit of 44,200 tons of potatoes, having produced 21,400 tons but having consumed 65,600 tons. Labour shortages, and delays sending seed potatoes to Derbyshire, were the chief reasons for the deficit. To prevent a similar fate in 1918, a strong appeal was made for people to plant potatoes in any available piece of land.

In November 1917, Captain Boyd of the Board of Agriculture reported that surveying was still in progress but that land scheduled for ploughing was to be ploughed immediately, and more land was sought. In view of the world shortage of food it was a case of the farmers growing more or the people having less to eat, the farmers were told.

The ploughing caused complaints in Clowne, when the District Council bemoaned trails of mud on the roads. Farmers questioned why the council did not have more important things to concern itself with.

On 28 November 1917, a meeting of the Derbyshire War Agricultural Executive Committee tried to address the urgent need for Derbyshire's full quota of land. Although the amount of pledged land was steadily rising, the rate of progress was too slow. General Chandos-Pole-Gell, who presided over the meeting, summed up the need as follows: 'The time has gone by for arguing, as every day brings us nearer seed time.' And so the committee issued more compulsory orders forcing the farmers to commence ploughing without delay.

At a meeting in Belper that same month, General Chandos-Pole-Gell warned that those who did not plough their land, when ordered to, would be imprisoned. A roll of honour was elsewhere suggested for those who volunteered land and a black list for those who had to be compelled.

94

Bakewell and its district was now considered to be a 'particular problem'. Approximately 3,500 more acres were needed to be ploughed in and around Bakewell but this could not be achieved because of the shortage of horses. The Board of Agriculture was able to provide horses but for the high price of 30s per head. This was despite the fact farmers in and around Bakewell had their horses requisitioned during the summer of 1914.

Despite the seed problem having been eased, in November 1917 there was still a seed shortage of 25,000 quarters for all the extra land that was to be cultivated. Land would be ploughed, it was said, with great difficulty, only for there to be no seeds to sow that land.

As the final year of active war opened, stronger demands for cooperation were made for Derbyshire farmers. During January the Derbyshire Agricultural War Committee issued a further 375 orders for the breaking up of grassland, this bringing the total to more than 2,200 orders issued since the policy of compulsion was introduced. Of the 30,000 acres required, so far only approximately 10,000 acres had been ploughed, which left a significant deficit resulting in a lack of food being produced. Although the hard weather had hindered ploughing this was not considered an adequate excuse. The new orders would, when followed, bring the number of acres ploughed much closer to the quota demanded of the county.

Although there had been an offer to plough up fifteen acres of the Duke of Devonshire's land at Hardwick Park, it was on a number of conditions and there was some reluctance from the Duke's agent to cooperate. At the meeting of the Chesterfield War Agricultural Executive Committee later in January, there were calls to force the Duke to comply. There were also calls to force F.C. Arkwright to plough of thirty acres of Sutton Deer Park. Arkwright had been unwilling to plough up grassland because farmers brought their cattle to the park to graze. It was argued that Arkwright and the Duke should not be treated any differently to other landowners. It was agreed that the land at the Sutton Deer Park should be broken up for corn and it was agreed that further diplomatic discussion should take place with the Duke's agent, the Duke himself living in Canada.

By the end of February 1918, 25,000 acres were scheduled for ploughing under orders by Derbyshire War Agricultural Executive Committee, but it was still short of the total required.

As 1918 progressed most farmers continued to do all that they could, either out of patriotic duty or through compulsion, to meet the government's demand for more crops.

In the weeks leading up to the armistice it was not only the lack of labour and machinery that was causing farmers difficulty. Nature played its own cruelty when corn in Derbyshire ripened a week earlier than usual, leaving farmers unprepared for its harvest as they were still busy hay-making. It was spoilt by rain during one of the wettest Septembers in living memory.

Although the issue of breaking up the land, and other problems affecting arable farming dominated the proceedings of the Agricultural Committees, and appeared most frequently in the newspapers, there were of course concerns also for pasture farmers. The shortage of labour on farms with livestock, whilst not as significant an issue as on arable farms, was a problem which was quickly recognised in the weeks following the outbreak of war, and a problem which grew as the war progressed.

However, it was not until 1917 when meat shortages in Derbyshire and across the country began to be a threat, and talks of the reduction and fixing of prices of, and eventually rationing of, meat began, that pasture farmers began to seriously worry. As milk, butter and margarine became scarcer, and the fixing of prices for these produces began, with eventual rationing in the case of the latter two commodities, further strains were placed on dairy farmers.

The fixing of meat retail prices was first discussed in September 1917. The Prices of Meat Order was introduced in January 1918, although some reduction in prices took place before that time, and it was quickly realised that this would have an impact upon how much farmers were paid for their slaughtered livestock. Some farmers complained that if the prices to come into operation in January were not withdrawn they would have no choice but to stop feeding their cattle, because with the price of cattle feed it would not be viable to keep them at the price for which they would be worth when killed.

A meeting of the Derbyshire War Agricultural committee in September 1917 also expressed its opposition to the meat prices order which, when combined with the cost of feeding livestock, meant farmers stood to lose on average about £9 for every steer that they fattened ready for slaughter over the course of the next winter.

Mr E. Edge of Hilltop, Ashover, wrote that pigs were very expensive to feed and as a result, 'Pork is very scarce. It will be much scarcer unless the price is altered at once. It's not a question of being unpatriotic. If a businessman finds a certain line does not pay he drops it and goes in for something else.'

The cost of feeding the livestock was a serious problem that affected not only the price and availability of slaughtered meat, but also the costs and availability of dairy products. By September 1917, dairy farmers were making a loss on the sales of milk and it was argued at a meeting of the Derbyshire War Agricultural Executive Committee that unless the government reduced the cost of cattle feed by £4 per ton the price of milk would have to rise to at least 2s per gallon. It was a problem that had been recognised back in February 1915 when Cutts had told farmers in Alfreton that dairy farming was 'near to the point of breaking down' because of the high costs of food for the cattle. It was in 1917, however, that the problem became a crisis.

Consequently some farmers across Derbyshire also ceased to produce butter and margarine, it requiring three gallons of milk to produce a pound of butter. At the November 1917 meeting of the Derbyshire War Agricultural Committee it was argued that if the government's policy of fixing the prices at which farmers could sell their produce continued for much longer the country would be faced with a serious problem due to the absence of certain food supplies. They were right, and in 1918 rationing of butter and margarine was introduced nationwide, with milk also in short supply.

The fixing of meat prices, and the high prices of cattle food, was clearly an issue that threatened the livelihoods of many a farmer in Derbyshire and during the autumn and early winter of 1917 farmers could only hope that the policy would be reconsidered before its full effect was felt in January.

However, the concerns and protests of farmers and butchers (for it impacted upon the profits of butchers, which is discussed in a later chapter) across the country failed to prevent its implementation. At the meeting of the Derbyshire War Agricultural committee in Derby on 9 January 1918 it was said price fixing had led to a 'serious diminution in production' and was a greater danger to the country's food supply than the U boats.

Immediately prior to the introduction of fixed meat prices, a 'wholesale murder' of animals took place, with animals killed which were not fit for slaughter, before price fixing was introduced, so they could be sold at a price considered, by the farmers, to be more reasonable.

It had been hoped that by the time of the full introduction of the Prices of Meat Order the Government would have reduced the cost of feeding stuffs for livestock. Lamentably this had not occurred. It was said that in January 1918 in Derbyshire that dairy farmers with large herds of cattle were unable to purchase more than 15cwt of animal feed per week. Even with the most stringent practice of economy this was considered 'totally inadequate'.

Chesterfield's MP, Barnet Kenyon, sympathised with Derbyshire's farmers. At a meeting of the Derbyshire Farmers' Union on 5 January 1918 he told farmers he understood their frustration when 'crank' schemes were introduced. However, he hoped they would recognise the schemes were part of emergency legislation and new to everybody, not just the farmers but also the administrators. He believed there was a glimpse of hope on the horizon with regards the war and that if the farmers hung together and did all that was humanly possible to feed the nation it would be worth it, even if it meant a few months of real sacrifice.

Other farm produce that became increasingly scarce in 1917 and 1918 in Derbyshire, as elsewhere, were jam and marmalade leading to rationing. The short supply of jam and marmalade was due to the shortage of sugar from 1917 and the failure of fruit crops the following year.

Despite their difficulties, farmers contributed to the war effort not only by producing food and milk, and hay for the war horses, but also by raising funds for worthy causes. For example, in February 1915 farmers in Alfreton held a jumble sale of livestock to raise funds for the Prince of Wales Relief Fund and the Belgian Refugees Fund. In Chesterfield, in May 1915, a Derbyshire Farmers' War Sale was held in aid of the War Relief Fund. 'Golden ducks' and a 'perfect mannered pony' were among the fares at the 'jumble sale'.

CHAPTER 12

The Role of Women

Just weeks before the outbreak of war, during a national incendiary campaign by suffragists, a plot to destroy one of Derbyshire's most famous landmarks was uncovered. Churches across the country had been set ablaze as part of the increasingly militant campaign by women to obtain the vote and a telegram from Sheffield to the church keeper at the Chesterfield Parish Church warned that suffragists intended to set the church, and its famous crooked spire, ablaze. The church was locked up and guarded; and thankfully no effort was made to cause it damage. In that town suffragettes occasionally addressed crowds from the pump in the Market Place. In May 1914 a window at Mr Sowter's millinery shop in Derby was smashed and 'votes for women' scrawled on walls. A fire at Breadsall church on 5 June 1914 was suspected to be the work of suffragettes. In Derby in June, three suffragettes tried to hold a meeting in the Market Place but crowds of angry men would not let them speak, hooting and jeering at the speakers. The women fled to the police station, were followed by a mob, and had to escape via the back door.

The militant suffragist campaign ran alongside a more peaceful campaign of suffragettes, who had been active in Derbyshire, as elsewhere, for decades. During the spring months of 1914 Mrs Pethick-Lawrence had addressed crowds in Derby.

The popular tactic of going on hunger strike when imprisoned was debated in the House of Commons shortly before the outbreak of war, when Sir A. Markham MP, the member for Mansfield who was born at Ringwood Hall in Chesterfield, argued that they should not be force-fed but that these 'malignants' should be left to die.

With the outbreak of war, and departure of thousands of men, the opportunity arose for women to make a contribution to prove their worth and display patriotism, and it was decided to abandon militant campaigning. Women of the suffragette movement, and those with no association with the campaign for female suffrage, began to carry out work to help men who had enlisted.

Suffragettes in Chesterfield's Market Place prior to the war. *Courtesy of Derbyshire Libraries and www.picturethepast.org.uk*

They formed comforts committees, mainly producing items for the Red Cross Society for the benefit of soldiers and sailors, with branches of the Society formed across the county. They wasted no time in knitting warm clothing, or purchasing articles of clothing where possible.

Such was the enthusiasm of women that by the end of February 1915 91,533 articles were sent by Derbyshire women; and during a one-year period between August 1917 and August 1918 the number of garments bought or made by women in Derbyshire was an impressive 1,167,880.

Local women also washed the men's clothes in towns and villages where soldiers were billeted, and some cooked meals for the men.

The collection of eggs was also a key campaign by women, with tens of thousands of eggs being collected across the county for the benefit of wounded soldiers in Derbyshire's hospitals, as well as soldiers in hospitals in France. In Derby alone women collected 2,168 eggs over the course of three Fridays. A national campaign during August and September 1915 aimed to obtain one million eggs; and Derbyshire women helped exceed that target.

There were many opportunities for women to help raise funds for the war itself, as well as for organisations such as the War Relief Fund, the Red Cross, the Belgian Refugee funds and local hospitals. Flag Days and Flower Days were frequently held to raise money for local charities. The events were largely organised and executed by women who were keen to remind people from 1915 onwards that Derbyshire folk generally, and especially those in the towns, had more money than ever before and so they should be generous.

Women helped implement and administer some of the new schemes to alleviate difficulties on the home and war fronts. For example, when the National Register was set up to aid recruitment to the army, women organised the delivery and collection of the forms and the compilation of the data, although it was felt 'advisable' in Chesterfield that women should not deliver or collect the forms; instead they were required to prepare the forms, work in the Recruiting Office and compile the information to send to the War Office.

Women also helped produce and distribute rationing cards and books when local and national rationing schemes were introduced.

Women also took part in paid employment. Although there had been some female teachers in Derbyshire before August 1914, it was a male dominated profession. As male teachers across the county left their jobs to become soldiers there became an opportunity for more women to take on the role of educating children. More women would have joined the profession, it was said in April 1917, if the schools were not so dirty, only being cleaned once

Women in Whaley Bridge, during a fundraising event for the Red Cross. *Courtesy of Derbyshire Libraries and www.picturethepast.org.uk*

a quarter, and if it were not for the dirty condition of the children, with one in ten children in Derbyshire being described as 'verminous' in a report by Dr Barwise, the School Medical Officer for Derbyshire.

In June 1914 a statue of Florence Nightingale was unveiled by the Duke of Devonshire on London Road in Derby. It was quite apt because although women had been nurses prior to the war commencing, with the almost constant flow of large numbers of wounded servicemen in Derbyshire's pre-established and makeshift hospitals, many more nurses were required.

There were lots of volunteers from the early stages of war in Derbyshire's Voluntary Aid Detachment (VAD) hospitals. Vera Brittain, who worked for a short time at a VAD hospital in her home town of Buxton, writes very critically of the women of that town, with the 'ladies of the Buxton elite' attempting to 'provincialise the war' for their self image. 'At the First Aid and Home Nursing classes they cluttered about the presiding doctor like hens round a barnyard cock, and one or two representatives of "the set", who never learnt any of the bandages correctly themselves, went about showing everybody else how to do them', she recalled in her book *Testament of Youth*.

Brittain started working as a VAD nurse soon after an urgent appeal, in April 1915, for 3,000 nurses. Women were needed for VAD hospitals at home and overseas. The nurses were required to have First Aid and Nursing certificates. A trial of one or two weeks was offered and if they were deemed suitable they were given further work.

The following year, in March 1916, the Duchess of Devonshire, president of the Derbyshire Red Cross, appealed for even more nurses when announcing the establishment of the Derbyshire Nursing Association, which was based in Chesterfield.

The Association was needed due to a greater need for nurses due to war wounded but also because the war had highlighted the poor health of the civilian population, with so many men being deemed unfit for military service, and in particular the health of infants with a higher rate of infant mortality in Derbyshire at this stage of the war than in the recent years preceding its outbreak.

Furthermore, women helped produce bandages and dressings for the patients, with ten miles of flannel and 1¼ tons of wool sent round to workers in the county every month by September 1918.

Women also took on roles that had previously been carried out solely, or largely, by men. As increasing numbers of men joined the forces a shortage of labour led to companies employing women, such as bus and tram conductresses, factory workers, shop workers and clerks.

In November 1915 women began delivering the post on some routes in Derby. The following month women began working as tram conductresses in Derby but there was tremendous opposition. The Town Council stated special considerations had to be given due to the effects of the weather on their health and the effect that running up and down stairs might have. The Tramways Committee made it clear it had only reluctantly decided to introduce women conductresses because they had failed to find sufficient male labour. The Committee was congratulated by the council for having held back the introduction of female labour for so long.

As women were paid less than their male counterparts, men began to worry that women would soon be taking their jobs as companies used the war as an excuse to save money on wages.

At a meeting of the Railway Clerks Association on 1 February 1915 at the Clifton Hotel in Chesterfield, the chairman, Mr T. Clarke, said he had read in the January issue of *Railway Clerk* that all railway clerks between the ages of 50 and 60 were being replaced by girls. He told the meeting he would rather have a Zeppelin in their midst than see the introduction of lady clerks who would, he believed, do far more damage than a Zeppelin.

Despite concerns by Clarke and his colleagues about women entering their ranks, there were soon positive reports of female involvement in another

A female tram conductress at Codnor during the First World War. *Courtesy of Wood Collection and www.picturethepast.org.uk*

section of railway work. In April 1915 it was reported that the 'experiment' to replacing some of the 4,000 railway porters, nationally, who were joining the forces, with women, was 'meeting with considerable success' on the Great Central Railway. Before the war there had been between fifty and sixty women employed on the Great Central Railway, as carriage cleaners, but by April 1915 there were approximately 400 women working at stations, fulfilling roles including ticket sorters, typists, shorthand writers, telegraphists, telephone operators and secretarial work.

There was even stronger opposition in one of Derbyshire's key industries when attempts were made to integrate women into the collieries. At a meeting of the Council of the Derbyshire Miners' Association at Chesterfield on 4 March 1916 there was heated discussion about 'certain colliery companies' including the Waleswood Colliery, who were seeking female labour. A resolution was passed 'strongly deprecating' the initiative and that if attempts to employ women were not halted the members of the Association would consider strike action. Women continued to be employed in some collieries and quarries, such as those of the Stancliffe Estate Company, crushing gritstone and cutting stone blocks.

Despite the concerns held by men about the threat women posed to their own positions, and the perceived inability of women to carry out 'men's work', as more and more men joined the Colours there was a serious labour shortage across all industries.

As part of Queen Mary's fund to help women find work, the Mayoress of Derby, Mrs E. Hill, held a conference with Derby employers in March 1915 to encourage them to take on women. Funding was needed for the scheme to pay for training and to ensure the women's wages were decent.

Towards the end of March 1915, mass employment of women within industry, agriculture and clerical work commenced, with a Register of Women for War Service set up by the Board of Trade.

Women interested in paid employment within industry, agriculture, or clerical work were encouraged to have their details entered in the Register. 'Any woman who by working helps to release a man or to equip a man for fighting does national war service', it was said. The appeal to the patriotism of women would certainly have encouraged them to do what they could and would have been particularly appealing for those who had worked prior to marriage and having children, but due to their husband or other males on whom they financially relied, being at war would have needed a better income. It would also have appealed to those who lost their jobs at the beginning of the war. Whilst War Relief Funds and the continuation of some companies paying wages for staff who had joined the Colours had eased some of the financial problems, the relatively high wages paid, particularly in some of the factories, were a much more acceptable alternative even if they were still paid less than men doing the same work, even if it meant long hours, strenuous work and entering a male orientated world which was, in most cases, completely alien to them.

In January 1916 training classes began in Derby to teach women skills in clerical and commercial work. Women were especially needed in banks, railway offices and commercial houses to replace men. There were two courses, one lasting four weeks (teaching commercial arithmetic, correspondence, business methods and bookkeeping) and another lasting eight weeks (teaching the same as the four week course but also shorthand and typewriting). Students had to be well educated and aged over seventeen and were required to undertake a test and interview to assess their suitability.

Women helped feed Derbyshire at a time when there were fears of famine. As shown in another chapter, labour shortages on farms were contributing to food shortages. After hopes to secure adequate child labour failed, and when attempts to overturn decisions for the calling up of male farm workers also failed, and with demands for increasing amounts of land to be cultivated, farmers began to turn to women.

Strong opposition remained. For example in March 1916 a farmer from Gleadless (which at this time was part of Derbyshire) applied for military exemption for a farmhand. He was asked if he would employ women in the man's place, but responded that he had given two women a chance in January but they had only worked two half days in a total of seven weeks.

Attitudes began to slowly change and more women were employed on the land as farmers recognised their potential and due to the continued depletion of the male workforce. Women were employed out of necessity, but reluctant and sceptical employers soon found very pleasing results. Increasingly, there were some farmers who wanted to employ women and teach them how to carry out useful work, but there were others who were reluctant to employ women unless they possessed some of the skills needed, and in this regard the Derbyshire Women's Agricultural Committee, organised by Miss E.B. Jackson of Stubben Edge Farm in Ashover, was pivotal.

During 1916 the Committee, assisted by the Derbyshire Education Committee, began teaching farm work at Dronfield Woodhouse, on the farm of Mr Oldman. The scheme was reported as being successful with enthusiastic instruction in basic farm skills including milking, sharpening tools, pulling and dressing turnips, hoeing and weeding. The classes were held only once a week, and lasted just two hours, but this was considered sufficient, by the organisers, to enable women to work on farms, full-time. It was hoped further training centres could be set up on working farms ad greater cooperation from farmers.

In January 1917 elements of Derbyshire County Council believed women should not work on farms because they may cause jealousy from farmwives. They also questioned the effects of farmwork, working with men, on their physical and moral well being. Dr Barwise, however, pointed out that his niece worked on a farm and her physical health had considerably improved.

Fitzherbert Wright MP urged farmers to change their attitude towards women if they were to resolve the labour issue. He knew from experience on his own farm at Yeldersley, that the women worked hard. Approximately 200 women offered themselves in Derbyshire to work full time on farms but many more were needed.

Despite continued hostility, women applied themselves well to farm work when given the opportunity and they began to be more sought after, especially as harvest time approached. At a meeting of Ashbourne Women's War Agricultural Committee in June 1917 it was said farmers were overcoming their prejudice.

According to Jackson in a report produced in July 1917 to show the work of the Derbyshire Women's Agricultural Committee, in addition to basic farm work an increasing number of women in the Buxton area of the county began carrying out more arduous work including felling trees, building walls, making roads, joinery, as well as working towards cultivating several hundred acres of new land. In Youlgreave and district pit props were being made out of the timber, to help colliery workers who had opposed women workers in their pits, and women also helped load and transport the timber as well as carrying out administrative duties such as keeping stock records. Thirty women were sawing the timber and it was said that five women could do the work of four men. Women also worked in brickfields, quarrying clay. It was remarked that they worked in all weathers, having worked in the woods in the snow during the previous winter, and often walked up to four miles a day before commencing work.

Jackson appealed for more women to join their ranks and also appealed for farmers to contact her if they were willing to help with training. Lots of farmers were still sceptical, especially regarding the relatively short nature of the training, which now lasted a maximum of five weeks. At a later meeting, in September 1917, Jackson said that whilst progress had not been great due to farmers' resistance, they needed to be given a chance, and they needed support. 'There is no fear of the women of Derbyshire funking work even under disagreeable conditions. Give us a helping hand and we shall be able to do a good deal more for you than we have done in the past.' This plea was certainly persuasive because immediately afterwards a South Normanton farmer asked for women to assist in potato harvesting.

In a report of the work of the Derbyshire Women's Agricultural Committee for the year ending 31 December 1917, Miss E.B. Jackson described how selection committees at Ilkeston, Chesterfield and Derby selected suitable women from those who had offered themselves as recruits for the recently formed Land Army under the National Service scheme. An instruction committee then took responsibility for training the women and by the end of 1917, fifty-eight women had been trained and were working on farms. New training farms were running at Mr Wall's farm in Rowsley, Mr Bowler's farm at Matlock, Mr Richardson's farm at Dalbury Lees near Ashbourne and Captain Fitzherbert Wright's farm at Yeldersley. An autumn demonstration had been held to showcase the abilities of the women, at Mr Richardson's training farm and also at a farm in Clay Cross. The women were found to be working in a 'satisfactory manner'.

Women's Institutes were established in Ashover, Chinley, Lea and Holloway and Handley. The Women's Institute was formed in 1915 to revitalise rural communities by producing more food and encouraging women to learn new skills.

In May 1918 a campaign was established to get more women on the land, to meet a new government target of 30,000 across the country. Due to soldier labour which had been promised no longer being available, and men released to farm work being recalled, due to increased demands on the Western Front during the Spring Offensive, women were needed in numbers larger than ever before, especially as the hay harvest approached. Minimum wages were fixed by the government at £1 per week for unskilled women and £1 2s when they had passed an efficiency test.

Mrs Kellett, the travelling inspector of women's work under the Board of Agriculture, spoke to women at Derby Technical College on 7 May 1918, to encourage them to join the Land Army. They were told the Land Army was a mobile force whose members agreed to work in any part of the country, although most worked in their own county. Women were able to sign up for six months, with no training required, or a year, with a six-week training course. A rally was held in Derby from 30 May to 1 June to recruit women.

Another role which women in Derbyshire played during the war, which also helped the nation's food stocks, was in educating people in food economy, especially as food shortages became more serious.

In November 1917 a women's subcommittee of the Food Control Committee was formed in Chesterfield to provide allotments to women, give cookery demonstrations and to produce and distribute leaflets and other literature promoting food economy. It was suggested speakers visit places of worship on Sundays to encourage congregations to be sensible with food.

In February 1918 the sub-committee set up the first communal kitchen in the country, where people could buy wholesome meals at affordable prices, at a time when certain foods were scarce and/or rationed. Women in other parts of the county followed suit.

Women worked in increasing numbers in all of the factories detailed in the 'Derbyshire's War Workshops' chapter and in some instances women made up the majority of the workforce, notably at the Locomotive Works in Derby and the munitions factory at Langwith.

The introduction of women in many of the factories, in particular those making munitions, was scoffed at but it was not long before managers were recognising the abilities of their new workers.

Women workers at the Langwith Munitions Factory in 1916. *Courtesy of Derbyshire Libraries and www.picturethepast.org.uk*

The War Budget,
December 30th, 1915.

The Girl Behind the Gun

The Girl Tommy Atkins left behind-him has enlisted in the great Munition Corps with " barracks " all over the country. There are now few processes in shell and cartridge manufacture with which women cannot be trusted. Above, percussion caps are being fitted, and below is a section of the testing room, where girls are gauging the shell cases as they pass along on a travelling belt.

201

This page appeared in the 30 December 1915 issue of the war magazine *The War Budget* and shows women in English munitions factories. Above: percussion caps being fitted. Below: final inspection of shell cases on a travelling belt. *Author's Collection*

The women were often required to work in extreme heat, with fumes and smoke, carrying out difficult work over lengthy shifts, sometimes travelling several miles each day to get to work (indeed many women, and some men, travelled daily from Derby to Chilwell to work in the munitions factory there). It was understandably very trying and they were usually paid less than their male colleagues. Chemists made available phosphorous tablets to women workers, which were advertised as making 'nerves strong and steady, restoring vigour, vitality, endurance and strength to the weak and aged and making long hours and hard work seem easy'.

At Chilwell the women were known as 'canaries' on account of the chemicals they were working with turning their skin yellow and their hair green.

Companies began training women to enhance their skills. For example, at the Robinson & Sons company in Chesterfield, towards the end of the war a Factory School was set up to provide four weeks of work experience to girls aged under sixteen prior to them commencing full time work.

Although most women lost their jobs as men returned from war, they had proved themselves to be important members of society and for this reason as early as February 1918 the Representation of the People Act was granted royal assent, giving women aged thirty and over, the vote, but only if they were either a member of, or married to a member, of the Local Government Register, a property owner, or a graduate in a university constituency, which meant that many women who had worked in the war effort were still not eligible to vote. Nonetheless, it was a step in the right direction and in a little over four years they had achieved more through peaceful participation in war than in decades of defiance, disturbance and destruction; and in Derby alone 24,470 women became eligible to vote in the 1918 General Election and 24,498 could vote in local elections. At the same time the voting age for men was reduced to twenty-one in order to allow more of those who had fought in the war to have a democratic voice.

Women in Derbyshire were told the vote was now a right, but with it came responsibility. At a meeting of the Derbyshire Branch of the National Union of Women Workers in the month that the Act went on the statute books, Mrs Ogilvie Gordon, president of the union, spoke about citizenship. She urged women to look into issues such as housing, education and divorce reform in light of bills being presented before parliament. She asked women to use the power of the vote and to stand for election for town councils. A scheme of Women's Citizens' Associations was being drawn up, she added.

Launching the Association in Chesterfield, Mrs Fisher, wife of H.A.L.

Fisher (Minister of Education) addressed a large crowd of women in the Market Hall. The war had made them all think what a wastage there had been on the women power in Great Britain, she said, and now they had got the vote they meant to use it in the best possible way for the country. She hoped women would be consulted on housing matters, especially the design of homes to make them comfortable and conveniently arranged and help improve infant welfare, and be involved in issues such as assistance for children of unmarried mothers, venereal disease and education.

In an article in the June 1918 issue of *The Link*, a magazine for employees of Robinson's & Sons, an employee named Betsy wrote, 'it is up to us now to refute all the misrepresentations as to our capabilities which have been against us in the past, and it behoves all of us who will shortly become fully-fledged members of the community to study all matters of interest to ourselves, in so far as local or Parliamentary conditions prevail. The next election will be fought with grave issues at stake respecting many years to come. After war problems will require urgent attention, and the care of the widow, orphans and children of those killed in this terrible war, are by no means least among problems where women will be able to prove their worth as citizens.'

Prior to the war some women in public life were only known as the wives of prominent men and they spoke at events because of their association to those men. During the war they obtained prominence in their own right by leading the way with comfort committees and other important work outlined above. As a result they began obtaining public office themselves.

On 25 September the Mayoress of Derby, Mrs E.J. Hulse, was unanimously elected a councillor at a meeting of the Town Council following the death of John Dean.

While women voted for the very first time, in December 1918, Chesterfield-born Lady Violet Carruthers was amongst the women who tried to become MPs, although not in Derbyshire. She hoped to win the Mansfield seat which had been held by her brother before his death in 1916. It was her brother, Arthur Markham, who was so outspoken about the 'malignant' suffragettes prior to the outbreak of war. She provided many reasons why she should be elected: she had been a member of the Executive Committee of the National Relief Fund, a member of the Central Committee of Women's Training and Employment and Deputy Director of the women's section of the National Service Department. She was also a staunch ally of the working class, despite her privileged background and had been one of the first recipients of the order of the Companions of Honour, in August 1917.

However, Mansfield was not ready for a female Member of Parliament or at least not ready for Carruthers to represent them. She came third in the poll.

However, Carruther's political activities continued. In 1924, she became a Chesterfield town councillor and in 1927 became the town's first female mayor. She also continued to involve herself in issues affecting women, holding positions on several national committees, including the Lord Chancellor's Advisory Committee for Women Justices.

CHAPTER 13

1915

As the first full year of war opened, people across Britain and indeed in the Allied nations in Europe, joined together to pray, with a Day of Intercession on Sunday 3 January. Regular churchgoers were joined by those who rarely, or indeed never usually ranked among members of the congregation, as people sought an end to the war and protection of their loved ones. Great emphasis was placed upon the importance of attending church. As H.C. MacKenzie of Old Brampton put it in a letter to the *Derbyshire Times*, 'Only three kinds of people will be absent from places of worship on Sunday; the sick, those who do not believe in God, and those who do not love their country.'

Despite the worries and need for prayers there was also a need to allow children to be children and to keep up their spirits, especially if they had a father in the armed forces.

In Derby, more than 400 children of Rolls-Royce employees enjoyed a New Year party, with food, entertainment and music. A christmas tree with hundreds of electric lights proved highly popular.

On the afternoon of 5 January there were parties for the children of Chesterfield's soldiers. The parties, organised by the Chesterfield War Relief Committee, were held at the Central Schools. They were funded by the mayor who was described as 'the children's friend' and were attended by approximately 800 children aged between five and twelve. Those under five were given a toy in their own home. The decorations were of 'fascinating colour and light', and cotton wool hanging from the ceiling gave a snowy appearance. For the younger children there was a huge christmas tree, and for the older children a scale model of HMS *Arethusa*, which was known as 'the destroyer of destroyers'. The model was constructed at Bryan Donkins, but the water tubes of the actual ship had been manufactured by the Chesterfield Tube Company.

A large amount of food was on offer and after eating, the entertainment commenced. Archdeacon Crosse played the role of Father Christmas, and other characters present included John Bull, a British Admiral, a clown, a jester, a Hindu and Father Time. Conjuring tricks, ventriloquism, a Punch and Judy show and a band performance were highlights. The children sang patriotic songs and the Mayor read a reply to a telegram he had sent to the King offering New Year's greetings on behalf of the children. The reply read: 'I am desired by the King to thank you for your telegram and for the loyal assurances and good wishes to which it gives expression on behalf of the children of the soldiers and sailors of Chesterfield.' After reading this 'ear-splitting' cheers were given to the Mayor and the King.

At the conclusion of festivities each child was given a toy and a bag containing two oranges, two tangerines, two apples and a packet of chocolate. The fruit was provided by the Mayor, who was a greengrocer by trade. After the children left, approximately 300 adults danced as the band played on.

Whilst the adults present at the children's party were able to enjoy some celebrations, there was increasing discontent in Derby and Chesterfield and their districts due to public houses being forced to close at 9pm, on account of soldiers being stationed in those towns, which came into force on 8 January.

Landlords of public houses argued the 9 o'clock closing order was not warranted. It had been introduced to prevent drunkenness among soldiers so that they would be more alert should an invasion take place. Licensees argued that landlocked Derbyshire was more remote from invasion than most other parts of the country yet it had the earliest closing times in the land. In Mansfield, pubs closed at 11pm, in Sheffield 9:30pm; and in Buxton, which was the headquarters of one of the battalions of the Sherwood Foresters, the pubs closed later than in Chesterfield.

In Chesterfield Councillors joined the call for a later closing time. Councillor Lancaster, Chairman of the Markets Committee, pointed out the earlier closing time was having a detrimental effect on the Saturday market (markets being held on Saturday evenings). A brief extension to the closing time was allowed, with public houses being permitted to remain open until 10pm whilst the decision was reviewed.

A deputation of councillors met with Lieutenant-Colonel Becks on 18 January to discuss the 'considerable criticisms' to the early closing times. Although special functions or special gatherings in connection with societies or clubs could continue until 10pm, with the Chief Constable's consent, it was necessary that pubs should close at 9pm, the councillors were informed, because soldiers were billeted in the town and the rule would also have to apply to civilians because it would be wrong to treat civilians any differently to soldiers.

Following the meeting, the opinion was sought of Lieutenant-Colonel WK Emslie, the Officer Commanding the 13th Battalion Lancashire Fusiliers who were quartered in Chesterfield. He had no objection to a later closing time because there had been no trouble from his men due to drink.

Emslie's support was conveyed to the Northern Command in York but achieved nothing. If the town felt hard done by because neighbouring villages and towns where troops were not quartered had public houses that could close at 10pm, the magistrates in those places could impose the 9pm closing time.

The earlier pub closing hours helped lead to a reduction in the number of convictions for drunkenness. In his annual report to the magistrates on 13 February, the Deputy Chief Constable (Mr R Faulkner) revealed there had been no convictions in Chesterfield for drunkenness following the introduction of the 9pm closing order, although a conviction did occur on 27 February; but generally drunkenness fell.

An increase in beer tax in January led to a fall in beer drinking, as it was intended, but the tax backfired because the drinking of cider and spirits significantly increased.

There were reports at this time of wives of soldiers spending their separation allowances on drink and neglecting their children. The NSPCC in Derby said it was no truer to slur the reputations of wives on the basis of a few isolated cases than to say Britain was a cruel nation because a small proportion were cruel and neglected their children.

During March 1915 the earlier closing order was extended to the whole of Derbyshire for public houses and clubs. This ensured there was equality because previously licensed premises just outside the restricted areas had benefited at the expense of the others.

Soldiers and sailors stationed in Chesterfield, or receiving medical care in the town, were able to enjoy a 'homely, cheery, attractive rendezvous' when the YMCA rooms opened on Knifesmithgate. They were informally opened on 7 January 1915 but the official opening ceremony took place on 3 February. A well-stocked reading room was provided, along with games. Whist drives were held and there were some gym facilities. The Elder Yard Mission was converted into a concert hall providing regular entertainment to the men. Between the informal opening and the official ceremony, approximately 6,100 visits had been made, for relaxation, recreation or to use the various services available, which included the provision of light refreshments, a savings bank and a post office. Letters written at the rooms were sent free of charge, and almost 3,000 were sent in the four weeks preceding the official opening. Appeals were made for the generosity of Chesterfield folk to help fund it.

YMCA rooms on Glumangate were later opened for the benefit of wives and mothers of soldiers and sailors, so that they would have a venue to socialise in. The rooms became known as the Tipperary Rooms.

The official opening of the Knifesmithgate YMCA rooms coincided with the official welcoming to Chesterfield of the 13th Service Battalion of the Lancashire Fusiliers, who had arrived on 5 December 1914 and whose presence was responsible for the earlier pub closing hours. There had been some claims, which appeared to be baseless, of bad behaviour by the troops. It would seem some of the Chesterfield people disliked the soldiers on account of their Lancashire customs. Archdeacon Crosse urged Chesterfield folk to give the soldiers hospitality by inviting them into their homes and in doing so strike up acquaintances. He emphasised that the Lancashire men came from homes that were just the same as many in Chesterfield.

On 5 February, further Lancashire Fusiliers arrived in the town and they were described as being 'an exceptionally fine body of men' with 'exemplary behaviour'. Gradually they were more warmly received, but they left the town in April 1915.

New YMCA rooms opened in March 1915 at Eden Lodge, Spital and Wesleyan Schools, Hasland, due to the arrival of two companies of Army Service Corps from Aldershot, who were quartered at Highfields and Hasland Hall. Appeals were made for decorations, pictures, books, magazines, music books, a gramophone and records, sports equipment, boxing gloves, fencing sticks and any other recreational items, as well as comforts such as socks and mittens.

As the men of Lancashire and the Army Service Corps arrived there were concerns that Derbyshire men were not doing enough and that there were too many shirkers in the county. Speaking at a meeting to establish a battalion of the Home Guard, Archdeacon Crosse told of the hundreds of young men who were 'simply shirkers'. It was a sorry state of affairs, he added, when three quarters of volunteers were married men. He wanted it to be widely thought that Chesterfield did not want young men staying in the town if they could go and fight.

In order to encourage more Derbyshire men to fight, F.C. Arkwright of Willersley, Cromford, promoted a scheme to identify the bravest village in the country. In order to be eligible the village would have a population between 150 and 7,500. The winner would be the one which had the highest proportion of its residents enlist to the armed forces and would have a special village cross built as a tribute to the men. Knowlton in Kent was the eventual winner.

In January 1915 the men of the 1st/5th and 1st/6th Battalions of Sherwood Foresters prepared to leave Britain for France. The Reserve 2nd/6th Battalion stationed at Buxton left Derbyshire in order to train further so that its members could replace those who were to be wounded or killed. The people of Buxton were sorry to see the men leave, because their conduct over the three months of their stay had been exemplary, and local tradesmen had benefited from the soldiers' custom. The seventeen officers and 768 men of the 2nd/5th left Swanwick, where they had been training, on two trains on 3 February.

Owing to the expectation of significant casualties, an appeal was made for 300-400 men to form a second reserve battalion, to be known as the 3rd/5th Battalion, and 400 men were needed to form the 3rd/6th Battalion, with training commencing as soon as weapons were received. By 30 January, more than 100 men had volunteered for the 3rd/6th and it was said they were of a very good class.

By 6 February, more than 300 of the 400 men sought for the 3rd/6th had volunteered and prospective volunteers were urged to hurry up and enlist otherwise they would find that the full number had already been achieved and they would have to enlist with another battalion. It was said that lots of married men were signing up, putting young single men of the county to shame.

In order to reach the desired figures for both reserve battalions, recruitment campaigns continued across the county. In Alfreton the town became a 'sort of military camp' for a week in February when the 300 men of the 3rd/6th Battalion thus far recruited were billeted in the town. When they arrived they received a 'hearty welcome'. There were 'impressive' marches in the town and opportunities for the men to 'fraternise' with the local civilians. Speeches and parades took place throughout the week, with the men visiting surrounding villages, with the primary intention of encouraging others to join the two new reserve battalions, as well as allowing the men to practice their marching. It was particularly hoped that men in the surrounding villages such as South Normanton and Tibshelf would be stirred into action.

The men marched throughout Alfreton, through South Normanton, Somercotes, Lea Brooks, Greenhill Lane, Codnor and Ripley, 'picturesque and old-world' Pentrich, Swanwick, Pye Bridge, Ironville, Codnor Park and Jacksdale. There was generally 'glorious weather' which encouraged men to watch the marching and join up, although on one day a severe snowstorm occurred but did not prevent the march. When not marching and undertaking training, the men enjoyed concerts and games and other amusements in reading rooms, provided by the Church of England Men's Society.

The week's events were considered successful, with approximately 100 new recruits. The first eighty-four were paraded on the Tuesday morning and were dispatched to Derby, with eighty-two of them joining the 3rd/5th Battalion. Before leaving Alfreton for Wingfield Station to travel to Derby, Major Heathcote reminded the new recruits that they were making the first stage of their journey to Berlin. On the Thursday morning, a further twelve men left for Derby to join up.

Prior to their return to Chesterfield, the soldiers gave a concert to the townspeople by way of thanks for their hospitality. When it was time to leave hundreds of residents saw them off at King Street. Pupils from the National Schools were said to be particularly loud in their enthusiastic cheers for the soldiers.

Shortly after the military visit to Alfreton, a woman of that district signed her husband up without his knowledge. He knew nothing of it until he got a letter telling him to go for a medical. She told him, 'Brother Jack's gone so you've got to go too. Besides I promised to love, honour and obey and isn't this an honour for you?'

As more and more men were needed for the Army, towards the end of February the War Office further reduced the height requirement for certain regiments to 5ft 1in, although this did not apply to the regiments of the Sherwood Foresters. The age requirement of 19-38 remained the same, as did the chest measurement of 34 inches.

It was announced in February that 500 men of the Army Service Corps and twenty-one officers were to be billeted at Matlock Bath, but this number was soon massively increased and preparations had to be made to house 4,500 men within Matlock and Matlock Bath. Four hundred were lodged in Matlock Bath, with accommodation in private housing and in the Old and New Pavilions. Four tons of straw for bedding and hundreds of blankets were delivered. Joseph Hardy, the vice-chairman of South Darley Urban Council did well out of the arrangements. As a butcher whose premises were in Matlock Bath he secured the contract to provide meat for the troops. Other catering was provided by John W. Boden of South Parade, Matlock Bath. A canteen was open daily.

As Joseph Hardy and others gained large numbers of new customers due to the war, there was discontent across the county at the escalating prices of food. However, the complaints were not entirely justified according to the editor of the *Derbyshire Times*. In an editorial of 20 February he wrote, 'During the Napoleonic War, and at the time of the Crimean campaign, the prices of to-day would have been hailed with thanksgiving, and even a year ago if politicians had been told that after six months of world-wide strife, the cost of living would be no more than it now is, they would have found it difficult to credit such an optimistic forecast.'

This was of little consolation to the small shopkeeper who found that there was growing support for the Cooperative movement as a cheaper alternative to dearer independent retailers.

'Struggling Tradesman' wrote to the *Derbyshire Times* in February to express the difficulties smaller retailers faced. 'When the little shopkeeper has passed out of existence, sad will be the day for England, Ireland and Scotland! We pay three times the rates of a dwelling house. I ask the public to think of us, especially in this time of trouble! Don't take all your ready to the Co-op and leave us with the "nod" ... Brothers don't forget us. We do our best for you.'

During February there were warnings of spies in the Midlands. Two men in khaki had gained access to a works carrying out naval work and had made enquiries regarding the presence or absence of anti aircraft guns.

With the imminent departure of the 1st/5th and 1st/6th Battalions there was an appeal to fund field cookers enabling the men to have hot meals whilst on marches. The government could not provide the cookers, which were especially needed during the colder months.

When the time came for the men to leave Britain, on 25 February 1915, the Bishop of Southwell wrote a letter to the *Derby Mercury* and *Derbyshire Times* in which he said 'In many a home today there will be a mixed feeling of pride and anxiety.' The letter was accompanied by a prayer which he wrote to be used by relatives of the men of the 5th and 6th battalions, as well as members of the 7th (men of Nottingham and district) and 8th (men of Newark and districts) battalions of the Sherwood Foresters. Part of the prayer read, 'O merciful Father, we commend to Thy care all those who have now gone forth to serve their country. Thou knowest the places where they are, and the dangers which beset them. Be Thou to each one a shield and defence. Give unto him courage and patience, and at all times a knowledge of Thy presence.'

According to one of the Sherwood Foresters, in a letter printed in the *Derbyshire Times* on 6 March 1915, they were given a 'hearty send off' when leaving Braintree, with large numbers of people lining the streets. When they arrived in Southampton the vast number of men and all their kit resulted in it taking two hours before they could board the ship. Immediately upon completion of boarding they set sail and the men 'gave a silent goodbye to England'. Many of them would never return.

Rumours of significant casualties spread throughout Derbyshire in the days following the arrival in France of the 1st/5th and 1st/6th battalions. The *Derbyshire Times* contacted the War Office to establish if there was any truth to the rumours only to receive a reply stating, 'Particulars of recent casualties not yet available.' Relatives of loved ones were advised to ignore any rumours, with facts being printed in the newspaper based on official War Office news.

To crush 'reckless rumours', of major casualties amongst the 1st/5th Battalion Sherwood Foresters, which had caused great pain and anxiety amongst the families who had loved ones in the regiment, the Chief Constable of Derby made enquiries and received a telegram from Colonel Mosley, the Officer Commanding the 1st/5th Battalion Notts and Derby Regiment, 'Please contradict statement that casualties have occurred in the 5th Battalion. No casualty has occurred except Sergeant Ware.'

News, from a soldier serving with the 1st/6th battalion, was printed in the *Derbyshire Times* on 13 March 1915 to put the minds of relatives at ease. Captain A.J. Hopkins wrote to his father of his journey to Belgium which despite travelling in cattle trucks with forty men in a truck, the men were 'cheerful and contented' and that the food was 'really very good'. His company, he wrote, in a letter printed in the *Derbyshire Times* on 13 March, were billeted in a deserted chateau and although they lay on straw, they considered themselves lucky. 'You can tell the Chesterfield people that the men they have sent are all cheerful and well', he added.

In a further letter he described arriving at the trenches where the noise of the guns resembled 'a continuous thunderstorm except that when a shell drops near there is a considerable shaking and one feels the concussion of the atmosphere'. Despite the war being fought around them the local civilians continued almost as normal, Hopkins claimed, with women remaining in the village and farmers continuing to plough their land. Trying to put his father's mind at rest, and thinking of the need for more men, he ended, 'The men are all splendid and none of them groans about their lot and all are keen to do their little bit, but in the midst of discomfort in everyone comes the memory of many enjoying home comforts who should be here.'

A week later, further news was received of Derbyshire men on the war front, from Sergeant R. Holmes of the 1st/6th Battalion, who said he was in

Belgium and was quite well. By 8 March 1915 there had only been one accident when a soldier was shot in the arm. 'One thing you will be pleased to know and that is there is plenty of food for all. I mention that lest you should hear from some misguided individual that our rations are short', he added.

Shortly before the 1st/5th and 1st/6th battalions left Britain, nearly 20,000 men of the West Riding Territorials, from Halifax and Huddersfield, arrived in Derby in three trains. They received a cordial welcome at the Midland Station and were billeted in schools and other large public buildings.

Some men were billeted in people's spare rooms. However, there was some disquiet that the military were taking advantage of peoples patriotism. Alf S. Hall complained that they were told they would receive an allowance for accommodating soldiers, but they were not given as much as promised. Householders found themselves having to supplement the men's meagre rations and were often out of pocket.

The YMCA hut at Victoria Hall in Derby was increasingly used by the new arrivals, as well as by those recovering in the Royal Infirmary and other local military and VAD hospitals. On 6 March, 100 wounded soldiers arrived in Derby, some of them considered very serious cases, and most of them showing signs of 'the intense stress and strain of modern warfare'.

There were, of course, continued appeals for more men. A meeting was held in Belper on 16 February to obtain more recruits. Alderman G.H. Strutt, presiding, said he could understand why young men were not forthcoming to join the army given the poor conditions, but now that the weather had settled he hoped they would come forward in large numbers. Mr Rhys added that there were some men who had been in the trenches for 100 hours at a time when there were men back home who could relieve them. He asked whether it was right that these brave soldiers should have such an unfair share of the war. Any man who could go to war, but refused, he remarked, was standing on the dead bodies of the men who had been killed. They should fight for their democracy and to smash Kaiserism. John Hancock MP described the situation in Belgium following the German invasion and how that country had looked to Britain for help. He added they had to fight for truth and justice and destroy the Kaiser so that further war was impossible. This could only be achieved if more young men came forward, he ended. Concluding the meeting Strutt stated that Derbyshire had responded well to the nation's call but that the 'sponge was not yet squeezed dry' and he hoped more young men would think about what they had heard that evening and come forward to serve their country.

In Tibshelf in late March a recruitment meeting was held during which John Hancock MP said that any man who could shoulder a rifle and hit a bullseye should enlist. He said miners in particularly had enlisted and it was very much a miner's war. He was told miners are excellent at digging trenches. Another speaker, Mr Rhys, urged men to come forward and said in the future there would be only two classes of men; those who did their duty in the country's hour of need, and those who did not.

With the 1st/5th and 1st/6th battalions at war and the 2nd/5th and 2nd/6th battalions having left the county, whilst the 3rd/5th and 3rd/6th grew in number, more troops arrived in Derbyshire. By April there were approximately 3,000 soldiers of the Royal Medical Corps and Army Service Corps camped in the Darley Dale district, living in what was almost a tented village. A YMCA hut was erected for their recreation and comfort.

In April, it was announced that no county cricket or Derbyshire League matches were to be played during the coming season. So many players had joined the colours and it was for this, and for financial reasons, that no cricket would be played. The costs of renting the cricket ground and hosting the matches were too expensive given that the club's income had greatly fallen as a result of so many of its subscribing members joining the forces. It was also considered unthinkable to have cricket played when so many of those who had played the previous summer were at war. However, occasional 'casual' games were played, including games involving soldiers. Soldiers overseas asked for any unused cricket equipment, as well as footballs, to be sent to the Front.

At the April meeting of Derbyshire County Council, held in Derby, it was agreed that financial support could be offered to the family of Dr W. Lewis Thomson, a distinguished bacteriologist who undertook bacteriological examinations of troops quartered in South Derbyshire and South Nottinghamshire, who had contracted cerebro-spinal meningitis as a result of his work and had died.

By the end of May there were concerns about the water supply in the north of Derbyshire. Due to low rainfall the reservoirs contained approximately only eighty days worth of water. People were advised not to waste water.

Colossal sums of money were discussed in May with regards to the war. The Chancellor of the Exchequer's budget revealed that if the war was to last until March 1916, at a cost of £2,100,000 a day it would cost £1,132,654,000, with ongoing costs in peacetime. If the war was to be won in only six months it would cost £787,000,000. The nation did not have this money, and even if it was to last another six months the country would be in debt by

£514,346,000. For people earning at most only a few shillings per day these figures were incomprehensible.

People in Derbyshire could better understand the human cost of war and soon there was increased discussion about this, as conscription began to look more likely. During May the Derbyshire Recruitment Committee requested censuses be taken of men of military age. Men were wanted for the army and to make munitions of war in 'practically unlimited numbers', councils were told.

Tradesmen received circulars asking for particulars of their men aged between nineteen and thirty-eight, giving details of the number that could be released to the Army, whether replacements would be required, as well as details of men and women over military age. The employers were also asked whether they would offer a guarantee to their workers that they could return to their jobs upon completion of military service.

Soldiers on the Front joined the calls to persuade men to enlist. In letters printed in newspapers they urged Derbyshire men to enlist and 'exterminate the rascals' with numerous letters stating there was 'plenty of room at the Front'. A regular message was that men should be men and not 'funks'.

Archdeacon Crosse had much to say about funks in Derbyshire and how more men were needed in the army. At a meeting of the clergy he argued here was no reason why the church could not support the war, even though the Bible taught that 'thou shalt not kill.' If a man entered someone's home with the intention of committing murder it was not wrong to use physical force, he argued, and as it is with the individual so it is with nations. Continuing his speech, he turned his attention to funks or shirkers: 'If, as I believe, the cause for which we fight be justice, honour and the common rights of man to man, it is not only honourable to volunteer and to fight and kill, but it is the common duty of every man to take his part in the conflict … For this reason we ought, I think, to demand universal conscription …'

In June, a new means by which civilians could help the war effort was devised, in the form of a War Savings Loan (commonly referred to as the 'Victory Loan'). By selling War Bonds and War Savings Certificates it was hoped to raise £910,000,000 towards the colossal cost of the war, with promises of interest at rates never before seen. According to the *Derbyshire Times* it was an 'undeniably gilt-edged investment' which appealed to the patriotism of all classes and was designed to meet the means of most. It was acknowledged that following the war there would be financial difficulties and people were encouraged to save for their own future and in doing so generate the money that would help win the war.

That same month a soldier wrote to the *Derbyshire Times* urging men to join the Army. 'If they only knew of the fun they miss they would down their tools and soon enlist', he said.

His call came at a time when there was a need for men in higher numbers than ever before, and a time when the rate of new recruits had dropped. Kitchener wrote to councils in Derbyshire in June and July 1915 thanking them for their efforts in terms of recruitment. In his letter he urged those who had not already enlisted to come forward 'to keep our force in the field at the maximum strength'. He added he wanted to know of any excuses men gave for not enlisting.

On 15 July the National Registration Act was passed and it was announced a new National Register was to be established to better organise Britain's human resources. It would reveal the number of men of military who had still not joined the Army or Navy and who among them were available for armed service, or for other essential war work such as munitions work. Announcing the scheme in the *Derbyshire Times*, the editor told readers that those who had not yet enlisted would have to answer searching questions as to why this was the case. 'The need for more men and still more men continues ... Vast reserves are necessary to make good the wastage of battle and to free for service abroad men who are completing their training ... Now is the supreme hour and from our use of it "all future results might be reckoned", he added.

As part of the drive for more men, a recruiting demonstration was held at Matlock on 17 July, when Colonel Herbert Brooke-Taylor, Lieutenant Glossop and Captain H.R. Seymore addressed a crowd. Seymore drew attention to the fact that within a hundred yards of the meeting young men were playing bowls. He hoped the audience would give a cold shoulder to those who thought bowls was better than bullets. He announced the maximum age limit had been increased to fifty in some circumstances, and he was sorry it had not been extended to sixty-one; otherwise he would happily return to war. Men who were not quite fit were now allowed to enlist, and they would find a place for anyone who came forward. For example, a man with a glass eye was given a role in a military hospital.

Speaking of the men playing bowls, and other 'slackers', Brooke-Taylor added that when you are at war and there is fear and anxiety, you become bitter at slackers at home. He told the meeting that some men had said to him that the war did not appeal to them. 'A man who talks like that is a coward', Brooke-Taylor said, 'and if I say so, a damned coward too. Cowards of that type have no right to live in the country at all, and if they are not prepared to carry out their responsibility as citizens, I would send them to the South Sea Islands and let them die of fever and their souls die afterwards.'

In order to fuel the already extreme hatred towards the Germans, Lieutenant Glossop told the crowd that the German 'beasts' had put arsenic in the water from which the 1st/6th Battalion drank, killing three of the soldiers. The Germans were also, he claimed, using young girls as human shields. Furthermore, he said, they had bashed the brains out of several dying British soldiers using rifle butts. He wanted 1,000 Sherwood Foresters to march into Berlin and bring the war to an end. When the war was over, he added, there would be a great gulf between those who did their duty and those who did not.

An interesting consequence of the war was a diminution in crime. It was remarked in July that across the county serious crime was on the decline. At the Derby Summer Assizes there were only twelve prisoners awaiting trial, with the offences described as being of a 'comparatively mild description'. This was in contrast to the twenty-four cases held during the Summer Assizes of 1914, prior to the outbreak of war, and the seventeen and twenty-two cases in the Autumn and Winter Assizes of 1914 respectively. 'It seems to me that it is another indication that during the terrible period through which we are passing crime has diminished in a most extraordinary way. Whether it is due to the war or not, I know not. It may be that in the terrible state in which the country finds itself, people's attention is fixed upon matters much more important than robbing their neighbours and committing crime. Let us hope that when the trial has passed, this country may still be marked by that excellent feature which we may trust is one of the good features of the many unhappy matters connected with the war now going on', Mr Justice Horridge remarked.

This trend would continue, with only five cases at the quarter sessions of the Autumn Assizes in October. Mr Henry St John D Raikes who presided over that session said, 'The quickening of the sense of citizenship which has been brought about by the present disastrous war is no doubt to a large extent responsible for this happy state of affairs.'

As the first anniversary of war grew nearer, further restrictions were placed on public houses and clubs to further curtail alcohol consumption. It was announced on 24 July that under the Defence of the Realm Act that public houses and clubs would only be open 10am to 9pm.

From early August soldiers were prevented from buying alcohol from railway refreshment rooms to take off the premises. Furthermore, the times during which alcohol could be sold to anyone in the military were changed, with an extension of half an hour during the daytime and a reduction by half an hour in the evening.

The alcohol restrictions continued to see a reduction in drunkenness, with a 40 per cent fall in convictions in North Derbyshire, according to the Chief Constable's quarterly report in August 1915. Similar statistics were cited regarding a fall in drunkenness in Derby.

In July, the Chesterfield races were abandoned and during that summer other sports followed suit. The Football Association suspended its Challenge and Amateur Cup competitions and the Midland League was restructured taking professionalism out of the game to create a series of friendly matches. Although expenses could be paid to players it became illegal to pay wages, with the belief that there were more important jobs than playing football and so if football was to be played it should only be done so when players were not working. To overcome issues of a lack of players, especially as more players began working long hours on farms and in industry, guest players were allowed to join teams to fill any gaps.

This had a huge financial impact on the clubs and as a result Chesterfield FC was wound up on 6 August. However, just weeks later, on 14 September, C.W. Everest bought the lease for the grounds and announced he was to form a new team and it was not long before matches began once again.

Derby County FC, based at the Baseball Ground, continued to play in the Midland League for the 1915/1916 season.

On Bank Holiday Monday, 2 August, a recruiting pageant was held in Derby, along with a National Patriotic Association demonstration, providing great interest to holiday makers. The Home Guard were inspected in the Market Place by the Duke of Devonshire before the procession led to Normanton Barracks. It was considered a 'complete success'.

As the first anniversary of war approached, the editor of the *Derbyshire Times* reflected upon the changes that had occurred during a year at war: 'A great change has unquestionably come over the British people. The Nation has been tried in the fires of a terrible emergency … We have passed from idle overconfidence, through anxious despondency, to a calm, steadfast, and characteristic resolve at all costs to "see this thing through".

On the weekend preceding the anniversary, cars drove through the streets of Chesterfield bearing signs such as 'The nearest way to Berlin is to stop this car', 'Stop this car and don the khaki', 'For the sake of your women and children stop this car' and 'Any man desirous of helping his country in this hour of need will stop this car'. Several men stopped the car and were driven to the Drill Hall. A band performance at Queens Park was held on the Sunday, with recruiting sergeants mingling among the crowd.

To the mark the anniversary, in Derby there was a 'great patriotic meeting' which was addressed by the Duke of Devonshire. He told the huge crowd that although Germany's empire was now a 'negligible quantity', almost all of Belgium and a large portion of Russia were in the hands of the enemy. He was confident the German advantage could be overturned, but only if every man, woman and child did their utmost. Warning men to join up soon he said, 'And mark you, if he does not come, and if he does not come very quickly I think he will find himself under very different circumstances to what he may have expected.'

A 'crowded meeting' in the Market Hall in Chesterfield was organised by the National Patriotic Association, where a resolution was passed stating, 'On this anniversary of the declaration of the righteous war, this meeting of the citizens of Chesterfield records its inflexible determination to continue to a victorious end the struggle for the maintenance of those ideals of liberty and justice that are common and sacred to the cause of the Allies.' The Mayor spoke of how 4 August would be celebrated for centuries to come once the war was over. There would, he believed, be rejoicing throughout the British Empire that Britain had been part of a war for the freedom of the whole world. Similar meetings were held elsewhere in the county.

The Duke of Devonshire's words at Derby alluded to conscription and this did take a step closer to being introduced in August, when the scheme of National Registration, which had been announced the previous month, came into being. Every person between the ages of fifteen and sixty-five (with certain exceptions) was required to fill in and sign a form of registration stating their name, place of residence, age, and certain other particulars.

Within days of the information being compiled and sent to London, the Ministry of Munitions selected men who it thought ought to work in the munitions factories, with many from Derbyshire being selected for that purpose.

During the week commencing 16 August a recruiting march took place in towns and villages across Derbyshire when men of the 14th Battalion Sherwood Foresters left their quarters at Lichfield and marched to Derby. Over the course of the week they visited Mackworth, Kirk Langley, Brailsford, Kniveton, Wirksworth, Cromford, Matlock, Darley Dale, Rowsley, Bakewell, Ashford, Taddington, Buxton, Chapel-en-le-Frith, Tideswell, Stoney Middleton, Baslow, Chesterfield, Staveley, Barlborough, Whitwell, Pleasley, Heath, Normanton, North Wingfield and various parts of Nottinghamshire.

Encouragement also continued from the men in the trenches who continued to write to the local newspapers. Letters in September told the people of Derbyshire that the men were 'having fun at the front' and that they were glad they went to war.

The National Patriotic Organisation also continued its efforts to assure people of the need to continue the war to a victorious conclusion and the need for more men. On 29 August approximately 1,000 people flocked to Chesterfield Market Place to see its war van and obtain information.

By the summer of 1915 there were 393 men from Derbyshire among the Sherwood Foresters who were known to be prisoners of war in Germany. They received weekly parcels of food and comforts to make their experience a little more bearable, at a time when stories of poor treatment, indeed even abuse, at the hands of the Germans became more prevalent. However, more money was needed to fund parcels for Derbyshire men from other regiments. In July the Mayoress of Derby launched an appeal to increase the amount of work and funds thus far achieved, and stories of the scant and poor quality food made available to the prisoners by their captors helped encourage generosity. Parcels of food had been sent, but many of them were not received because the prisoners kept being moved between different camps. The difficulty in sending food was that it soon 'went off' but experiments were conducted to bake a type of bread that would last six weeks.

On 4 September, the same submarine, with the same captain, which sank the *Lusitania* struck another passenger ship; the RMS *Hesperian* just hours

School children in Creswell holding parcels to send to Derbyshire's prisoners of war abroad. *Courtesy of Derbyshire Libraries and www.picturethepast.org.uk*

after it set sail from Liverpool for Quebec. On board were 814 passengers (mainly British and Canadian) and 300 crew members. Lifeboats were quickly manned and efforts made to rescue all the passengers and tow the ship, although it succumbed to the sea on 6 September. Although the loss of life was not as significant as the *Lusitania*, thirty-two people died when a lifeboat capsized. Among the passengers who were saved were Mrs Reeves of Darley Dale and her three young children. The attack on a passenger ship so soon after the sinking of the *Lusitania* further fuelled anger towards the Germans, although there was some pleasure in the knowledge that the Derbyshire passengers had been rescued.

A week after the *Hesperian* was torpedoed, members of the 3rd/6th Battalion Sherwood Foresters left Chesterfield for Grantham. They marched to the Great Central Station at the Market Place, where the public were not allowed to view the 'fine body of men' until they had boarded the train. The train departed with enthusiastic waving and cheering from both soldiers and well wishers.

Yet still more men were needed and so recruiting rallies were held across the country on 2 October, under instructions from the War Office.

In Chesterfield, there were two meetings in the New Square. At the first, Captain C.E. Brown of the ASC said he could not understand why men were holding back when each week Derbyshire men were making appeals in the newspapers. Major W.B. Robinson asked the women of Chesterfield to play their part in making their men enlist. It would be a large sacrifice for the women, he said, in sending their sons, brothers and sweethearts to defend Old England. However, he added that if they did not go now, under a voluntary system, they would find it much more difficult to cope when they were forced to go. 'Don't look at or have anything to do with a boy unless he is in khaki', the Major told the women, 'and if he is a munition worker ask him if he is there to shirk his duty as a soldier?' If it had not been for shirkers, he argued, the Germans would have been pushed back on their own soil by now. Robinson added that for every man who joined up, the lives of three British soldiers would be saved.

At the evening meeting the Sherwood Foresters were praised and Mr W. Glossop told the crowds that more recruits were needed from Derbyshire to assist in the successful prosecution of the war against what he described as 'the greatest tyrants in Christendom.'

With the pressing need for more recruits, the Lord Derby Scheme was introduced, which was a final push to encourage men to join the forces voluntarily with the recognition that if it failed some form of compulsory service would follow. Lord Derby became Director-General of Recruiting in October 1915 and immediately set about asking every man aged between eighteen and forty-one whether he would attest (to pledge his services to King and country if called for, but until that time continue as before with work and life), with all men being divided into two classes; married men and single men, with the classes divided into twenty-three groups depending upon age (based upon the information compiled in the National Register). When required the younger single men would be called up first, with married men being called up last.

In a letter to newspapers, Lord Derby encouraged employers to allow employees to enlist and keep their jobs open for when the war ended. If by leaving the company it would cause tremendous difficulty, the employee could be put into a later group.

In November another appeal was made for more men of the 6th Battalion of Sherwood Foresters. The editor of the *Derbyshire Times* found it 'somewhat surprising' they wanted more men, who were to receive the shortest of training. Clearly the War Office anticipated lots of deaths and needed reserves who were ready to fight even if they were not fully prepared.

It was the death of so many men in a war with no end in sight that caused some despondency and depression on the Home Front. Reverend Father Daniel Meenagh, the Roman Catholic priest for Clay Cross became so depressed by the war that he suffered a nervous breakdown and cut his own throat on 21 October.

On 19 November a memorial service was held at St James' church in Derby for the war dead, with special reference to the Sherwoods. The Bishop of Southwell remarked it was essential to hold such services to show the sacrifices being made.

Yet patriotic Derbyshire men continued to rally to the nation's call and pressured unwilling men to do their bit. During Christmas 1915 a story of patriotism in 'a certain Derbyshire mining village' was recounted. In that village two brothers of military age owned and ran a shop. Both had refused to enlist and had been heard to make disparaging comments about those who had. Eventually the villagers grew so angry that a meeting was held and it was decided the brothers would be told one of them had to enlist, otherwise their shop would be wrecked. Within twenty-four hours one of the brothers enlisted. Pleased with such action the *Derbyshire Times* noted that 'a little persuasion is a wonderful aid to voluntary recruiting'.

'Wonderful voluntary recruiting' was discussed in the House of Commons in December 1915, as the effectiveness of the Derby Scheme was questioned.

Mr Hohley, MP for Chatham, asked whether if insufficient unmarried men answered the nation's call on a voluntary basis, whether compulsion would be used. The Prime Minister responded that it was his hope and belief that the question of coercion would not be needed. He believed the request that men should carry out their patriotic duty would be enough to obtain the numbers needed, from all classes and especially young, unmarried men. A review of the number of unmarried men who had yet to attest would settle the matter. If only a negligible number of unmarried men had failed to attest then conscription would be unlikely, but if a significant number of unmarried men had not attested then they may have to be compelled to do so.

Soldiers joined the call for men to enlist before they might be compelled to do so. Fred Conley of Borrowash, who was serving in France, wrote to the *Derby Mercury* in December, 'Now then, you slackers, come on! Let's see you take up arms at your own free will. Let's have you all in at the death. You have not long to go now. And then what? Hurray! Compulsion! I can tell you straight, and speak with authority, for the boys in the trenches will welcome the order as soon as Mr Asquith feels inclined to issue it ...'

In addition to worries about conscription, in the run up to Christmas there was potentially worrying news for those reliant upon the Derbyshire War Relief Fund, money in which was reportedly close to exhaustion. It was much needed, with 1,483 cases on the books in Chesterfield alone, with hundreds of enquiries and requests for money weekly. This demand had drained the resources and although people had given very generously towards the beginning of the war, but due to the many other requests for money, people were not giving as generously by the end of 1915.

Furthermore, worries were raised a week before Christmas for those in groups 2, 3, 4 and 5 of the Derby Scheme when Lord Derby announced they would be called up to serve from January, although they could apply to join a later group if they were engaged in important war work or if there were other exceptional circumstances. There was evidently a great need for men and this only fuelled the belief that conscription was to be introduced in 1916.

For those soldiers and sailors from Derbyshire, efforts were again made to provide each with Christmas gifts.

In the run up to Christmas there was some festive cheer for licensees and drinkers when pub closing hours were extended to 9.30pm on weekdays as of 4 December in Derby and some other parts of the county.

The Christmas of 1915 was rather 'subdued', according to the *Derbyshire Times*, which was hardly surprising with worries that conscription could be on the horizon. Christmas of 1914 had seen the people of Derbyshire hopeful of a fairly speedy outcome to the war but one year on the optimism had somewhat waned. There were hearths and dinner tables across the county with vacant chairs and a gloomy atmosphere prevailed, with what the *Derby Mercury* described as a 'keen anxiety' for those at war.

In Derby it was a quiet Yuletide due to worries over the war, as well as heavy rain. Few ventured outdoors except to attend church, and a football match between Derby County and Barnsley had only a 'negligible' crowd. Cinemas were also almost empty.

At the Derby Royal Infirmary an enjoyable Christmas was had, with gifts showered on patients which included 120 sick and wounded soldiers and 200 civilians. The wards were decorated in a simple but 'charming' fashion and the patients were entertained by the Littleover Church choir, carols and concerts. On Christmas Day the soldiers were given a substantial breakfast. With intense excitement in the children's ward toys were given. Fruits and sweets were given to female patients, tobacco and pipes to the men. Following a turkey dinner, the Mayor and Mayoress visited and gave cigarettes to the soldiers.

At the Chesterfield Hospital the wards were 'tastefully decorated' and on Christmas Eve nurses sang carols. On Christmas Day patients enjoyed a dinner followed by singing from the Parish Church choir. On Boxing Day a concert was held on the Devonshire Ward and other concerts in the proceeding days. On the Tuesday afternoon Archdeacon Crosse, dressed as Father Christmas, distributed gifts from the 'well laden and beautifully illuminated Christmas tree'. Similar scenes were enjoyed at the hospitals across the county.

Special efforts were made for the county's children, particularly those who were the children of soldiers and sailors. In Chesterfield approximately 1,600 children were 'lavishly entertained' on 29 December with large parties held in various schools across the town, funded by members of the Prince of Wales Fund Committee. It was described as a 'very pleasant sight to watch the light hearted children and the scene, bright and consoling, was in striking contrast to the dull miserable weather.' The children had a feast, and a Punch and Judy show, a ventriloquist, comedien and a conjuror were among the entertainment. The Punch and Judy show proved extremely popular, with 'tears of laughter' from the children.

The Mayor and Alderman G.A. Eastwood addressed the youngsters in a 'homely and heart-reaching' manner. At the Mount Zion School the Mayor said, 'We hope the next time you come to tea it will be to celebrate the return of your fathers after a glorious victory.' Eastwood told the children that the town was proud of their fathers and promised that as soon as peace was declared there would be another tea. As the children left they were each given an orange, an apple and a penny.

A party for 130 children of soldiers and sailors was held at the old Normanton Congregation Church in Derby. A larger children's party was to be held in Derby early in the New Year and contributions to its cost were sought.

On Boxing Day a hurricane swept across the nation. Although Derbyshire fared better than some parts, with relatively minor damage, there was extensive damage in Wirksworth and the Ecclesbourne Valley. There, stone walls, railings and roofs were damaged and trees uprooted. A torrential downpour of rain led to 'raging torrents' and flooding.

Whilst Wirksworth dealt with floods, elsewhere after the festive break life resumed, with hard work in the factories, on the farms and down the pits as men and women returned with renewed energy.

Although an official statement was not to be made until early in the New Year, it was 'confidently stated', as the *Derby Mercury* phrased it, that the Derby Scheme had failed and that compulsion was inevitable. Unmarried men in Derbyshire who had not wanted to fight now realised that what they had feared but had hoped would never happen, now would. Of course, a reasonable proportion were unfit and another significant proportion were employed in war work, but another significant proportion were what the government and the country as a whole regarded as shirkers.

CHAPTER 14

1916

As the second full year of war began three days of intercession services were held in all churches across the county. At All Saints' Church in Derby Reverend J. Howell told the congregation that taking a broad view of the military position of the Allies there was abundant cause for thankfulness, but that people in Britain were not practising their religion as strongly as they ought to.

In Chesterfield, Archdeacon Crosse considered that it was a time to look to the future, and not the past because that would only cause disappointment. He pleaded for the congregation to attend church more frequently.

Early in the New Year the continued fall in crime in Derbyshire was noted, with only four cases at the Derbyshire Quarter Sessions on 5 January.

On 6 January approximately 1,050 children of servicemen were entertained at Derby's Hippodrome, with toys and sweets given after a 'delightful concert' to celebrate the Twelfth night. A huge Twelfth Night cake was presented, which weighed over a hundredweight. Many children were not able to attend because there was insufficient room but they each received a gift.

'Dramatic entertainment' was held in Alfreton for sick and wounded servicemen. The entertainment was organised by Captain R.C.A. Palmer-Morewood of Alfreton Park and Mrs Salmond of Langton Hall, Pinxton. 'A capital audience' assembled in the town's Assembly Rooms to watch several talented amateurs with 'more than the average histrionic ability' perform comedy plays.

There were suggestions the Ashover Shrovetide match should not be held but it was decided to go ahead with the annual event on account of it raising money for charity as well as providing pleasure for the locals and the men of Ashover who were fighting overseas. Indeed, it was held each year of the war despite some criticism.

The main issue dominating life in Derbyshire as 1916 commenced was the introduction of conscription, following the failure of the Derby Scheme in providing sufficient men. The number of unmarried men who had not attested had been found to be 651,160, which was not considered to be 'a negligible number' and therefore compulsion was necessary. The 'lack of patriotism, or culpable thoughtlessness and selfishness', as the editor of the *Derbyshire Times* put it, of the 651,160 unmarried men who had not attested caused anger across Derbyshire. On 5 January a Compulsion Bill was presented at the House of Commons. Derbyshire men were warned that the word 'conscription' would be a 'standing disgrace for all time' and they were urged to attest under the voluntary scheme whilst they still could before they were forced to join up.

George Gibbons, a Chesterfield baker and confectioner, was concerned about being called up to the army because he would have to leave his disabled father, who was dependent upon him. He had wanted to join but his father objected. Depressed by not being able to volunteer, Gibbons hanged himself on 13 January.

That same month Lord Derby contacted the mayors of Derbyshire again asking that they urge men to join up voluntarily before conscription began.

A popular jingle as the date of conscription approached was 'Will you march son, or wait till March 2?' The editor of the *Derbyshire Times* said there would be no sympathy for those who woke up on the 3 March to find they had 'forfeited the proud right to enter Britain's Army as volunteers' and were forced to do so as 'conscriptees'.

At this time Wirksworth was disappointed that its attempts to have troops billeted in the town were unsuccessful.

Meanwhile, there was much interest from 22 January when a captured German gun went on display in Chesterfield for a week. The gun, captured in Loos, was escorted into the town by Home Guards and a detachment of convalescing soldiers from Ashgate Hospital. It arrived from York by train and left the Midland Station, from which a procession was led to Alpine Gardens where the gun was positioned and was visited by thousands.

There was concern at the war news, with reports on 16 February of British troops losing around 600 yards of trenches. That day Gyte recorded in her diary: 'I do wish the terrible war was over but it does not look at all bright.'

The Military Service Act, which introduced conscription, became law on 27 January and from midnight on 2 March all single men who had not already joined up were automatically enlisted if, by 15 August 1915 they had attained the age of nineteen but were not yet forty-one. However, there were exceptions for men who were married (and had been prior to 2 November 1915), men who were unmarried or widowers who had dependant children, those serving in the regular or reserve forces or territorial forces, those serving in the Navy of Royal Marines, regular ministers of religion or members of Holy Orders, men who had served with the military or Navy previously and had been discharged for ill health or termination of service, and men who held a certificate of exemption or who had offered themselves for enlistment since 4 August 1914 but had been rejected.

Men who did not meet the criteria outlined above could claim exemption if they satisfied one or more of the following grounds: they were serving in a reserved occupation carrying out essential war work, or training to carry out such work, and it was in the national interest for them to continue doing so; if serious hardship would result from a man being called up to the Army either for the business for which he worked, if he could not be replaced, or for his domestic circumstances (for example a man with elderly parents or sisters to provide for); ill health or infirmity; those who genuinely opposed war on the grounds of conscience.

Military Service Tribunals were established in each town to assess the cases of men who sought exemption. They consisted of between five and twenty-five members, who were representatives of business and each tribunal had a military representative. It was the role of the tribunal to scrutinise each claim, usually with an emphasis on showing the applicant would be better suited in the army unless he was able to prove his exemption on one of the above grounds. A frequent criticism of the tribunals was that they did not understand the work of the applicants, and there are numerous examples of this in the chapters which follow.

It was not just war in Europe that Derbyshire men were fighting. Whilst battles raged in Belgium, a lesser known conflict was occurring closer to home. Prior to the outbreak of war with Germany there had been disturbances and bloodshed in Ireland. In the years that had followed news had understandably been dominated by events in Europe but the problems across the Irish Sea had continued and came to a head in April 1916, when Derbyshire soldiers of the 2nd/6th Battalion were among battalions sent to Ireland to quell what is known as the Easter Rising. The Irish situation put extra pressure on Britain's already overstretched military resources and indeed in Ireland the Sherwood Foresters suffered heavy losses. In total, 116 British soldiers were killed, 368 wounded and nine were reported as missing. It was a particularly bloody Rising, with 318 rebels and civilians killed and 2,217 wounded.

The overstretched resources meant that more men had to be compelled to join the army and so on 2 May it was announced that general conscription would take place for all married and single men, with the exceptions noted

The members of the Derby Military Tribunal prior to the start of a hearing.
Courtesy of the Derby Evening Telegraph *and www.picturethepast.org.uk*

earlier in this chapter, and that people would be enlisted as soon as they reached their eighteenth birthday. The new Military Service Act received Royal Assent on 25 May. This came as a great surprise to married men who had believed, from Asquith's pledge less than a year earlier, that they would not be called upon to serve their country.

Another change that affected life on the home front at this time was the introduction of British Summer Time with the Daylight Saving Act. On 21 May clocks were put forward an hour for the first time.

In June 1916 it was recommended by the Prime Minister that the Duke of Devonshire be appointed Governor General of Canada. The King approved the recommendation in August and so the Duke, the Duchess and their children left the country, remaining in Canada until 1921. In their absence Chatsworth

House was unused, leading to dereliction of the great conservatory which had to be demolished in 1920. Although the Duchess continued to take an interest in the work of the Red Cross in Derbyshire, and retained the position of President, it was impossible for her to have anything but an honorary role. The Chatsworth Estate ceased to offer working space for the Red Cross. However, the naval convalescence hospital continued its work until December 1918. Whilst the Duke was Governor of Canada and Commander in Chief of the Militia and Naval Forces of Canada, his responsibilities for the territorials in Derbyshire were deputised to F.C. Arkwright.

Food prices continued to cause worry, with prices having risen on average 55 per cent between July 1914 and May 1916, with sugar a particular problem, having risen 152 per cent.

A correspondent to the *Derby Mercury* accused those who complained about food prices of being childish. In a letter printed on 14 July, he wrote: 'The whining we hear about dear food is childish. Good bread only 2d per lb! Any old people will tell you they have paid more for much worse quality in peace time. And if the farm labourer is to have a living wage - and he will have it now or change his trade - he must receive higher pay. Good milk at 4 1/2d per quart is much less than mineral waters or beer, with four times the nourishment of either. Do the grumblers want their food for nothing? Why their poor old grandmothers would laugh at their childish ignorance.'

Nonetheless, there was hardship in Derbyshire, with 2,415 wives of servicemen on the books of the Prince of Wales Relief Fund, with 4,686 children and 696 other dependants (most probably elderly parents), and the cost of food was a particular concern to them.

It continued to be a concern for the majority of people especially the price of bread with complaints in August that the price of bread, and all other foods, would lead to starvation.

There was 'steady though not uninterrupted progress' on the Western Front according to the editor of the *Derby Mercury* on 21 July, with the 'enemy compelled to act on the defensive'. This was a somewhat positive view of events, with the Battle of the Somme having commenced on 1 July, with approximately 57,500 British soldiers killed on that day. News of deaths and injuries provided a more truthful account but still the official view was one of British successes.

On 21 July another convoy of 124 wounded soldiers, including fourteen Australians and six Canadians, arrived in Derby. Fifty of the men were taken to Egginton Hall, with the remainder being treated at Derby Royal Infirmary. The increasing number of wounded servicemen led to the Derby Royal

Infirmary starting a subscription list with people being urged to give a penny a week.

By now people had begun to realise the huge losses being suffered and they were warned that the August Bank Holiday was to be postponed so that more munitions could be produced and shopkeepers and other workers were asked to continue working because Lloyd George believed it was not a time for any sort of holiday atmosphere. Holidays were instead held in October or November in different parts of the county. Still, however, the editor of the *Derby Mercury* remained overly positive with an editorial on the anniversary of war stating, 'We are entering upon the third year of this war with a higher spirit of hopefulness and confidence than has before been experienced.'

On the anniversary of war, patriotic meetings were held in all towns and villages, with resolutions passed expressing inflexible determination to continue the war.

It was at this time that Reverend Joseph Martyn Simmons of Crich resigned, saying he could no longer be part of a national church with his private convictions. No further details were given but it is likely he opposed the church's stand on the war, especially in light of the losses at the Somme.

Whilst lives were being lost in Europe, Matlock was reported as experiencing great prosperity with lots of tourism and 'splendid entertainment'.

During August the football season began. Derby County did not play during the season, but in Chesterfield the club began to play matches in front of an average of 4,000 spectators, with some discontent that so many spectators were not in khaki. During the season it was established Chesterfield were cheating by paying players when rules stated football games should be played on a voluntary basis with only expenses paid. Forty-four players were suspended and Chesterfield was later barred from playing games in the 1917/18 season; and only recommenced matches after the war.

During August there were petrol shortages in Derbyshire, as in other parts of the country, and so bus services were curtailed.

There was also a shortage of beer when government restrictions led to decreased production. Some pubs completely exhausted their supplies.

There had been calls throughout the war for prohibition and at the 30th annual meeting of the Derby Temperance Society on 6 November it was argued prohibition would considerably shorten the war.

Appeals were made for food for prisoners of war in Germany and for jobs for discharged soldiers. One man, who was frequently seen hobbling around Derby, had been well paid in his work before going to war but could no longer perform that trade. A trade unionist found him a job and suggested that as men come back they should replace the temporary women in munitions factories.

Motor car and motor cycle owners across Derbyshire were asked to give 1s for the benefit of the YMCA hut fund.

In pursuit of more men for the army, the police visited Cromford Wakes during September. All men of military age who were present, and who were not wearing khaki, were asked why they had not enlisted. Six men were unable to provide a satisfactory response and so they were arrested and handed over to the military.

During October a requiem mass was held at the Chesterfield Roman Catholic Church in memory of twenty-three members of the congregation who had lost their lives in the war. Officiating, Father Hassan said it was rare to have black vestments in use on the altar on a Sunday but the Catholic Bishops of England and Wales had asked Pope Benedict XV for permission on account of all those killed. The town's representatives, including the Mayor and councillors, were there to show their respect and sympathy for the bereaved families and honour the memory of the dead, who included John Kelly, a brother of my great grandmother. Kelly died on 16 September 1916 from wounds sustained a week earlier, having only been on the Front for three weeks. He left three children, the youngest of whom he had never met.

A storm hit parts of the county on 27 October, with thunder prevalent, and a cyclone in Chesterfield causing much damage.

Two days later there was a storm of a different kind, with a protest meeting in Derby regarding food prices. The event, organised by the Derby Trades Council, passed a resolution protesting against the prices and calling on the government to make the essentials of life within the reach of all.

In November it was announced there would be a new type of bread produced in the New Year due to new flour being introduced. It was quickly believed the bread would be inferior, on a par with that given in gaols and workhouses and so people flocked to shops to stockpile white flour whilst it was still available.

On 6 December a 3-day Christmas market opened in Derby to raise funds for the YMCA. Stalls and concerts helped raise money for huts and comforts for the men overseas and those who were training in England.

The YMCA agreed to open a soldiers' room at Derby railway station because soldiers, especially the wounded, often had long waits while their train made a break at the station, and also soldiers had lengthy waits for trains when on leave. It was funded by an anonymous donor.

It was not just for soldiers that funds were needed. Shortly before Christmas fetes were held for the Blue Cross, the charity helping horses that have been maimed in the war and those on war work at home.

There was a sombre mood across Derbyshire for this, the third Christmas of war. In Derby it was described as was one of the quietist on record, with snow and ice alone providing a festive atmosphere.

The picture halls in Derby were open on Christmas Day providing music, and a few theatres were open providing entertainment largely for children, but they were not well attended. Church services were well attended but otherwise most people remained in their homes. There was some joy in the homes, in Derby and across the county, of soldiers who had returned on leave but as in previous years there was anguish in the homes of those who had lost relatives and anxiety in the hearts of those who had loved ones who were still at war.

In Chesterfield, Christmas was spent, according to the *Derbyshire Times*, in a 'less boisterous' manner than usual and the same can be said for every other part of the county. In her diary Maria Gyte noted the day had Christmas weather 'but nothing else. No singing in the night or going round. I think everybody is depressed and war weary. We did not decorate a bit as we are accustomed for Xmas.'

Christmas carols and other entertainments were enjoyed at the county's hospitals for the benefit of wounded soldiers and ill civilians. However, it was noted decorations were not as lavish as previous years.

Entertainment for the county's children continued. In Derby there were parties held in the schools and other public buildings for the 7,000 wives and children of servicemen, with tea being served and entertainment in the form of a concert.

School-aged children were entertained in the central schools in Chesterfield on Christmas morning. Whilst snow and ice covered the ground outside, inside there was 'warmth and good cheer' and a formidable feast.

As people enjoyed dinners of turkey or whichever meat they had been able to procure, there was some thought of enforced meatless days which were to commence in the New Year, with shops being prohibited from selling meat on Thursdays and people strongly encouraged not to eat meat on those days. It was anticipated due to meat shortages there would even have to be two meatless days each week.

There would also have been some discussion over the Christmas period about Lloyd George having just become Prime Minister, and new hopes that the change in government would lead to progress in the year ahead.

CHAPTER 15

Conscientious Objectors and Pacifists

As outlined in the previous chapter, with the introduction of conscription, which came into force on 2 March 1916, all men who, on 15 August 1915 had attained the age of nineteen but were not yet forty-one, were recruited to the army, with the exceptions noted previously. Subsequent Acts in May 1916 and April 1918 required the attestation of married men, and increased the upper age limit to fifty-one. However, among groups who could claim exemption from military service were men who genuinely opposed war on the grounds of conscience.

When describing the criteria for exemption on the grounds of conscience in January 1916, the Prime Minister, Asquith, said genuine conscientious objectors were 'persons who satisfy the prescribed authority that their conscientious beliefs do not allow them to bear arms'. This included certain religious groups, including the Society of Friends (the Quakers) and Jehovah's Witnesses, whose religion expressly forbade the bearing of arms. However, such objectors would not automatically be considered exempt from non-combat roles such as minesweeping, which was a means of preventing death rather than causing it, or ambulance work. Certain other types of factory work, as well as farm work were also alternatives for those who were able to justify exemption on this ground.

At the Military Service Tribunals claims for exemptions for conscientious beliefs (who were often scornfully referred to as 'conchies'), were thoroughly scrutinised. It will be shown the tribunals were often composed of members working on the assumption that the applicant's claim was false and had been conceived to 'shirk' their duty to got to war, unless there was definite proof of a deep conscious opposition to war which existed prior to conscription being introduced. It was not enough to simply claim to be religious because, as has been shown, church ministers of most Christian denominations supported the war and encouraged recruitment.

If a claim for exemption was refused at a Military Service Tribunal, the applicant could appeal at the County Appeal Tribunal in Derby. If the appeal was lost and they were called to the army, it became an offence to refuse to join and there were numerous instances of conscientious objectors being court martialled and imprisoned for being absent from the army. Even if the appeal was successful the objector faced a difficult time during the war, being the target of abuse and often losing their jobs because their bosses did not want to be seen employing someone who was considered unpatriotic. An image of patriotism meant everything for businesses during the First World War.

The following cases are typical examples of hearings of the cases of conscientious objectors at Military Service Tribunals in Derbyshire between 1916 and 1918. They represent a minority of the cases, with many more examples featured prominently in the local newspapers.

On 8 March 1916, just days after the Military Service Act came into force, Dronfield saw its first conscientious objector claim for exemption. The townsfolk eagerly followed the case of Harold Edees who worked in a colliery as he sought exemption from both combat and non combat roles on the grounds of 'religious and moral' beliefs. Questioned by the chairman of the tribunal, Dr Barber, he said he did not believe in fighting at all. If ever roused to fight he said he, 'should go off on the spur of the moment then, but if folks let me alone, I shall let them alone.' Asked if he would defend his sisters if they were attacked he said he would, but he would not strike any blows. Asked if he would rather let his neighbours fight for King and country he responded, 'I do not believe in the King', in an announcement which would not have helped his cause, later adding, 'as far as the King goes I can't see what good he is doing.' When it was pointed out that he had been given many privileges by the country, such as free education, and that he ought to fight for his country in return, Edees replied, 'Well I think I am doing my duty for my country. I am a collier and you can't do without coal.' Barber remarked that Edees was not claiming exemption on the grounds that he was doing important work, but instead on the grounds of conscience. 'I have a conscientious objection to undertake military duty of any kind,' Edees responded. On being asked whether he would oppose the Germans if they came into the country, Edees replied with a simple 'No.' With such a response it was inevitable that his claim was refused.

Days later, an application for exemption on the grounds of conscience from G.T. Carter in Chesterfield saw a more probing investigation into his conscience. Carter, a clerk of a Chesterfield firm of chartered accountants, was a married man but was considered single under the rules of the Military

Service Act because he had married after 2 November 1915. Carter was a Methodist and a member of the Mount Zion Primitive Methodist Church in Brampton. At his hearing he was accompanied by Reverend W.J. Musson, minister of the Mount Zion PM Church. Musson did not have any objection to war on the grounds of conscience and he was expecting to be called up to be an army chaplain. He was brought by Carter, however, to support his claim.

Stating his case, Carter told the tribunal, 'I appeal for total exemption because I believe in the teaching of Jesus Christ, which is against the taking part in war. We don't want to get too much on the Bible, but I am against the war in any shape or form. I don't believe the war will help us in any way and I cannot enter into it in one particle. In the same way I believe drink is against the war. I could not more drink a pint of beer. I am as much against it as I am the war, therefore I cannot take any part in it. Not only my beliefs but my principles which I have stood by for twenty years, are against it, and I do not feel justified in allowing those principles to be broken by man.'

Captain Manly (the military representative) asked if Carter had any objections to working in non-combatant roles. 'Oh, certainly, a very strong objection,' he replied. When asked if he had any objection to having his breakfast, lunch or dinner he could not see the relevance of the question, but Manly told him, 'If it were not for the Navy and the Army you would not be able to have your breakfast, dinner and tea.' After further lengthy arguments about the role of the army and navy in protecting food supplies, Carter told the tribunal, 'If you take away a man's conscience, well, in my case you might as well take my life. My case is entirely in your hands and I hope you will see it is a just one. If I believed in war I should not have waited until 1916 but have enlisted early on.'

Carter was certified for non combatant work but said he would appeal the decision.

On 10 March 1916, James Frost, a quarryman, appealed for exemption at the South Darley Military Tribunal. Frost said he was opposed to the taking of human life. It was pointed out that Frost, who was also a United Methodist preacher, had never spoken about the sacredness of human life and how killing was wrong, during any of his sermons. When asked what he would do if the Germans invaded and murdered his mother, or took the honour of his sister, he responded that he did not know. His claim was dismissed although due to the nature of his work he was given exemption for two months, which was repeatedly renewed until the end of the war.

On 3 Jan 1918 a 'quartet of conchies' (as the *Derbyshire Times* labelled the men) had their cases heard at the Chesterfield Rural District Tribunal. The clerk of the tribunal, Mr T.T.I. Davies, explained that each of the applicants already had a Colliery Court certificate of exemption but they wanted to claim exemption on grounds of conscience. This was because the certificates of colliery exemptions could potentially be withdrawn, and the men compelled to join the armed forces if someone suitable could be found to replace them, whereas a successful application against conscience formed a greater guarantee of exemption.

Isaac Booth, aged twenty-four, was a boiler stoker at Pilsley Colliery who appealed for exemption. A member of the tribunal committee, Mr Handbury, remarked to Booth, 'You are drawing more wages since the war began than before that time.' He questioned why, if Booth was opposed to the war, was he happy to profit from it. Booth replied that he was no better off despite the pay rises. Although he did not specify he will have been alluding to the increased cost of living. He added, 'Whatever decision you arrive at I shall refuse to be a soldier under any circumstances. I object to killing my fellow men; I consider it is murder under any circumstances to kill a man.' Asked if he would fight the Germans if they invaded he answered, 'I should object to killing any man, no matter what nationality he belonged to.' Booth's case was dismissed and he was told he must rely on his colliery certificate for exemption.

William Miles, aged thirty-three, worked at Hardwick Colliery. In his opinion war was opposed to Christian teaching and the highest moral standard of human conduct, and therefore he could not take part in it. The chairman, Mr C.W. Kendall, opened the questioning by pointing out that Miles' work in the colliery was helping to 'further the war'. Miles could not see what this mattered. 'That is no concern of mine whether it is or not', he replied. After all, he had worked in the colliery before the war began so the fact the coal was helping the war made no difference to the work he had long carried out. He said he had no objections going on with his work in the colliery. Kendall told him, 'Well we consider that you are doing work of national importance, and as you are covered by your colliery certificate, we will dismiss the application.' Miles did not want to be covered by his colliery certificate because he did not want to hide behind it when he had a genuine conscientious objection to war.

Henry Hickling, thirty-one, was married and worked as a checkweighman at Williamthorpe Colliery. He lived at North Wingfield. When Kendall remarked the tribunal were seeing a good supply of alleged conscientious objectors that day, Hickling replied, 'And there's more to come.' Outlining the basis of his conscientious objection he said, 'Christ taught us to love our enemies and not to kill them.'

Kendall again pointed out that Hickling's work helped 'to defeat the Germans or to prosecute the war against the Germans'. Like Miles, Hickling did not see the relevance of this. 'I was helping to make the country successful before the war began, if anyone changes the course that is their look out, not mine,' he replied. His claim was dismissed and he was told to rely on his colliery certificate. On asking what would happen if his colliery certificate was ever withdrawn he was told he would have to appeal that decision.

William Butcher, aged thirty-one, a married miner at Pilsley Colliery, told the tribunal 'I have arrived at a conscientious objection to any form of military service, believing that it is contrary to Christian teaching to do it.' His claim was also dismissed and he was told to rely on his colliery certificate.

Not only could unsuccessful applicants appeal the decision of the tribunals, the military representative also had the power to appeal against a person being granted exemption. As more men were wanted to fight, tribunals were pressured into refusing exemption, and when exemptions were granted, the military representatives took greater care to appeal those decisions.

There are many examples of the military representative appealing decisions, but the following is a good example, although one where the decision of the tribunal was upheld. On 6 November 1916, Captain Mosley made a number of appeals at Alfreton for cases of exemption to be reviewed. One of the men was a conscientious objector and was referred to as being 'a well known motor mechanic and agent'. He was thirty-eight years old and from Somercotes.

The man said his church was 'The New and Latter House of Israel' and that his religion was based on 'The new era that is coming, the immortalising of this body, the second coming of our Saviour.' He was not baptised, he acknowledged, adding that he believed 'in the new baptism that is coming'. He believed the entirety of the Scriptures. On it being pointed out that the Old Testament permitted warfare he pointed out 'I know it says "He that takes up the sword shall perish by the sword."'

He had only recently married and there was much derisive laughter from the tribunal upon learning this. They believed he had only got married in order to obtain total exemption, although married men had not been exempt from the Army since May that year.

The objector said his religion was 'the oldest religion going' and he had 'embraced' it twenty years previously. One of the fundamental beliefs of his faith, he told the tribunal, was that they should not take any part whatsoever in active warfare. He had been opposed to war and violence all his life.

Asked if he was willing to do something for the country, he said he would but that he did not want a fighting job. Asked if he would be willing to do mechanical transport work, he replied, 'I would not like to do it at present' because it was 'against our creed for employment in cruelty or war. I am willing to serve my country as far as I can.' Asked if he would be willing to drive a motor ambulance as the work of mercy, he said he would if he was compelled to do so but it would be 'very awkward' to do so because his religion prohibited the consumption of pork. It also prohibited shaving and the cutting of hair. Furthermore, he told the tribunal that his religion expected that on two days per week he would have to spend an hour for prayer. The tribunal believed the man was a genuine conscientious objector, and they upheld their previous decision; and dismissed the military representative's appeal.

Much derision was directed at the conscientious objectors from many sectors of the community at home and also from the men of the armed forces overseas. The following letter written by and on behalf of soldiers from Chesterfield, printed in the *Derbyshire Times* in July 1918, summed up the feelings of men who wanted more soldiers in the trenches to help them have a better chance of success:

'Sir – We see in your paper of the 22 June where a young fellow named Harry Buckley, aged 18 years, applied for exemption on religious grounds and gets it, and in the next column we read where men, married and 40 and over get their marching orders while fit young men get off scot free. Well, sir, according to Buckley's remarks he must think nobody in the Army is religious, but there are thousands of cases where a man attended Church twice on Sundays, also in the week during peacetimes. In our opinion his heart is in the wrong place and what his conscience really is, is that he is afraid of getting a good hiding from these square faced fellows in front of us, who we have been battling against for over three years without our balls being knocked off. I dare say he claps his hands and shouts "Hurrah!" when he hears of the bombing of our hospitals and the killing of our brave nurses and WAAC's. There is plenty he can do at his trade out here, if it's only camouflaging and painting our steel helmets when we get out of the line. No Christian would have a conscience against fighting, as we are fighting for Christianity and justice, and if he would only practice what he preaches about he would be out here, where his place keeps still vacant. We town lads never thought we possessed and owned such fellows in our town. We hope when his appeal comes up again they make him a soldier and a man and stop listening to all this daft talk from such young men, who are not old enough to know the thorough meaning of religion, etc.'

Attitudes changed somewhat towards conscientious objectors following the war. In fact one of Derbyshire's longest serving MPs, George Benson, who represented Chesterfield from 1929-1931 and again from 1935-1964, had been imprisoned for refusing to join up when called for, on the grounds of conscience.

For some, however, the changing attitudes came too late. Henry Haston was employed as a coal miner, and also worked as a teacher at a Sunday school. As a conscientious objector he refused to join the army when called up. He was court martialled and imprisoned at Dartmoor Prison, notorious for its severe regime and brutality. On 25 October 1918, just weeks before the armistice, Haston died, aged just twenty-six.

In addition to conscientious objectors who often opposed the war as individuals, there were more active individuals who grouped together and campaigned for the end to the policy of conscription and these formed groups such as the No Conscription Fellowship, and those who wanted to bring the war to an end through peaceful negotiation.

From 1915 onwards members of the government attempted to persuade the Prime Minister and cabinet to reach a peace agreement with the Germans. The government agreed to end the war if independence was restored to Belgium and Serbia, Alsace and Lorraine were surrendered to France, frontiers were to be changed between Italy and Austria,

Henry 'Harry' Haston, a conscientious objector who died in prison in October 1918. *Courtesy of Ms A.P.Y. Gallon and www.picturethepast.org.uk*

148

Russia would be given an outlet to the sea, and if guarantees could be given by the German government that no such attempts would ever be made to wage such a war again.

In November 1916 a Joint Peace Negotiations Committee was formed in Derby to urge the government to begin negotiations.

Discussions with the German authorities, with US President Woodrow Wilson being instrumental, led to Germany offering a deal in 1917. Germany agreed to end the war provided it could occupy much of Belgium, have its border with France straightened so that it could take land rich in iron, it could have indemnity from France and provided it received full compensation for the commercial losses it had experienced as a result of war.

As Lloyd George later wrote, in his memoirs, the German terms 'assumed Germany to be victorious, and no peace could possibly have been based on them'. It was considered necessary that the war continue until peace terms agreeable to Britain and her allies were offered. However, across the country, and certainly in Derbyshire, there were individuals and organisations who thought Britain should make a deal with the enemy at the earliest opportunity particularly as men continued to die, men were compelled to fight in a war they did not agree with, and civilians continued to experience hardship in a war that had no end in sight and a war that, at times, it felt there was the real prospect that Germany would be victorious. This was especially the case when Russia left the war in 1917 and the German U boat attacks on merchant ships threatened Britain with starvation.

A meeting, which was described as being a 'peace meeting' was held in Creswell, at the Primitive Methodist Chapel, on Saturday 14 January 1917.

The meeting was arranged by the chairman of the parish council, Samuel Smith, who was well known as a pacifist, as were the other organisers and speakers. The well publicised meeting attracted a large audience of villagers, and people from surrounding villages and towns, including a number of soldiers. Although some supporters had gathered, the audience was largely composed of what were described as 'patriots'. Tempers had been raised by an anonymous letter to the family of a killed soldier in which the writer's opinion of the futility of the war was described. There were plenty of people ready to vent their tempers.

The crowd was sufficiently vociferous that the speakers could barely be heard. 'You will have your opportunity shortly', the speaker said to a soldier who interrupted the opening remarks. The 'hero of Flanders', as the *Derbyshire Times* described him, responded, 'I took my opportunity two years ago. Why didn't you take yours?'

The crowd began singing 'war songs' including *Keep the Home Fires Burning* and *Pack Up Your Troubles in Your Old Kit Bag*. Union flags were unfurled and eggs were thrown at the speakers. Eggs were very expensive in January 1917 but this did not deter so many of them from being used. Windows were also smashed in what would later be described by the pacifists as 'hooliganism'.

Despite the hooliganism of the 'patriots', it was the organisers of the meeting who were described as being 'a disgrace to the village'. A follow up meeting was held on the Monday, organised by the patriots where it was said that 99 per cent of Creswell was loyal and generous to the war. A resolution was passed calling for Smith's resignation from the chair of the parish council.

The Creswell meeting sparked debate for several months, both within the village and its council and in the letters page of the *Derbyshire Times*, which at least enabled the organisers to finally have their messages heard.

Mr S. Sales wrote that the crowd of anti-pacifists had been responsible for 'hooliganism of the worst type.' Indeed, he described it as the same mob mentality that condemned Jesus Christ to crucifixion. He had been present at the meeting and had had an egg thrown at him, which had hit him in the eye. 'Eggs are so scarce surely he could have found a better use for it,' he wrote, adding that a man had stole a handful of hair from him but he could keep it as a momento of that Creswell 'victory' and feel pride in what he had done during the war. 'When he gets old and wants to relate to his grandchildren deeds of heroism and valour he displayed in the one and only battle he fought in, what better to make their eyes sparkle than to be able to show them the trophy of war.'

Sales criticised the police for watching and doing nothing. And he condemned the anti-pacifists for eroding freedom of speech. Why should people fight for liberty, he asked, when people will return to a society that was less free, where pacifists are assaulted rather than being given the chance to be heard?

Another correspondent named William Miles, who was presumably the same William Miles featured earlier in this chapter, said that the anti-pacifists had 'joined the German hymn of hate'.

A participant of the war, in the form of a signaller of the Sherwood Foresters, wrote that he was 'absolutely disgusted' by reading the news of the meeting and that no punishment could be too harsh for those who had organised it. 'Those responsible persons don't seem to realise there is a war of life and death on, and brave boys are losing their lives every day for the sake of such … We all know how welcome peace would be but you must understand we don't want it in disguise, and peace now, as you have heard, would probably be broken up in a few years time and perhaps there would be a war far worse than this. What good can be had from the "peace" meetings I am at a loss to understand. They can't get a hearing, and have very few sympathisers. People poke ridicule at them and regard them as maniacs. They make themselves objectionable to everyone they come into contact with.'

Pressure was put on the council's chairman to resign his position at the February parish meeting. Smith was asked to vacate the chair on the basis of the resolution passed following the peace meeting. After much debate he refused, but succumbed to pressure the following month.

On 30 June 1917 another peace meeting was attempted, this time in Crich, with its organisers being similarly treated to those in Creswell, by crowds of patriots who fiercely supported the war and were not afraid to use violence in order to justify it.

Leaflets had been distributed promoting 'a great demonstration' in Crich Market Place under the auspices of the Derby and District Independent Labour Party Federation.

Part of the leaflet read, 'Is it really necessary to go on? Are we, by continuing the war, actually preparing for that world without war which we all long to see? Are we not rather multiplying evil and planting the seeds of bitterness which can never bear the fruit of peace?'

Prior to the meeting the organisers and participants had tea at the Mount Tabor Chapel. The *Derbyshire Times*, in reporting the events of the day, placed great emphasis on the fact the 'considerable force' of people had tea with sugar. This was a time of shortages of sugar and although the use of sugar with tea was quite ordinary, the emphasis of the fact seemed to suggest the organisers were being unpatriotic not only in opposing the war, but also by using a scarce commodity.

By the time they converged on the Market Place an angry crowd of several hundred had gathered and more arrived as the speakers took their positions.

The first speaker was able to say a few words but then could not be heard, as the crowd of what the *Derbyshire Times* described as 'loyal and patriotic populace' shouted, jeered and sang patriotic songs, with some throwing missiles in the form of tin cans, grass sods and any other item they could easily find. The speakers persevered for around two hours, but the verbal and physical abuse they faced caused them to retreat.

Several of the speakers headed to Fritchley where a crowd formed.

However, the reception was no better than in Crich. The hat of one of the speakers was removed from his head and placed on a lamppost in the centre of the market place. A spike on the lamppost pierced the hat, making it resemble a German helmet. There it remained for some time as a reminder of the opposition to pacifism.

On 12 May 1918 Derby Councillor Reuben Farrow made a pacifist speech in Mansfield in which he made remarks said to cause 'disaffection to his Majesty and to prejudice recruitment' by condemning the war. He was imprisoned for four months.

On 28 October 1918 there was a packed courtroom in Eckington to see Sylvia Pankhurst, charged under the Defence of the Realm Act that on September 28th at Creswell she did unlawfully commit an act 'calculated to cause mutiny, sedition and disaffection' among His Majesty's forces or among the civilian population.

A reporter from the *Derbyshire Times* had been present at the Creswell meeting, which had been organised by the local Labour Party, and had written a shorthand record of what Pankhurst had said, despite the accused being an unusually rapid speaker.

During the speech Pankhurst said that it looked like they were coming to the end of the war and it was high time. It had been the greatest crisis in civilisation and rather than being a war of freedom and liberation it 'was absolutely a capitalists' war' and a 'sordid scramble between two rival groups of capitalists who were struggling to get control of the world's raw materials.' She argued that Britain was continuing the war claiming for better terms of peace but was really interested in the German colonies where there was rubber, oilfields in Mesopotamia and steel and iron in Alsace Lorraine.

Alluding to the police strike in London, she remarked that a soldiers' strike could happen, adding, 'I advise the Government to be a little wiser in the way it manages this war or the soldiers will take the management of it upon themselves.'

PC Edger said he recalled many of the comments in the reporters account, but many of Pankhurst's supporters said they heard nothing which led them to believe she advocated mutiny or sedition. Pankhurst argued she had merely expressed freedom of speech and made fair criticism of the current system, which she argued was not illegal and was her duty as a socialist. She was found guilty and was fined £50 plus costs.

Pankhurst returned to Creswell on 2 November as part of a protest meeting against her trial and fine. Prior to her arrival a speaker declared that the prosecution had been a blow to free speech. At one stage the crowd, part of which comprised soldiers in khaki, became angry and someone threw a potato, remarking that eggs were too expensive for a demonstration of that kind. When Pankhurst arrived she was greeted with cheers from supporters, mingled with boos from the opposition. She told the crowd she would not pay her fine and would willingly go to prison if she had to, and if that happened she would go on hunger strike. A collection was taken to help cover the costs of her fine.

Thoughts of the possibility of military disaffection and mutiny were unnecessary because the war news looked very positive, with indications of an imminent end to hostilities.

Verbal and physical attacks were common against pacifists but as shocking as these acts were they paled into insignificance when compared to the efforts to interfere with a pacifist movement in Derby ...

CHAPTER 16

The Derby Sensation

Towards the start of 1917 'great excitement' and 'commotion' was felt in Derby when three women and a man were arrested for what was known as 'the Derby sensation'. Such was the magnitude of the story that it dominated the Derby newspapers more greatly than any other news story during the war, including the Zeppelin raid of 1916 and even the armistice and peace celebrations.

It was alleged the group, consisting of Alice Wheeldon (a second-hand clothes dealer who had a shop in the front of her house at Pear Tree Road, Derby), her daughters Harriet Ann Wheeldon (a teacher in Ilkeston) and Winnie Mason (also a teacher) and Winnie's husband Alfred (a chemist employed at Southampton University), had intended to derail the war effort in one of the most dramatic of manners: by assassinating the Prime Minister.

In addition to plotting to murder David Lloyd George, it was alleged they had planned to kill Arthur Henderson MP. Henderson was leader of the Labour Party and part of Lloyd George's war cabinet. The murder plot, it was claimed, had been orchestrated between 26 December 1916 and 11 January 1917 and it was intended that the Prime Minister would be killed by firing an air rifle, with a pellet dipped in curare, a poison used in Central American countries, whilst playing golf at Walton Heath.

On 31 January, the day after their arrest, the four were brought before the Mayor and magistrates in Derby. At the hearing Alice argued it was a trumped up charge to punish her for her son being a conscientious objector. Winnie added that the allegations were a concoction against her family and husband. Despite their vociferous challenges to the accusation, given the nature of the allegations it was inevitable the four were remanded into custody.

The claim that the group were being held prisoner due to conscientious objections was not without evidence, and indeed Winnie's granddaughters are attempting to overturn the convictions, claiming they were prisoners of conscience who were convicted for political, and not criminal, actions.

The Wheeldon and Mason families were highly active in the conscientious objection movement, being members of the No-Conscription Fellowship, as well as the socialist movement. Alice was also a strong feminist and ardent campaigner for female suffrage. The shop at Pear Tree Road was a place of business. However, men who were on the run from the military authorities, having refused to join the armed forces on grounds of conscience, were given temporary lodgings there.

Alice's own son, William, who had been employed as a teacher, was a conscientious objector and was on the run, having been called up in 1916 and having lost his appeal for exemption. He was assisted by a group of Quakers, who moved him from house to house in order to avoid capture.

The family also attended hearings (tribunals and court martials) to investigate the validity of conscientious objection claims, offering support to the defendants.

The case against the four, was based upon evidence provided by a man calling himself Alec Gordon. Gordon had arrived at Alice's shop on 27 December 1916, claiming to be a conscientious objector on the run. He stayed at Pear Tree Road and, two days later, introduced Alice to a man who used the nom-de-plum 'Comrade Bert', who also claimed to be a conscientious objector.

It was claimed by Alice that within days of their first meeting, Gordon persuaded her to obtain poison from Alfred, who had access to curare and other types of poison as a chemist working at the university. The family's defence was that it had been requested in order to kill a dog used at a prison camp where conscientious objectors were held. Gordon, it was claimed, had wanted to have the dog poisoned so that he could facilitate a friend's escape. Correspondence between Alice and Alfred was used at trial to show that curare had been requested with the intention to cause death by poisoning, and the curare and several other deadly poisons were intercepted en-route from Southampton to Derby. The correspondence did not refer to any assassination plot and indeed one letter referred to 'the bloke that owns it' which suggests the target was something that was owned, such as a dog, rather than senior politicians. The claims of an assassination conspiracy were based on Gordon's account of conversations he had with Alice, which was read out at the trial (Gordon himself did not appear as a witness).

In fact Alec Gordon was really William Rickard. Both he and 'Comrade Bert' were members of the Parliamentary Military Security Department 2 (PMS2), the intelligence unit of the Ministry of Munitions. PMS2 was responsible for protecting munitions factories from espionage and sabotage, and to make enquiries with regards to aliens coming into munitions work. However, within months of being set up it was given additional responsibilities of gathering intelligence on the labour movement. By infiltrating groups, it was intended that strikes could be prevented and that individuals who were plotting to cause damage to factories, could be identified. It has since been argued that in the case of the Wheeldon/Mason families the unit was used to hinder the harbouring and escape of conscientious objectors. It ceased to operate when questions were asked about its methods and its work was taken over by MI5.

Whatever the truth of the allegations, and indeed it seems some evidence was questionable, the case progressed through the legal process. In early February when the four were brought to court to face the Grand Jury, their guilt was a foregone conclusion. Indeed, before the trial commenced, the judge, Mr Justice Rowlatt (who, in 1918, headed the controversial Rowlatt Commission), told the court, 'It is a most serious crime to conspire to murder at any time. To conspire to murder a Minister of the Crown for a supposed political object is at any time a most sinister thing. At the present moment to conspire to murder, and to murder by poison, the First Minister of the Crown and one of his associates seems to pass beyond the description that I have applied to the crime in general, and become a felon blow attempted against the safety of our country. When you see the letters and observe the levity of the writers, not only the levity but the violence and obscenity in places you may be tempted perhaps for a moment to think that this is mere froth and foolishness on the part of misguided and light headed people. I am sure on second thoughts you will not take that view...'

The Grand Jury agreed that there was sufficient evidence for the case to progress to trial. The four were again remanded into custody to await their trial at the next Assizes.

When the 3-day trial opened, at the Old Bailey, in March 1917 there was much drama as the evidence was heard. In addition to the claims outlined above, it was argued that Alice had said, referring to Lloyd George, that she wanted to rid the world of a murderer. It was also argued she was involved in the fire at Breadsall church.

Upon the conclusion of the defence and prosecution cases it was time for the jury to consider their verdict. However, one of the jurors took ill with influenza and the judge refused to allow a verdict with only eleven jurors, so the trial began again with a replacement juror. Following the conclusion of the second trial the jury required less than half an hour to reach guilty verdicts for Alice, Winnie and Alfred. Hettie, however, was acquitted. Alice was sentenced to ten years' imprisonment, Winnie five years and Alfred seven years in prison.

However, none of the sentences were completed. Alice was released in December 1917 due to suffering from valvular disease of the heart, brought about by an eight- day long hunger strike, at the request of Lloyd George himself, who did not want her to become a martyr to her cause if she were to die in prison. She returned to Derby but was considered a traitor to her country and never regained any degree of respect. She died of influenza in February 1919.

Winnie and Alfred were both released in January 1919 and moved to London. It has been suggested all three convicts were released within two years because even Lloyd George did not believe the validity of the allegations.

Hettie died in childbirth in 1920. As for William, in 1919 after an amnesty was issued to all conscientious objectors, he tried to resume his life but because he had been in prison he was not allowed to return to teaching. After a brief period working at a dairy he emigrated to Russia in order to escape the vilification that his family received as a result of the convictions where he continued his socialist activities. He was executed in 1937 during the Stalinist purges.

A Blue Plaque created by Derby Civic Society, placed on the home of Alice Wheeldon. *Photograph taken by Russ Hamer*

CHAPTER 17

The Defence of the County (August 1914–January 1916)

At the outbreak of war no one knew what to expect but the naval battles of the North Coast led to fears of a possible invasion. In addition to the regular police force more special constables volunteered to increase a police presence and maintain order. By 16 October there were 200 special constables in Derby, including a King's Councillor.

From November 1914 lighting restrictions began to plunge Derbyshire into darkness. No electric flashlights were allowed and Bonfire Night celebrations were kept to a minimum that year and were actively discouraged.

All prominent external lights were subdued to prevent enemy aircraft from identifying built up areas. Coming just eleven years after the Wright brothers first flew, the suggestion that flying machines could cause damage to Derbyshire was somewhat inconceivable to many of the county's folk. Even some of their representatives argued that the Home Office's rules were unnecessary.

For example, in Chesterfield in December 1914 there was a 'long and tedious' debate in the monthly council meeting regarding whether or not to follow the Watch and Lighting Committee's recommendations to have street lamps fully lit on Saturday nights only. Councillor Lancaster argued that by having limited lighting there was a danger to traffic and pedestrians. He believed that until it could be proven that the lights could cause an air raid, they should be kept lit. Councillor Robinson agreed, adding that there was no point having streets in darkness when the blast furnaces at Sheepbridge, Clay Cross and Staveley were so bright that they lit up the whole countryside. Councillor Woodhead, however, argued that as a loyal town the council should comply with Home Office rules and it was eventually agreed, begrudgingly by a number of the councillors, that the rules should be followed. In time the restrictions would become much more severe.

The German naval attacks on Scarborough, Whitby and Hartlepool in December 1914 led to initial hopes of an end to the war by Christmas, being replaced with pessimism and concerns about defence. The authorities remained outwardly positive, to maintain morale, and this was reflected in the public statements and press reports. In the *Derby Mercury* it was stated, 'At all three places there was an entire absence of panic, and the demeanour of the people was everything that could be desired.' A somewhat overconfident editorial in the *Derbyshire Times* on 19 December 1914 stated: 'If the main object of the German bombardment of the east coast towns of Scarborough, Whitby and Hartlepool, was to strike terror into the hearts of the people of this country it has failed ignominiously ...'

The *Derbyshire Times* also claimed there was no panic and as soon as the bombardment ended people returned to their normal duties but were more resolute towards fighting the Germans. The fact so many fled, some to Chesterfield, showed people were scared at the coast. The fear was not absent in land-locked Derbyshire.

A more checked attitude followed the limited bombing raid on Dover, with readers of the *Derbyshire Times* being given some advice of what to do in the event of an air raid. They were particularly warned about danger from shrapnel. Upon hearing the sound of enemy guns or explosions people were advised to keep under cover, and go into a basement if possible. There were no dedicated air raid sirens in Derbyshire during the First World War, with factory sirens used to warn the workers in those factories, and the surrounding populations of impending enemy aircraft. The sirens became known in some areas as 'bulls' because they resembled the sound of the farmyard animal.

In a comment that would be proven to be very wrong, the editorial ended, 'We think that the prospect of a successful air raid on these islands is small, but that is no reason why the widest possible advertisement should not be given to precautionary instructions. So far as the lay mind is competent to judge, it appears that German's great fleet of Zeppelins is proving "a white elephant". The colossal balloon-suspended creations of Count Zeppelin were to work all manner of wonders when "the day" arrived. "The day" has come, and, so far as German prospects of success are concerned, it has gone, and the Zeppelins have accomplished nothing of practical military value.' The Allies had caused great destruction in Germany and with this in mind, the editor ended, people should have no fear.

However, people did have fear. Suddenly they were beginning to realise that there was a potential threat of an air attack, or an invasion by sea, although there remained a significant level of complacency. There still remained a large number who believed the Germans would not be able to reach as far inland as Derbyshire.

Nonetheless, fears did remain due to the attacks on the east coast and the belief that invasion was possible. On 18 December 1914 the Duke of Devonshire chaired a meeting in Derby to establish a strategy in the event of a German invasion (a circular regarding the meeting is part of the Derbyshire Record Office archives: reference D331/1/48). It was decided that the existing volunteer groups such as the Derby Physical Training and Rifle Club, the Midland Railway Rifle Club, the Matlock and District Rifle Club, the Duffield Rifle Club and the Clay Cross National Reserve and Old Comrades Association (who practised rifle shooting on the Gas Works Range in the village) would be coordinated as a defensive force. In the early stages of war the military had opposed home defence units but groups were set up anyway, by men who felt they needed to do something.

However, it was soon determined that a more substantial body of disciplined men, under one command, would be required in the form of a civil defence force and action was taken very early into the first full year of war to establish such a force.

Eight battalions of a new Derbyshire Volunteer Regiment of the Home Guards were formed in the county. These were to be known as the Derby Borough, North Derbyshire, West Derbyshire, North East Derbyshire, East Derbyshire, Mid Derbyshire, South East Derbyshire and South Derbyshire battalions. Men were required to complete forty drills of an hour in duration to obtain a certificate of efficiency. Costs were to be minimal and subscriptions were sought. In the event of an invasion the fittest men would go to the coast and dig trenches to hinder the enemy and assist the local territorials in any other way to repel attempted landings. Those who were less physically fit could assist in dealing with crowds of people driven in and from the coast (by helping women, children and goods from being moved inland, and to assist in getting troops to the coast), deal with food supplies, keep roads clear for military purposes, protect bridges, tunnels, telegraph wires, and vulnerable points in the county, act as dispatch riders, and help preserve order and prevent panic.

On 17 January 1915, the first of the eight battalions, that of East Derbyshire, was created in Chesterfield, under the command of C.P. Markham. Colonel Brooke-Taylor, who conceived the idea of the Home Guard, explained the scheme to a well-attended meeting.

Brooke-Taylor said that a few weeks earlier he had heard a rumour that the enemy was bombarding Skegness. Presumably the rumour was based upon the actual bombardments of other coastal towns. Upon hearing the rumour he began wondering what would happen if Britain was invaded.

He explained that any able-bodied man aged over thirty-eight would be welcomed, as would those aged under nineteen who were fit. Additionally, men aged nineteen to thirty-eight could join up if they agreed to join the regular army if called upon. There were to be concerns that people were joining the Home Guard as a means of doing their bit when they would have been better suited to join the army itself; and Brooke-Taylor was keen to minimise the chances of this happening. Additionally membership was open to men who were aged nineteen to thirty-eight who had been refused by the military due to poor health, married men with dependants and men aged nineteen to thirty-eight who were engaged on government contracts and so were not allowed to leave their work.

He spoke to the married man telling them that if they wanted their wives and children to be protected it was about time they did something, such as join the Home Guards.

The Mayor, Shentall, told the large crowd that he knew what the Germans had done with some mayors in Belgium and if the Germans invaded and came to Chesterfield he would want defending. An 'influx of men' responded favourably, with 246 men signing up.

A pamphlet (Derbyshire Record Office reference D3772/T38/10/34) produced in 1915 explained the aims and objects of the Home Guards and included the information outlined above. It also stated the belief that the Home Guards 'would greatly strengthen the hands of the War Office' if there were already a large body of men who had some experience in drill and rifle practice, which would be particularly useful in coastal defence in order to liberate men who could then fight abroad. 'EVERY loyal citizen should join, as by so doing he adds to the strength and resources of his Country and thus helps to bring the War to a speedier termination', the pamphlet ended.

On 25 January the Derby Battalion was formed at a crowded meeting in the Drill Hall. That same day a Home Guard was established in Ashbourne where it was said invasion was unlikely, but recent events had shown the need for preparation.

A Belper unit of Home Guards was formed four days later. G.H. Strutt said the invasion of England might be unlikely but people should not be overconfident.

A renewed appeal issued through the press by Colonel Brooke-Taylor in April 1915 aimed to encourage further recruits to the Home Guards. The minimum age was now sixteen and a half. The colonel again made it clear that each man enlisting for the Home Guards was required to sign a Red Slip agreeing to join the armed forces if requested to do so, or leave the Home Guards, unless he had a very good reason.

He warned readers the Germans would 'burn and slaughter in a manner unknown even in Belgium'. He thought that few Derbyshire men would take such brutality and they would resist the Germans 'even with pitch forks'. The Home Guard was a means of organising this determination.

The appeals and meetings soon bore success. More than 4,000 members were enrolled by 26 June 1915, with new units established at Peak Dale and Wormhill, Church Greasley, West Hallam, Brimington, Darley Dale, Grassmoor and Holmebrook. By 21 August 1915 there were 5,500 members in Derbyshire and this figure continued to rise, with 6,235 members as of 18 September and 6,431 by 27 November that year.

Numbers fell slightly by the end of 1915, as more men enlisted to the army and others worked in factories and had insufficient time to drill due to the long hours and physical exertion of their work. However, there were healthy contingents across the county. The West Derbyshire Regiment had 1,160 men; the North East Derbyshire Regiment had 1,003 men in its ranks; Derby Borough had 800 men; East Derbyshire 756 men; North Derbyshire 672 men; Mid Derbyshire 552 men; South Derbyshire 538 men.

These men needed uniforms and weapons if they were to be an effective and disciplined force. With the government's focus on the army, it once again fell to the people of Derbyshire to cover the costs. An appeal was made in

The Darley Abbey contingent of the Derby Home Guards. *Courtesy of Derby City Council and www.picturethepast.org.uk*

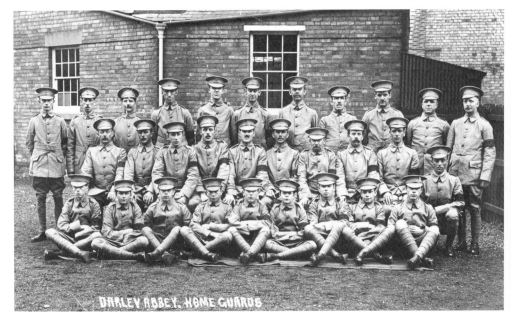

Members of the Chinley and Bugsworth contingent of the West Derbyshire Home Guard during an inspection on 19 May 1915. *Courtesy of Jane Goldsmith and www.picturethepast.org.uk*

July 1915 for money to equip the 500 men of the East Derbyshire Battalion, with £2,000 being sought. Similar appeals were made elsewhere in the county for the duration of the war. In the end many of the members had to buy their own uniforms.

There was some comfort for the establishment of a Home Guard in January 1915 when it was reported that in the early hours of 17 January a policeman saw a searchlight in the sky and a noise that he thought was an engine. Police Constable Frederick Allen watched the light for some considerable time and concluded it must have been an airship or other flying machine. A sentry at Normanton Barracks also heard the engine. There were other sightings of the light. The sightings were attributed to an enemy aircraft although this could not have been the case; no Zeppelins were in the region that night.

On the first anniversary of the establishment of the East Derbyshire Battalion, in January 1916, a special anniversary event took place at the Corn Exchange in Chesterfield. By this time the battalion consisted of 756 officers and men.

The battalion Commandant, C.P. Markham, was presented with a sword by Colonel H. Brooke-Taylor, who described Markham as a strong leader of one of the strongest battalions in the county. Brooke-Taylor added that every commander requires an emblem of his authority and so he handed Markham the sword, making clear that it should never be drawn without good cause.

The Home Guard were organised to respond to an emergency borne out of the war such as an invasion or an air raid where damage was caused to property, lines of communication and potentially human life. In March 1915,

E.V. Afrey appealed for the formation of a women's volunteer reserve for Derby for those aged eighteen to forty. The women learnt skills in signalling, ambulance work, camp cooking, drills and route marching, so they could be of use in and emergency. However, measures were set up in Derbyshire, as elsewhere, to prevent such an emergency arising.

Following the restrictions discussed at the beginning of this chapter, in 1915 even stricter lighting rules were imposed by the military. Street lamps had to be half covered and house windows covered. By September 1916 there was no street lighting.

Flagrant disregard for the lighting regulations by those who remained sceptical of the air threat, was at first challenged by verbal warnings in the hope they would not repeat their wrongdoing. It soon became apparent that legal action was necessary in order to tackle the problem.

In June 1915 the first prosecutions took place in Chesterfield for contravening the Lighting Order. Tom Gillyat had little excuse for breaching the regulations given that he owned a drapery shop and it was two very bright lights seen emitting from this shop, with no attempt of shading, that led to him being summoned. Gillyat pleaded ignorance of the effect of his lights outside and would have altered them if only he knew. It was pointed out to the court that a month previously Gillyat had been cautioned for using bright lights in his shop.

The court found that because it was the first prosecution under the Lighting Order, Gillyat only had to pay the costs. Such leniency would not be afforded to others in the future. The complacency continued and resulted in tragedy the following year.

Lighting restrictions in homes and businesses proved to be an inconvenience, but the reduced street lighting proved to be dangerous. For example, in August 1915 two soldiers were killed, on separate occasions, in the darkness. The first soldier was knocked down by a taxi cab. Within hours of his funeral, Private Frank Hibbert of Barrow Hill was run over when two cyclists went down Brimington Hill with no lights. They rang their bells and it was later established by the evidence of a witness at the inquest into Hibbert's death, that they had not been cycling with excessive speed. Unable to see in the darkness one of the cyclists hit Hibbert, resulting in a 'terrible crash' and his khaki-clad figure was seen huddled on the ground.

Other such fatalities occurred across the county in the war years. In January 1916 John Sharp was struck down by a tram in Crowton when its driver was unable to see more than four feet in front of him due to the road being 'absolutely black'.

And this situation became more serious with increased restrictions. On Christmas Day 1915 people in Chesterfield learnt of new restrictions which were to come into force on 10 January in the town of the crooked spire as well as in Sheffield, Rotherham and Doncaster. It was announced that the majority of street lights in those towns would be extinguished, with the Chief Constable having the power to decide upon which lamps should remain lit. Shop lights were dulled and windows in private residences had to be completely covered to ensure that 'no more than a dull light is visible from any direction outside'. The same rules applied to all places of worship and entertainment.

It was realised that factories, especially those with blast furnaces, could not prevent light from being emitted, and due to the work being undertaken throughout the night, other arrangements had to be made. Where government work was being undertaken, lighting was maintained but managers had to be informed immediately of any approaching enemy aircraft so that lights could be extinguished. However, the decision to extinguish lights in the works was left to the owner or manager and, as will be shown in the following chapter, this was a costly oversight.

The new regulations further stated that lighting of railway stations and goods yards was to be reduced to a minimum and that the lighting up time for vehicles was to be half an hour after sunset, with all vehicles showing a lamp at the rear, emitting a red light.

The new restrictions led to a flurry of activity. People flocked to drapers to buy curtains, green calico and blinds. For those who could not afford to buy, people produced their own makeshift blackout curtains by stitching brown and green paper inside curtains to stop light escaping. At Chesterfield parish church the windows were treated with dark green distemper on the outside, to reduce light from escaping and other places of worship in the town followed this example. The new restrictions would bring such change, the *Derbyshire Times* claimed, with 'The public lighting of the town will after the week be reduced to almost a vanishing point.'

On 29 January 1916, Colonel Butler Bowdon presented Sergeant Major W.H. Skelton of the Clowne Unit of the East Derbyshire Battalion of Home Guards with a gold watch to commemorate the unit's first anniversary. Addressing the men he remarked: 'I believe shortly that we shall have a duty to perform which I daresay many of you won't care about. But one never knows when the Germans might run amok, and our duty will be in connection with an emergency which I hope will never arise.' How prophetic his words would be proven to be when, just two days later, Derbyshire experienced its first air raid.

CHAPTER 18

Derbyshire's First Air Raid

Many articles and chapters have been produced regarding the 1916 air raid on Derbyshire. However, these have focussed on the bombing of Derby. The following chapter provides a more complete picture of the impact of the raid on Derbyshire and reveals some of the little known details of that tragically eventful night.

On the night of Monday 31 January 1916, and during the early hours of the following morning, parts of Derbyshire experienced some of the horrors of warfare on the Home Front, when Zeppelins intent on destroying homes, industries and the morale of the civilian population arrived over the county; and over towns and cities elsewhere in the Midlands, and the North of England, as well as attempting raids on Paris and Salonika (Greece).

Following the raid, the German authorities boasted of the devastation they had caused. They had sent a fleet of airships, with the intention of bombing key cities including Birmingham and Liverpool. Liverpool was a particular target due to its docks receiving supplies from the USA. A report from Berlin claimed:

'On the night of January 31 one of our naval airship squadrons dropped large quantities of explosives and incendiary bombs on the docks, harbour, and factories in and near Liverpool and Birkenhead, and on the iron foundries and smelting furnaces at Nottingham and Sheffield and the great industrial works on the Humber and near Great Yarmouth. Everywhere marked effects were observed in the gigantic explosions and serious conflagrations. On the Humber a battery was also silenced. Our airships were heavily fired on from all directions but were not hit, and safely returned.'

The German claims were erroneous in every respect. The locations cited were far from the true flight paths of the aircraft and the effects of the bombs were wildly exaggerated. This led to the British War Office concluding that, 'The utterly inaccurate report in the Berlin official telegram of February 1st … affords a further proof of the fact that the raiders were quite unable to ascertain their position or shape their courses with any degree of certainty.'

Erroneous as the Berlin reports were, however, damage was still done and human lives were lost as Derbyshire experienced its first ever air raid.

It was remarked in the *Derbyshire Times* on the Saturday after the raid that even in those areas where bombs were dropped, the local populace acted 'very calmly' and added that if the aim had been to bring fear, the German plan had completely failed. The claim was made to maintain morale, and for the benefit of any Germans who might happen to be passed the information. Certainly given the nature of the descriptions from eyewitnesses, the raid was a terrifying experience.

In that same edition of the newspaper the editor claimed that only where the lighting precautions were not followed had material damage occurred, and therefore even the relatively little damage that had been caused could have been reduced further. This information was based upon official information from the War Office, which had issued a statement on the morning after the raid, that read: 'A Zeppelin raid by six or seven airships took place last night over the eastern and north eastern and midland counties, and a number of bombs were dropped. Up to the present no considerable damage has been reported.'

Whilst the initial information suggested the raids had scarcely caused damage, as more information was obtained a picture of greater devastation began to emerge.

The perceived failure of the raid was attributed to thick fog, which hampered navigation, according to a War Office statement issued at 6pm on Tuesday 1 February, although it was acknowledged the raid had been attempted an 'an extensive scale', affecting parts of Derbyshire, Leicestershire, Lincolnshire and Staffordshire. It was also said that fifty-four people had been reported as dead and sixty-seven injured as a result of the raid.

Less than two hours later, at 7:55pm, a further statement was made, based upon updated information. The raid was now said to have affected a larger area than on any previous occasion, with parts of Norfolk, Suffolk, Lincolnshire, Leicestershire, Staffordshire and Derbyshire being hit. It was thought approximately 200 bombs had been dropped, but that the only material damage caused was in one part of Staffordshire. The death toll, however, was rising: thirty-three men, twenty-two women and six children were reported as having been killed; and fifty-one men, forty-eight women and two children injured. It would later be established that more than 300 bombs had been dropped and that nine airships were probably involved, rather than six or seven as originally believed. The number of airships remains uncertain, with speculation in 1918 that as many as twenty-five were involved, although historians agree the figure was almost certainly nine.

Despite admitting that sixty-one people had been killed, the official government news still did not portray an accurate representation of what had taken place. For such information we must rely upon some of the accounts of people who witnessed the raids and the local news reports, including a report of the raid printed in the *Derby Mercury* following the armistice.

It was a policy not to reveal the locations of Zeppelin raids, so that the Germans would not be able to establish which towns and cities they had hit. In doing so it was hoped the enemy could not learn from any mistakes, or successes, they might have made to refine their navigation skills. It was, at the time, suffice for the War Office to say that the bombs were not dropped on Liverpool, Birkenhead, Sheffield, Nottingham, the Humber and Great Yarmouth, instead giving vague location details such as referring to places such as Derby as a 'Midland town'.

In one such Midland town, which is known to have been Derby, news was received of the approach of the Zeppelins at about 7pm, and hooters and buzzers began to sound in order to alert people of the potential danger. Street lights were extinguished, windows were 'blacked out', all factories ceased work and cut off their lights, and trams and trains were brought to a halt. Ambulance men, doctors and special constables were summoned to their headquarters. Approximately half-an-hour later in parts of Derby people saw and heard the airships a distance away, most from what they believed to be the safety of their homes, whilst others ventured outdoors to try and catch a glimpse of the monstrous flying machines.

The ships were an imposing 163.5m in length and 18.7m in diameter. A Derbyshire correspondent described one of the Zeppelins as looking 'like a corridor train in the sky'. Another described 'brilliant searchlights' being cast down from airship, which enabled the airships to be seen despite the darkness and fog. It is easy, in the 21st century to fail to realise the spectacle of seeing a large vehicle in the sky. The aeroplane had only been invented thirteen years previously. Airships had been around a little longer than 1903, and a few flyovers of aeroplanes had occurred in the county, including three days of air displays over Ashgate in April 1914 when BC Hucks looped the loop with his Bleriot plane; and Gustav Hamel performed the same trick during early May 1914 over the area of Nottingham Road cemetery in Derby;

A Zeppelin similar to those which caused fear, damage and death in Derbyshire. *Author's Collection*

but there will have been many in Derbyshire who had never seen any 'flying machine' in the sky.

In addition to their large size, which would have brought terror upon those who saw them, their four engines produced a loud 'menacing drone ... like an irregular drum beat', as one witness in Derby later recalled.

Seeing only darkness whilst over Derby, the ship's crew continued their journey, as did the crews of two other ships which passed nearby. Another town, having been notified of the approaching aircraft, also entered a state of near complete darkness, and with the fog, its residents heard the Zeppelin but not a single bomb was dropped on the town.

In other places, including Middleton, Darley Dale and Matlock the Zeppelins were heard. In Middleton it was assumed they were British aeroplanes. People swarmed the streets of Ashbourne to see the aircraft and when bombs later fell on Derby, Ashbourne folk, it was claimed, experienced what felt like an earthquake and windows rattled although the distance involved makes this claim somewhat suspect. It was also claimed the same happened in Duffield and Dalbury Lees. There was great alarm in the surrounding villages.

Meanwhile, a Zeppelin, having passed over Derby, targeted a neighbouring town, to the west, which its crew believed was Liverpool, but was in fact Burton-on-Trent, and bombs began to fall. That town had failed to follow air raid precautions, being well lit and very visible from the air. It was later stated that no warning had been given to the town.

Detonations could be heard for two hours as bombs continued to fall on the brewery town, with the explosions being heard up to twenty miles away. It is also likely explosions in Loughborough could be heard, from a distance, as bombs were dropped there. Certainly in Derby people listened to explosions in horror but with an air of complacency that was to cost some areas of the town dear.

At around midnight, believing the danger to have passed with the distant explosions having ceased almost two hours earlier, Derby began to return to normality, and some lights were once again lit, notably in the factories which became a blaze of light as work was intended to continue through the night. The tram cars were sent to their depots. These were actions that would soon result in tragedy, as Derby was once again approached by a Zeppelin.

Just minutes after midnight (reports vary between 12:07am and 12:20am) the sound of the engines of the L14 Zeppelin, under the command of Captain Alois Boecker, could be heard and it was followed quickly by the first explosions. Then in five or six intervals, approximately two or three minutes apart, more bombs fell. The final set of bombs was described as causing explosions of a 'particularly vicious character'. It was thought the bombs, consisting of high explosives and incendiaries, were dropped in twos or threes, but it was believed to be possible that as many as five or six were dropped in the final instalment.

Despite the 'vicious character' of the bombings, relatively little damage was done. Three fell around the Rolls-Royce factory, with only one on the grounds of the factory itself, hitting a car-testing track, causing no damage other than a few shattered windows and a crater in the ground; three fell on the Metallite Lamp Works on Gresham Road, almost destroying it; others fell on the Carriage and Wagon Works; incendiaries fell on Fletcher's lace mill; and more incendiaries hit the road at Horton Street, causing one house to catch fire. Two bombs fell in a garden on the corner of Bateman Street, one of which did not detonate, the other creating a crater into which it was later remarked a horse and cart could have disappeared, and damage was caused to roofs and windows. Several bombs were dropped on the Locomotive Works, killing three men outright and mortally wounding a fourth; and at least two high explosive bombs and one incendiary were dropped over the gasworks but failed to cause any damage. In most cases the damage to buildings largely consisted of shattered windows, although the cost of the damage was estimated at £13,000.

Rolls-Royce Motor Works in c.1912. *Courtesy of Derby City Council and www.picturethepast.org.uk*

At an inquest held in Derby on 5 February, the circumstances of the deaths of those who were killed in Derby were investigated, although it was not revealed in the press that Derby had been attacked; instead the location merely being described as a 'populous and very busy' town. The deaths concerned were those who died at the Locomotive Works. Upon hearing bombs being dropped the men attempted to flee the area but when they heard the explosions getting closer they took cover but a bomb fell only half a dozen or so yards away, killing three of the men outright and seriously wounding the fourth, who died three days later. A fifth man, who was nearby, was knocked to the ground but not hurt.

The bodies were so badly mutilated that they were described as 'mangled beyond recognition'. In fact the coroner was given the names of three men who were believed to be the men who died at the scene, but two, if not all three (reports are contradictory) of the men who were supposed to have been killed presented themselves to work the next day. It was not until the Wednesday morning that the identities of the deceased were established.

At the inquest, the trade union representative questioned why the lights at the Locomotive Works had been put back on. The lights had been extinguished earlier in the evening, when lights were extinguished across Derby, but after a few hours they were relit and work recommenced. Then bombs were heard and the lights were briefly extinguished again, before being relit after a short while. It was almost immediately afterwards that bombs started to fall in quick succession. The jury found that the deceased were killed by a German Zeppelin and that it was their opinion that the Chief Constable should have control of the whole district in regards to lighting and deciding when it was safe to light up again.

At the end of the inquest the jury handed a note stating the following: 'The Jury express their sympathy with the relatives and friends of the four victims of one of the most murderous and dastardly outrages the country has ever witnessed, and we hope that when the day of reckoning comes that England and her Allies will not forget these outrageous crimes that have been dealt out to their civil population.'

The four victims were not publicly named at the time of the raids. However, it is known that they were: William Bancroft, Harry Hithersay, James Gibbs Hardy and Charles Henry Champion. The latter was the man who died days after the raid.

In total, five people died in Derby as a result of the raids. In addition to those directly killed by the bombs in Derby, an elderly woman named Sarah Constantine, was so shocked that she suffered a fatal heart attack. She was approximately 200 or 300 yards away from the spot where the three men were killed and the fourth man mortally wounded. Additionally, a baby born without legs was considered a victim of the raid, with the shock suffered by his mother believed to be responsible for the abnormality.

After the last bombs fell on Derby, the Zeppelin headed east, over Nottinghamshire, Lincolnshire and the North Sea, returning to Germany to deliver the news that it had brought devastation to Liverpool.

Elsewhere in Derbyshire, bombs were dropped. In Swadlincote two bombs are recorded as having been dropped, at around 11:45pm, by Boecker's L14 Zeppelin en-route to Derby, though neither caused any real damage, with the blast shattering windows of a few houses. The following morning, according to *The Times*, a village constable found a bomb, picked it up and carried it four miles to his headquarters.

Only one other part of the county was hit by bombs that night. Bombs were dropped at the Iron Works in Stanton, near Ilkeston, by another airship in the fleet, the L20. The bombing was so loud that in Chilwell, just over the Derbyshire/Nottinghamshire border, the explosions could be heard. Mary Eliza Charlton, of Chilwell Hall, wrote a letter within days of the air raid, in which she described her experiences. 'What a loud motor bicycle', she claimed to have remarked when hearing the engines. Her husband, Geoff, responded, 'More like a train.' Two or three minutes later a 'terrific bang' was heard, quickly followed by similar explosions. The couple believed the bombs were being dropped over Nottingham but later discovered they were dropping over Stanton 'where they did very little damage, except for killing two poor men', Mary added. In fact fifteen bombs were dropped on and around the ironworks, one of which damaged a railway bridge crossing the Nutbrook Canal. The force of the explosion was, it was reported, so strong that windows in Lenton, Nottingham were shattered.

An inquest on 5 February looked at the death of a forty-one-year-old man in Derbyshire who, as the verdict recorded, 'was killed by the explosion of a bomb dropped by a hostile aircraft'. The raid referred to was at Stanton, where bombs fell at 8:20pm. The man, who was at work, tried to flee the area with his colleagues. As they fled, believing they were moving away from danger, two bombs exploded twenty yards away. The victim was found crouching up against a church wall, conscious, but complaining of severe pain in his back. In addition to injuring the man, the bomb had destroyed a parish room. He was carried to a hotel but by the time he arrived it was clear he had lost a lot of blood. He was conveyed to a hospital, and an operation performed but he died the following afternoon. The coroner, in recording the jury's verdict, described the raid as an 'abominable outrage'.

The second man killed at Stanton Iron Works was also horribly mutilated whilst he attempted to shelter from the bombs. The coroner described his death as a 'dastardly outrage' that carried German frightfulness into their midst.

The only other Derbyshire victim was a man killed during the raid on Burton-on- Trent, where many deaths had occurred because people had gone outdoors to look at the zeppelins.

During the course of that night, outside of Derbyshire, some of the towns of Leicestershire, Staffordshire and Lincolnshire experienced varying degrees of horror and these were reported in the Derbyshire newspapers in the days and weeks following the raid. Derbyshire had comparatively come off lightly, although that would have been of no consolation to those in the affected areas and the families of those who had died.

In addition to lighting restrictions not being adequately enforced, enabling the raiders to see and identify potential targets, there were criticisms of the anti aircraft measures in place. In Derby there were three anti-aircraft guns but one of these was not supplied with ammunition and the other two were evidently not used on the night of the raids. Following the bombing of his works, the General Managing Director of Rolls-Royce requested the government provide more guns as well as Royal Flying Corps aircraft to intercept zeppelins before they were able to cause any damage to built-up areas. Doubtless others joined his call for better defences.

There was evidence that spies were at work in the county. There were multiple sightings of a car at Stanton. The occupants of the vehicle appeared to be signalling to the airship. The car and its occupants were never traced.

The air raid was commemorated in the form of a plaque on the site of the Wagon and Carriage Works where the only deaths/mortal wounds in Derby caused directly by the bombs occurred.

It was also commemorated in the form of some Royal Crown Derby pottery. On the night of the raid a kiln was being fired at the Old Crown Derby China Works. When the warning of the raid was given, the kiln fire was extinguished. When it was safe to return to the works the contents of the kiln were examined and found to have fired well. To mark the occasion the bases of those vessels were marked with a Zeppelin and a crescent moon.

This was the first and only raid on Derbyshire during the First World War. There were further air raid warnings and when a Zeppelin unsuccessfully attacked the Midlands and North in September 1917 there were fears that the airships would return to Derbyshire.

CHAPTER 19

Further Defence of the County

Following the air raid of 31 January/1 February 1916 there were twelve further occasions when Zeppelins flew close to Derbyshire's borders, and within thirty miles of Derby, and air raid warnings were given. Having suffered a raid people in Derbyshire were generally more eager to follow precautions and so no more bombs were dropped on the county during the war.

There were, however, exceptions. Just days after the raid on Derby there was outrage that people were still lighting up the darkness. 'ISIS' wrote in the *Derby Mercury* of 'happy go lucky' displays of light in Derby from shop windows, places of amusement, public houses, public buildings and private residences too.

'Quo Jure', writing in the same paper, criticised the management of the Reginald Street Bath for allowing its 'brilliant glow' to shine through its glass roof.

To answer these concerns, a new order was received by the Chief Constable of Derby on 9 February and came into force one week later. The Chief Constable now had power to decide which public lamps should be retained for public safety, otherwise street lighting was to be kept to a minimum. There was to be no lighting for advertising and lights from shops were subdued so they were not visible from outside. Householders were also instructed to cover their windows so that no light could be seen from outside. In workshops and factories light was to be reduced to a minimum.

There was an understandable level of panic and fear that the Zeppelins would return. This manifested itself most notably each time the works' sirens and buzzers sounded at the end of each shift, leading some people to believe airships were in the vicinity. To remedy this, in February 1916 the factory managers were asked to ensure buzzers sounded for just five or six seconds.

That same month new detachments of the Home Guard were formed at Foston and Sheepbridge as more men wanted to do their bit in the event of another raid, and membership of the pre-existing units grew further.

The Chief Constable of Derbyshire set up motor control stations for which the Home Guard assisted. Following reports that the occupants of a vehicle had signalled to a Zeppelin at Stanton there was great desire to investigate the movements and intentions of all motorists in future raids. During a raid the members of the Home Guard were required to hold up all cars and bicycles, to inspect the driving licenses of motorists, take details of the vehicle and its occupants, questioning them on their intended movements, check lamps were fixed and could not be used as searchlights and check there was no signalling apparatus in the vehicle. As the Home Guard was not a statutory body each member was required to be sworn in as a special constable in order to be granted the power to stop vehicles.

Despite the new regulations and the knowledge that Zeppelins were capable of wreaking havoc in Derbyshire, some still refused to follow precautions. On 21 February 1916, Charles Henson of Belper Road, Derby, was found to have had his blinds up with lots of light visible from outside. He was prosecuted and fined £3 5s, although his case was not helped by the fact he assaulted the police constable who had asked him to cover his window.

In March 1916 many 'well known' residents of Matlock, including Reverend Heiliwell Thomas, were fined for breaching the regulations.

Littleover was a hotspot for those breaching the regulations and so it was targeted by the police, with a number of residents prosecuted in March 1916. The prosecutions are typical of those initiated across the county for this type of offence.

John Stone of Burton Road, Littleover, thought his blinds were sufficient but according to the police constable light could be seen from miles away. As it was the first case against the new regulations at Derby Magistrates' Court, the magistrates were lenient and imposed only a 20s fine.

Walter Evans was also fined 20s for not having blinds up. He thought the weather was 'too rough for a raid tonight' and did not think there was any risk.

Alwyn Arthur Andrews was fined 30s for having lights on and no blinds. He did not think it mattered if there was light because he was in the country not the town.

Other breaches of the rules continued for the remainder of the war. For example, in October 1916 two men were summoned to Derby Borough Police Court for striking matches outdoors after an air raid warning had been given, and fifteen people were prosecuted for having unscreened lights.

In October 1917 there was an unsuccessful raid in the Midlands and

Zeppelins were within the vicinity of north Derbyshire and warning was given. Following that raid a number of men and youths were prosecuted for failing to observe air raid precautions. Arthur Blood was fined for not shading the inside light of his house. A man was fined for striking several matches whilst outdoors. Five youths were fined for singing the song *Blighty* at the tops of their voices.

In October 1916 the battalions of the home guards were wound up, and men were transferred to the Derbyshire Volunteers Regiment, which had been established in June that year. In October recruitment to the Volunteers became a condition of exemption from the military, resulting in membership swelling.

By the end of that month there were 7,626 members of the Volunteers in Derbyshire, although some still did not have uniforms when almost 7,000 were inspected by Field Marshall Viscount French, at Derby, during October; and were described as a 'wonderful display of the country's latent military strength'.

The eight distinct groups that had been in existence since January 1915 were retained. The Derby Battalion became known as the 1st Battalion; East Derbyshire, the 2nd Battalion; South East Derbyshire, the 3rd; North East Derbyshire, the 4th; West Derbyshire, the 5th; North Derbyshire, the 6th; South Derbyshire, the 7th; and Mid Derbyshire, the 8th.

In April 1917 it was decided to discontinue the use of the factory sirens because their use caused panic, resulting in people fleeing their homes, placing them in greater danger. It was also remarked that their use led to women being off work for several days. There was much debate about the issue, especially at meetings of Derby Town Council, but they were never again used during the war as an air raid warning.

In October 1917 new air raid precautions were released by the Chief Constable. They advised people to take cover as soon as possible, go indoors if at all possible but if in the countryside lay in a ditch or behind a wall. Other guidance included not looking out of a window; planning an escape route in advance; not crowding into a basement with only one means of escape; having water and fine sand in buckets to help extinguish any fires; not to touch any unexploded bombs and to inform the police in the event of any fumes to leave the area; not to use telephones during or immediately after a raid because the lines would be required by the emergency services and the military. People were also reminded it was an offence punishable by fine or imprisonment to spread false reports of an air raid warning. Thankfully, circumstances never necessitated their use.

CHAPTER 20

1917

The third full year of war opened with much merriment. On New Year's Day a 'good humoured and hilarious crowd' surrounded the ropes at Chesterfield's football ground on Saltergate to watch two teams of women munition workers from Bryan Donkins and Chesterfield Tube Company, play in aid of the *Derbyshire Times* tobacco fund and the hospital, the game ending in a goalless draw. A match held weeks later played between teams of women from the Holmebrook Works and Wheatbridge Mills of Robinson and Sons', was watched by a 'large and boisterous but good humoured crowd'. The quality of football was said to be far superior to that of the New Year's Day match, with one goal being scored.

Merriment was also had by approximately 2,500 Chesterfield children of soldiers and sailors who were again treated to a party. The Mayor, Alderman G.A. Eastwood and Councillor Clark visited all schools and the promise of another tea when peace was declared was repeated, leading to cheers and one boy to exclaim, 'We want it tomorrow.' Entertainment included a Punch and Judy show and humorous songs and stories.

On 8 January, ninety-four wounded servicemen arrived in Derby, forming a reminder of the risks of war and around this time a shrine was erected at Dove Holes for the protection of the 154 men of the village who had gone to war.

Similar shrines had been set up in other parts of the county, and others were erected during the remainder of the war, including two at Brampton, bearing the names of men from the immediate neighbourhood who were in active service, along with a prayer to protect them from peril and for their spiritual well being. The soldiers' 'women folk' were able to leave flowers. There were three in Derby, regarded as a visible sign of patriotism.

The requests for God's protection had been frequently made, but as the war continued, without an end in sight, understandably people began to question the existence of a higher being and, if God did exist, they questioned why He had not stopped the war.

Reverend John Bradbury, of the Matlock Primitive Methodist Church, gave his opinion to a record congregation in March 1917. It was, he said, 'a natural question out of perplexity and pain'. He argued that people wanted God to intervene but why would He when so many people were absent from church? God would not stop the war, he continued, because if He did something far worse would happen. If God stopped the war, at that time, 'He would be admitting His mighty superiority had failed because He had created man with the greatest revelation of love.' The war would end, Bradbury concluded, when his 'eternal plan' had been worked out.

It was inevitable that a wave of atheism continued to spread across the county, but the frequently crowded churches showed there were still a large number of faithful in Derbyshire who continued to hope and pray for divine intervention and intercession services were once again held across the county at the beginning of 1917.

1917 was to be a year of economy in terms of money and food as the nation struggled to make do with what it had. Sugar was particularly scarce and so a tribunal to assess a confectioner's claim of exemption from military service was quite timely. The applicant, a thirty-eight-year-old married man with two children, was a partner in a Brampton firm of wholesale confectioners. When the war broke out the firm had eight men and two youths but now there were only two workers. His company would not be able to function if he were taken, he argued. Major Wardlaw thought it would be a good thing if his company ceased trading; the fact it used £14,000 of sugar was no argument for exemption at a time when sugar was scarce. The country needed soldiers, not confectioners, he argued.

Shortages of meat led to new regulations in February, allowing people in Derbyshire who had appropriate land to keep pigs, poultry and tame rabbits, even if they lived in urban areas. They would only be prevented from keeping the animals if the medical officer had any objection. Municipal piggeries were later considered in Derby and Chesterfield.

The shortages in food became pronounced in 1917 as a result of what was frequently named the 'submarine menace', with German U boats intensifying their campaign of sinking cargo ships carrying food. During 1916, according to government figures, 287 ships were sunk, with a loss of 1,237,364 tons of food. It was reported in the *Derbyshire Times* that during a period of nineteen days there have been forty encounters with enemy submarines. Although the situation was described as 'serious', between 1 February and 18 February 134 ships carrying more than 100 tons of cargo had been sunk, but 6,076 ships had arrived safely into British ports. This was said to be encouraging, and that fewer ships would be sunk due to the increasing use of arms on merchant ships.

Although public reports described the situation as encouraging, in Whitehall it was described as anything but. Indeed, in November 1916, according to Lloyd George's memoirs, it was estimated that a complete breakdown in imports would come before June 1917, and probably much sooner. If the facts as revealed to the public were sufficient to worry people, the truth would have been more concerning. According to Lloyd George's memoirs figures revealed in the press relating to the number of ships sunk were false, with the true figures being three or four times larger than stated. For every large steam ship leaving Britain's, twenty-five failed to return. It was at this time that the government believed the war could be lost unless the submarine menace was effectively dealt with.

In order to overcome the submarine menace farmers and civilians alike were encouraged to grow more food so the country could become more self-sufficient, and to use food more wisely. Allotments began to appear on every available piece of land. In Derby, more than 1,000 tenants began tilling their new allotments in February.

In addition to food economy, in 1917 increased emphasis was placed on financial economy, as the cost of the war continued to grow at a level inconceivable to almost all, and as the cost of living continued to rise.

People in Derbyshire were encouraged to save for their future and prepare for financial hardship whether Britain won or lost the war. If Britain was to lose, they were warned, it would be the working class who would suffer the most. People were encouraged to practice economy and in making self sacrifices they could afford to contribute to the cost of the war. If they could not afford to give 15s for a War Savings Certificate, they were encouraged to join a War Savings Association where individual savers contributed 6d each.

The appeals for this 'greatest loan of history' generated an impressive £1,000,312,950 nationally by the end of February 1917 and Derbyshire contributed its fair share of this sum. Remarking on the 'sum so large as to surpass imagination', the editor of the *Derbyshire Times* wrote that the people of Derbyshire had shown great patriotism and that if further money was needed, it would be found.

Money was required during 1917, to wipe out the £4,000 debt of the Chesterfield and North Derbyshire Hospital. The hospital had become increasingly used for the treatment of wounded servicemen, placing huge pressure on an already overstretched institution. To this end, a series of fund-raising events were held in the town. In June 1917 the Chesterfield Industrial

Exhibition raised £500 for the cause, as well providing an opportunity for the town to showcase its industries. Other small events led to £2,000 being raised by September.

In September a 4-day bazaar was held at Chesterfield's ice skating rink. The event, opened by the Marchioness of Hartington, saw the ice rink converted into thirty-five alcoves or open-fronted shops. In addition to stalls, there were concerts and entertainments, luncheons and teas. The official handbook of the bazaar highlighted the community effort that went into its organisation: 'The bazaar is a splendid example of the co-operation of all classes of the community, who have worked energetically and have spent many hours in self-denying labour to supply money and goods to the various sections.'

This cooperation helped generate more than £8,000 by 29 September and further efforts were made to reach £10,000. The hospital became debt free for the first time in twenty years and was granted royal hospital status in recognition of the efforts to clear the deficit, as well as its efforts in treating the war wounded.

There was another shortage in Derbyshire, in the form of children. In his annual report as School Medical Officer for Derbyshire in April 1917, Dr Barwise said the average number of children on the school registers of the county was 82,050 compared with 90,000 when the work of medical inspection was started around ten years earlier. The number of births was falling more rapidly than deaths and the number of children surviving to five was 1,000 fewer than in 1903. 'This is serious in view of the necessity for increased manpower in the nation, and makes the work of ameliorating the condition of the schoolchildren of paramount importance,' Barwise said. It would later transpire that for 1917 as a whole the birth rate in the county had followed the national trend by falling, and that the infant mortality rate, although lower than in 1916 and particularly 1915 which had seen a peak in mortality rates for young children, was still worryingly high, especially in the Ilkeston district.

In order to help preserve the lives of children a Baby Week was observed in Chesterfield in July to help teach mothers how to better care for their children. Forget-me-nots were sold to raise funds for child welfare.

The year 1917 witnessed military tragedies on the Home Front which, in addition to the presence of wounded servicemen in the county's hospitals, and the news of deaths abroad, helped bring home the human cost of war.

In February, Chesterfield had its first aviation fatality when a biplane piloted by Lieutenant W.H. Segrave crash landed in a field close to the Blue Stoops. News of the crash led to a gloom over the whole town, although curious spectators flocked to the scene. At the inquest it was established that Segrave had been flying across the town and for some unknown reason descended into the field belonging to Walton Hall Farm, hitting a tree, turned over and crashed. The incident was witnessed and Segrave was quickly found beneath the wreckage, with head injuries, but he died within a few minutes of impact.

Another tragedy occurred in May, this time at Chatsworth Park, where Major Lawrence Johnstone of the Canadian Infantry was experimenting with a new gun. The gun jammed and when efforts were made to fix it, it exploded, instantly killing him.

Just weeks after Major Johnstone's death, Chatsworth Park was the scene of a fete to raise funds for the Red Cross Society, with naval and military sports helping draw in the crowds.

There was mixed news in the spring of 1917, with revolution in Russia during February looking set to remove one of Britain's allies from the war arena. Although Russia remained an active participant in war for much of the year, with its internal problems it was unable to muster the full force of its military strength against Germany and its allies. In April the USA joined the war and there were some hopes that increased forces would take some pressure off the British army, but it was soon realised that the American forces would experience limited front line action until 1918.

As 1917 progressed the food shortages became more serious and the people of Derbyshire were instructed to exercise stricter food economy.

There was some criticism in May of the allotments committee in Derby for not providing enough plots, but the committee said it had obtained all the land they could. Ashbourne Road residents in particular complained, but it was pointed out they had been offered allotments a mile and a quarter away but refused the plots saying they were too far from their homes. Nonetheless it was recognised in Derby and across the county that more allotments were needed, but it was a matter of finding landowners willing to allow their land to be used for this purpose.

Whitsun events were held across the county but only in the form of sports and concerts, with no teas as in previous years due to food shortages. The government and Ministry of Munitions urged workers to forego Whitsun holidays until August.

One of the most important meetings to be held in Chesterfield took place on 19 June, when Captain Parsons and Henry St John Raikes, chairman of Derbyshire Quarter Sessions, spoke of the need for food economy. The conserving of food, especially bread, was a national service, it was argued.

One of many posters produced to encourage people to exercise food economy. *Author's Collection*

Captain Parsons spoke of the need for decreased consumption and increased production so that there were more stocks in the 'national larder'. The war had ceased to be merely a military question and was now also battle between the power of the civilians of the Allies and the civilians of the enemy. Britain would now only lose, he said, due to the apathy and self indulgence of the civilian population at large. He urged for greater food economy, but he said it was only a small sacrifice that was asked for; one fifth less bread to be consumed. He felt that it was no use blaming profiteers for the food problems. Instead it was better that they bought and consumed less and then the profiteers would make less profit, which was a good punishment, although he believed profiteers should be hanged.

The theme of shortages continued with a shortage of water in Wirksworth and district in June, and people there were advised to economise with water.

As the anniversary of war approached, a YMCA Hut Week, to finance huts on the Front raised around £1,250.

'We are entering upon the fourth year of the war with no definite hope that a decision is within sight, but with a firm determination that the duty laid upon us by civilisation and posterity shall be performed so far as in lieu,' the *Derby Mercury* wrote on the eve of the anniversary.

To mark the anniversary patriotic meetings were held across Derbyshire. At a meeting of Derby Town Council a resolution was passed stating Derby's inflexible determination to continue the war through to victory. Mr Farrow, a councillor active in the Pacifist movement, argued negotiation should start to bring the war to an end. He thought a victory on either side was only a victory for militarism. He was told to shut up and leave the building.

On 5 August services were held at all churches. At All Saints' in Derby, Reverend W.H. Green led prayers for a spirit of firmness and perseverance, as well as prayers for the fallen, and for the strength of all involved at home and at war.

A celebratory service led by Archdeacon Crosse was held at Chesterfield Parish Church. War was straining, he remarked, but they had got to see it through to the finish. He reminded them of the words from Isaiah 55: 'Say to them that are of fearful heart, be strong, fear not.' More sacrifice was needed to end the war but, he said by way of trying to keep up morale: 'I believe we are nearer the realisation of our goal than many of us think or dream to be possible.'

Later that month an appeal was made to Derbyshire boys possessing 'pluck, intelligence and initiative' to join the Royal Flying Corps as pilots or observers, because the War Office needed boys in large numbers. Boys aged between sixteen and seventeen-and-a-half years old were also sought, to train as mechanics.

A large cookery room at Herbert Strutt School in Belper was packed for a food economy demonstration on 27 August. As people in Belper, and elsewhere at other such demonstrations, began learning how to produce a wholesome meal without using unnecessary amounts of scarce food there were allegations that money was being made at the expense of the customer. A letter from *Pro Bono Publico* in August, claimed there had been much profiteering from grocers and short weights. One grocer, he claimed, gave

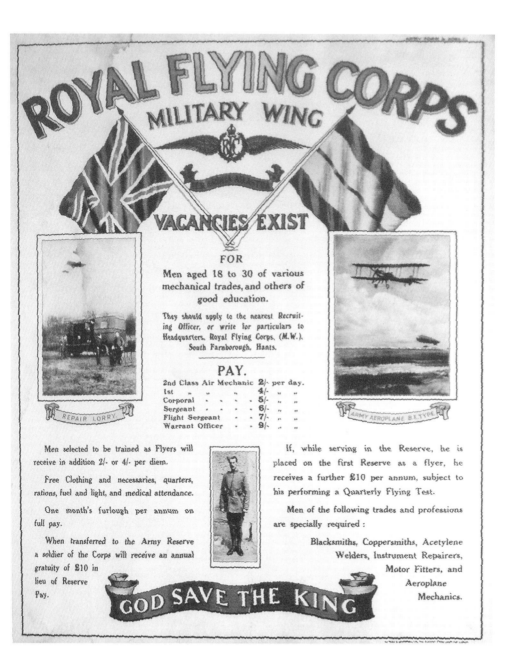

A poster encouraging people to join the Royal Flying Corps. *Author's Collection*

sugar short by three quarters of an ounce on average on each pound supplied.

The introduction of 'sugar cards' in Chesterfield and district was announced in September as a means of ensuring a fair distribution of the commodity. The fair distribution was not to commence immediately, however. It was a pioneering scheme and there was much administration attached to it, and so the distribution by sugar cards only began on 31 December 1917.

The prices and availability of meat and bread also required action, and in September a Food Control Committee was established in Derby.

In Derbyshire, and elsewhere in the country, it was announced that a schedule of decreasing the prices of meat and bread would come into full operation in January 1918, but that some benefits to the public would occur sooner. On 17 September the nine-penny 'quarten' loaf of bread went on sale and on 1 October a new maximum price was set for the sale of flour.

Soon maximum prices were fixed nationally for jam, government-imported cheese, milk, lentils, oatmeal, rolled and flaked oats, peas, haricot and butter beans, certain grades of tea, and chocolate and other sweet meats, Irish butter and the farmer's price for home grown wheat, rye, oats and barley. The produce of the 1917 harvest was also regulated. People were advised to inform the police of anyone who sold above the maximum prices.

Derbyshire butchers were 'much perturbed' when the limitation of meat prices was announced. Farmers shared their concerns (as detailed in the On the Farm chapter).

They felt hard done by as their profit margins were squeezed, but despite the efforts to reduce prices there were criticisms that the benefits were not being passed on to the consumer, with *Pro Bono Publico* writing in the *Derbyshire Times* in October, that customers were still paying 'exuberant prices'.

During October the wife of Chesterfield's food inspector acted as a mystery shopper to investigate the prices that butchers in the town were selling their meat, and to ensure the correct weight had been given. In several cases she was charged too much and it was decided that those butchers should be prosecuted and that further test purchases should be made, and not only for meat.

James Haslam of Chatsworth Road found himself becoming the first butcher to be fined. He sold 1lb of breast of mutton for 1s 2d per pound when it should have been sold for just 1s. James Middleton, who held a stall on Chesterfield market, was also fined for selling 1lb of best rump steak for 2s, which was 2d more than he should have charged. He pleaded ignorance of

Scott and Haslam's butchers in Brampton, Chesterfield, in 1912. Haslam would later be fined for selling overpriced meat. *Courtesy of Derbyshire Libraries and www.picturethepast.org.uk*

the new rules but it was argued they had been well publicised. Soon prosecutions commenced across the county.

Beer shortages were the latest problem for publicans. During July licensees in parts of the county complained there was no beer to sell. It was a frequent problem for the remainder of the war.

Exactly one year before the Armistice was agreed, Archdeacon Crosse held his final official service in Chesterfield, before moving to Whitwell. Cross told the large congregation that despite victory at Flanders and Palestine the outlook of the country was far from being as bright as could be wished for and there never was a greater time when the church was needed to point the way to hope. Cross was praised, with the Mayor saying he had done more than any to keep the people of the town in good heart.

Food shortages were the theme of 1917 and this was certainly the case as the year came to an end.

Sir Arthur Yapp's voluntary rationing scheme was introduced on 12 November and although it was not a scheme that could be enforced, it was expected that patriotic people would follow it. There were, the *Derby Mercury* reported, some people in Derby who visited a number of shops buying all that they could in what was described as 'skirmishing for food'. People often bought excessive amounts if they were able to, to ensure they had sufficient for when there were shortages. Indeed the same buying behaviour was exhibited across Derbyshire. Yapp's scheme was intended to combat the effects of such 'skirmishing'. The scheme appealed to retailers to ration their customers, with varying allowances depending upon occupation, gender and different amounts for children and adults. It had many flaws and it was expected it would fail and a compulsory scheme introduced.

There were shortages of butter in every Derbyshire town. In Wirksworth there had, for centuries, been a weekly butter market held on a Tuesday, with farmers travelling miles to attend. However, the lack of butter led to the market no longer being held.

In Ilkeston a scheme of equal distribution for butter and margarine was planned for January. Extensive queues formed outside shops across Derbyshire daily, with customers attempting to obtain commodities. Some households obtained more than they needed whilst others struggled to get anything.

Smaller retailers, particularly on the outer parts of towns and adjoining districts were often out of supplies of tea, butter and margarine, and so people flocked to the town centres to obtain supplies from the larger dealers, resulting in the very lengthy queues and disturbances, often requiring police involvement.

In Sheldon, Gyte recorded in her diary on 13 December, 'There is no getting anything scarcely and what a price everything is. There is such a shortage of the following articles viz. butter, bacon, tea, lard, margarine, sugar, jam, currants, raisins, candied peel, dates, figs. Eggs are 7 for two shillings.'

Councillor Varley, President of the Chesterfield Trades and Labour Council, caused tremendous controversy when he alleged that foodstuffs had been thrown on manure hemps at Chesterfield by men who had preached food economy. At a mass meeting of trade unionists in Chesterfield on 2 December he protested against high food prices, the 'half-hearted methods of the Food Controller', and the decision of Chesterfield Town Council in electing only one Labour representative on the Local Food Control Committee. Varley severely criticised the food profiteers and said no one should be allowed to gamble with the necessities of life. He added that if food prices were fixed on the basis of supply and demand then workers should demand any sum they desired because they were in demand.

The Chesterfield Food Control Committee continued its efforts despite

Varley's criticisms and introduced a scheme for the rationing of butter, margarine and tea in order to tackle the 'objectionable queue system' and ensure equal distribution. It was the first such scheme in the country.

A scheme on the basis of the sugar-card system was devised for the 36,000 who had registered for sugar who lived in the Borough, and 12,000 who came into the town from the outerlying areas to buy their sugar. It was assumed that these 12,000 would come into Chesterfield for other provisions and so they were needed to be included in the town's new scheme.

Each person who had registered for sugar was given a ration ticket for butter, margarine and tea. There was to be one ration for margarine or butter, so that people could not obtain a full ration of both.

The scheme was adopted voluntarily locally and later become a compulsory scheme for the whole country. People were informed they would be allocated 4 ounces of butter or margarine (or half of each) per person per week and 1 ounce of tea per person per week.

The Chesterfield rationing scheme came into force on 31 December and it was reported to have had immediate success. It had been feared there would be large queues on the day of its introduction, on account of shops being closed for the New Year. However, there were no queues to be seen. The only problems experienced in the town were 'one or two occasions' where shops ran out of supplies. However, these were replenished the next day they were open. Most customers were pleased to receive a higher than anticipated amount of tea; 1½ ounces.

Many mothers sent their children to get provisions, without the cards, having already gone themselves, in the hope they would be able to obtain double rations. However, retailers were firm and refused to serve anyone who did not present their card. It was thought the rationing card system would be free from fraud because unlike sugar cards, the card had to be stamped to show the customer had received their quota.

Some shopkeepers suffered abuse at the hands of customers who were not satisfied with their allowance. The scheme was generally regarded as successful, however.

Due to the successful implementation of the scheme the Town Clerk, Mr J.H. Rothwell, was head hunted by Lord Rhondda and became Director of a department within the Food Controller's Office for approving rationing schemes from various parts of the country. In his absence, Mr W.E. Waverley took on his duties, with Miss Marjorie Newton becoming Assistant Executive Officer as a result of her 'strenuous and efficient efforts', further showing the increasing role women were playing.

For the Christmas of 1917 there was no county effort to send presents to the troops, due to the organisational difficulties involved and the cost of sending parcels. Instead each town and village was encouraged to collect money and send each soldier and sailor a small sum so that they could buy themselves a treat.

On 23 December a constant stream of soldiers who had to break their journey home on leave at Derby railway station sought shelter and refreshment in the YMCA quarters. Such was the demand for food that supplies were quickly exhausted and further food had to be sought from a bakery until it too ran out, at which time food was obtained from the Midland Hotel. Over 1,000 sandwiches, 1,000 cups of tea and coffee and 500 cakes were sold at the YMCA room during a 6-hour period, in addition to other meals.

The lack of encouraging war news, with Russia having commenced peace talks with the Germans on 22 December, and the ever increasing food worries left a gloomy feel to the festive period. Maria Gyte, in recording the first Christmas since her son was killed at war, noted 'Xmas Day and such a sad one. My dear lad Tony was missing from the family circle first time for 20 years. Oh dear! What a dreadful war and what awfully sad homes there are this Xmas. The worst I have ever known. No singing Xmas hymns. No decorations. The singing will be in church.' These sentiments were widely shared.

Christmas in Derby was described as being virtually a 'fireside celebration' with an absence of merriment, although church services were well attended.

The 140 soldiers at Derby Royal Infirmary thoroughly enjoyed Christmas Day, with carols, a service in the chapel and 'charming schemes of decorations'. The Mayor and Mayoress presented cigarettes for the men and toys for the children. Following an 'excellent' turkey dinner there was entertainment, with some of the soldiers leading with singing. A highland fling by Private McMillan was a highlight.

Belper was described as 'very quiet'. In that town the workhouse inmates had a poor Christmas with their rations reduced.

As the year ended a grim discovery was made in the north of the county as Derbyshire suffered another casualty of the war, at home. A Shuttlewood man named Albert Mason had been so tormented by people demanding he join the army, that he killed himself. He had tried to enlist but had been refused on the grounds of poor health and he had been placed on substitution work instead. His body was discovered on the Great Central Line between Eckington and Killamarsh.

CHAPTER 21

1918

As 1918 began there were hopes there would be peace before the year ended, but it was considered unlikely. The editor of the *Derby Mercury* remarked the year had begun with 'an atmosphere which is gloomy and dark, and through which there gleams no light which gives us the sure and certain hope of the near approach of the dawn which we desire'.

It was gloomy not just metaphorically but also quite literally due to electricity shortages in Derby which necessitated curtailed shop lighting and reduced power for trams. The problem was due to the steam boilers in the electricity works needing cleaning and improving. A short supply of coal was also responsible.

On the first Sunday of 1918 churches across Derbyshire and the country joined in prayer once again as another day of intercession took place for an end to the war and protection of troops overseas.

In Matlock, in early January, plans were made for a war shrine, in the form of an inscribed sundial, to encourage prayer for protection of Matlock's men abroad, although discussions about it were still ongoing as the war came to an end.

In addition to prayers, 900 Sherwood Foresters who were prisoners of war in Germany and Turkey, each needed regular food supplies to be sent from home to compensate for the scant provision made by their captors. An appeal was made for funds to send each man six food parcels per month, with £380 spent on average every fortnight.

The main theme of early 1918 was the ongoing food shortages, food price fixing, and rationing, which was now underway in Chesterfield and was to be introduced elsewhere as the year progressed.

A Cattle Order was introduced to ensure a more equitable supply of livestock at each market so that butchers who had struggled to obtain meat had a better prospect of being able to supply their customers. The provision of livestock in the markets was based upon the amount of meat which butchers in the county had required in October 1917. It was decided that the markets should be supplied with half of the amount of meat that butchers had said they had needed. In the case of Derby this entitled the market to ninety cows per week. However, in practice due to shortages in other areas Derby often received a far lower number. In the first week of 1918 just sixty cattle were present, with butchers claiming they needed 165 in order to meet their customers' requirements, and so there was great competition for those cows and for sheep and pigs which thankfully had a higher quantity than usual.

Supplies improved slightly in the following weeks in Derby and there were good supplies of sheep, but there was a serious shortage of beasts, especially in Matlock and Wirksworth.

After a week of rationing of butter, margarine and tea in Chesterfield it became apparent the system was open to fraud, with some people buying supplies outside the town before using their ration tickets at their designated shop within the town, in order to get more of the restricted foods. This problem was alleviated when the rationing scheme was extended to cover the surrounding districts of Clay Cross and the communities of North East Derbyshire, affecting 173,000 people. Those found to commit this offence had their ration card withdrawn.

With Chesterfield's rationing scheme underway, a meeting in Derby of the Town Council considered rationing for margarine, butter and sugar during January.

Delegates went to Birmingham and Leicester to study their schemes. Derby wanted to proceed but the Food Controller said they had to wait until neighbouring district committees had discussed their plans.

On 11 January, Ashbourne Urban, Ashbourne Rural and Mayfield Rural councils also began planning rationing schemes for butter, margarine and tea.

From 17 January, on every Thursday afternoon, free lessons were given in war-time cooking, teaching people how to avoid waste and make the most of the food available, at the Co-op Lecture Hall in Chesterfield.

Meetings continued to be held across the county to persuade people to practice food economy. In Tibshelf on 17 January, Reverend G.H. Bartlett, told a meeting that he felt certain people did not mind being called upon to go short of a certain amount of food for those who were fighting. Mr White, of Matlock, added that they were now on the last lap of the war and a little self-sacrifice would help end the war and secure peace for all time, he believed.

The food situation in Derbyshire had 'distinctly improved' by 12 January according to the Derbyshire Times, with no prospect of famine in the area, provided that people put their trust in the authorities. However, it would appear the improvements were confined to the Chesterfield area where rationing was in force.

A meeting was held in January in the Central Hall, Derby to protest against food availability and the queues outside shops. People had to queue for several hours in all weather, across the county with the exception of Chesterfield, and this was considered detrimental to health and morale. A frequent complaint was that whilst the working classes waited in lengthy queues for several hours, motor cars would pull up outside a shop and within five minutes the driver succeeded in obtaining what food they required.

The Director of Food Economy wrote a public notice saying three British destroyers were sunk, with a loss of life, while convoying butter ships from Holland and people should remember that fact when grumbling about queues because the sailors in the Navy were quite literally dying in order to bring the food. He argued that the less food that was consumed, the lower the risk to those who brought it. Rich people were asked to use less butter to help ensure there was more for the poor who had to queue in the cold for it.

A casualty of the food queues was Mary A. Towey, a twenty-eight-year-old wife and mother from Canal Street, Derby, who drowned herself in the Erewash Canal in January. She had suffered from influenza due to standing in food queues for many hours and had become despondent that she was unable to obtain enough food.

People across Derbyshire were urged to grow their own food if they could, and owners of larger tracts of land were encouraged to provide space for allotments. Later in the year the *Derbyshire Times* ran a competition for the largest three potatoes grown in the county, in order to encourage people to grow their own, especially as there had been a deficit of 44,200 tons of potatoes grown in the county in 1917.

Supplies of beef were for a time exhausted in the Chesterfield area in early January and 100 frozen sheep carcasses had to be obtained from the government to provide an alternative. Due to this meat shortage there were recommendations from butchers in the north of Derbyshire for nationwide meat rationing but, in the meantime, it was decided to implement a local scheme, covering Chesterfield, Holmesfield, Dronfield Woodhouse, Coal Aston, Beighton, Killamarsh, Barlborough, Whitwell, Elmton, Bolsover, Heath, North Wingfield, Pilsley, Morton, Shirland and Wessington. The scheme ran along the same lines as the rationing of other foodstuffs, although different allowances were given based upon occupation (although women workers in munitions factories later complained they had not received the enhanced rations).

The local meat rationing scheme's introduction was delayed because butchers did not complete the paperwork in time. Additionally, when requested by the government to provide accurate figures of how much meat they had sold during October, in order to better ensure the government sent the amount of meat that was needed to satisfy customer's demands, many of the butchers gave untruthful figures believing the forms had something to do with income tax.

When the scheme was introduced in February all the meat available was divided between the butchers according to the number of people registered with them. Every butcher received sufficient meat to supply their customers with half a pound for each adult, with those employed in certain occupations receiving more, and quarter of a pound for each child (aged five to fourteen). The scheme did not include pork offals, rabbits and tinned meat.

With the shortages of beef and pork, at least one butcher attempted to sell horseflesh under the pretence it was beef. William Colledge of William Colledge and Sons, was fined the maximum £20 plus £5 5s costs for failing to comply with the Sales of Horse Flesh Regulations Act (1889). The Act required a sign bearing letters no less than 4 inches in length to clearly state the meat was horseflesh. Colledge claimed he had not been misleading his customers and that he did not realise it was not beef. However, he was not believed and as a butcher he ought to have been able to distinguish the two types of meat. The court room was full and the case had been the talk of the town for the preceding week.

Horse flesh proved to be a popular alternative to beef when it went on sale in February 1918, in accordance with the law, with the stall on Chesterfield market surrounded by crowds. There was great demand for the meat and so the other horses were quickly slaughtered. Depots for the sale of horse flesh were set up under the strict supervision of the health authorities. All horse flesh for human consumption was slaughtered at a central station and only approved retailers were able to sell the meat, which soon went on sale elsewhere in Derbyshire.

Although the problems in north Derbyshire were slightly alleviated by the efforts of the butchers and the local food committees, elsewhere difficulties continued to escalate. In Derby there was great anger that workers in Spondon were receiving excessive amounts of food at the expense of others. In fact there were some cases of people working in Spondon selling the food at a profit. One reason for the excessive supply in Spondon was the works canteens, where workers were able to eat wholesome meals at work and still obtain their full allowance for consumption at home. The problem was not unique to Spondon. It was suggested the allocation for the canteens should be reduced by at least a half. It was accepted that once the full rationing scheme commenced the problem would be alleviated.

There were also suspicions from workers in Derby that they were not receiving their fair share of food. At the February meeting of the Derby Town Council it was agreed that some workers should be elected as members of the Food Control Committee so that those suspicions might be eliminated by a greater understanding of the difficulties faced by the committee.

There was anger in Matlock also, that visitors who were staying at the Hydro were able to buy sugar from a Matlock grocer and also from a shop at which they were registered at home.

On 26 January captured German guns arrived in Belper. The guns, which were captured by the Sherwood Foresters, were part of a week long exhibition to encourage the purchase of War Bonds and Certificates. Other exhibits included: a German officer's coat, razor, watch and chain; used shells and shrapnel; German revolvers; a bayonet; a relic of the first Zeppelin shot down; a German gas mask; a small book containing a German will; other personal belongings taken from a German dugout.

The following day there were scenes of great excitement when 'Old Bill' arrived in Derby. Officially known as Tank 119, its presence was not to satisfy needs of pleasure or curiosity, but to satisfy the need for money to finance the war. Old Bill was one of six touring tanks which were often referred to as 'Tank Banks'. A massive £1,500,000 was needed from Derbyshire to pay for 300 tanks and War Savings Bonds and Certificates were sold to reach this figure. There had been disappointment that whilst in the county it had not gone to Chesterfield where, the authorities felt sure, a large amount of money could have been raised. There were also complaints from the Derby Free

Tank 119, affectionately known as Old Bill, one of the 'tank banks' which visited Derby. *Author's Collection*

Church that the machine of war had arrived on a Sunday. The Market Place and Corn Exchange became a 'maze of moving humanity', according to the *Derby Mercury*, as people tried to watch the tank's arrival.

The official opening of Tank Week occurred the following day when huge crowds assembled in Derby Market Place to see the war machine and to hear speakers including Mr E.J. Hulse (Mayor of Derby), Mr F.C. Arkwright (Vice Lieutenant), Ernest Shentall (Mayor of Chesterfield), Alderman A. Henshaw (Mayor of Ilkeston), Alderman J. Oakes (Chairman of Derbyshire County Council) and Gilbert Crompton (High Sheriff of Derbyshire).

Hulse opened the event by saying everyone knew the fighting abilities of the tanks and how the Germans ran when they saw them, but that Old Bill had come to Derby on a more peaceful errand: to find money so that more of his fellows might be sent to the front.

Mr Arkwright appealed to large employers, wealthy private individuals who, if they did not have enough money now, could borrow money to invest, and small investors. Even the ordinary working class could afford to buy, he said, given the higher wages they were now earning.

Alderman Oakes said they would have difficulty beating the amount of money Nottingham had raised, but Derbyshire was a wealthy county and he did not see why it should not do it. Ernest Shentall added that it was not a case of beating Nottingham but of beating the enemy. Alderman Henshaw called on every man and woman in Derbyshire to do their duty and invest what they could.

In order to encourage people to buy, the High Sheriff provided prizes to the value of £1,000. Upon buying a Certificate or Bond the investor was given a sealed envelope, some of which contained prizes in the form of further certificates.

A Children's Day was held on Tuesday, with more than 12,000 youngsters enjoying the spectacle. Children had been great contributors to the cause. In the county there were more than 350 school war savings associations, with a membership of 25,991 children who together had invested £21,000 by the end of September 1917.

To appeal to the women of Derbyshire, there was a special Ladies Day on the Wednesday, with speakers including the Mayoress of Derby. That day the famous actor Fred Terry, who was performing at the Grande Theatre, made an appeal from the tank for people to lend more than they could spare.

On Thursday, during Tradesman Day, there were scenes of amazement when aeroplanes flew over the Market Place, dropping 'bombs' in the form of propaganda cards persuading people to invest.

On Friday, a ceremony was held with speakers including Colonel Fitzherbert Wright MP, the mayor of Derby and Mr J.W. Cutts of the Derbyshire Farmers' Union. That same day decorated motor cars drove the streets, with people being able to buy War Savings Certificates from the vehicle.

Although the tank was only present in Derby, special efforts were made elsewhere in the county during the week. In Chesterfield, 1,000 War Savings Certificates were sold, with Alderman G.A. Eastwood personally adding 1s to the value of each certificate in order for people to be encouraged to invest. In Ilkeston, 1,000 certificates were purchased for the town's children.

During the week £1,309,514 18s 6d was raised and to thank the people of Derby a tank was delivered on 23 May 1919 and was kept on Normanton Recreation Ground where it remained until it was scrapped during the Second World War (an invitation to the arrival ceremony forms part of the Derbyshire Record Office archive: reference D3772/T38/10/5).

The famous actor, Fred Terry, who urged Derbyshire folk to invest more than they could afford during Derby Tank Week. *Author's Collection*

Following the armistice other Derbyshire towns including Chesterfield and Glossop also received tanks to show gratitude for their fund raising.

Following Tank Week, the county returned its attentions to the food problems. Schools were closed in Wirksworth to allow teachers to prepare cards for the rationing of tea, butter and margarine. The scheme began on 25 February affecting 3,205 people in Wirksworth and surrounding villages.

On 14 February the first communal kitchen in the country was opened in Chesterfield. The Glumangate kitchen was set up largely on the efforts of the Ladies' Sub-committee of the Food Control Committee. Affordable meals included soup, meat and potato pie and jam rolls. Sugar and fresh milk were also sold. It was remarked a housewife would have to be 'thrifty indeed' to be able to prepare such meals at the prices charged. It was emphasised that the kitchen was not a charitable institution, instead being run as a business and to buy from it was to be patriotic, by helping prevent food wastage. By buying from the kitchen a good meal was provided with vegetables as well as meat, something which it appeared many did not fully understand, thereby reducing the amount of meat consumed in a time of meat shortages.

Within a week of its opening the kitchen was considered to be a great success, with housewives of 'all classes' buying meals, with an average of 303 meals sold for the first five days. It was not long before a further two kitchens were opened in the town, on 30 March and 20 April.

The following week it was decided to open food kitchens in Derby, although there was some opposition from councillors who questioned if they were needed.

Plans to set up a Belper communal kitchen began in March although there was reluctance from councillors to go ahead unless the government covered the costs of the initiative. It was argued they had managed for four years without them.

The government had to be called upon to help provide more meat during March when the livestock at the Derby market was woefully inadequate. The government responded by sending frozen meat for two weeks to make up the shortfall.

Elsewhere in Derbyshire, and nationally, it was announced a meat rationing scheme was to be introduced on 25 March, although its introduction was later postponed until 7 April and so voluntary schemes continued. The postponement was for further arrangements to allow those who undertook heavy industrial work to receive larger rations.

The consequences of the prices and availability of meat on butchers was made stark in March when a Chesterfield butcher shot himself dead. Although grief for his son who had been killed at war in July 1916 contributed to his state of depression, Sydney Thomas Whitford became increasingly despondent due to the fixing of meat prices which left him unable to cope financially. Whitford was sixty-five years old and had kept a stall on Chesterfield Market for forty years. According to his daughter he was often seen brooding and rarely left the house. In the weeks before his death he had told his daughter he had pains in his head and that the war would kill him. 'The honest truth is the meat shortage has killed him. When he was reckoning up his meat he used to hold his head and say, "It's no use, I can't do it", she told the inquest into his death. The jury returned a verdict of 'suicide whilst of unsound mind.'

Food hoarding, in light of the food shortages, was a criminal offence. A gross case of hoarding occurred in Wirksworth in March, when a household consisting of eight persons were known to possess 56lbs of bacon at a time when bacon was extremely scarce and was soon to be rationed. In addition to the 56lbs, which had been obtained from Ireland, the head of the household had a further supply of bacon in cold storage and she had recently purchased a pig which had been slaughtered in Middleton. The Wirksworth Local Food Control Committee informed Mr Marsden-Smedley, a Justice of the Peace, but were frustrated when he wrote back saying that nothing could be done until they provided more information. The Committee wanted to search the property themselves rather than wait for the police to undertake initial investigations, by which time the bacon would be gone. One member remarked, 'Practically Mr Marsden-Smedley says it is quite right for a person to buy bacon in 56lbs, while other people cannot get 56 grains.'

The issue of hoarding meat was particularly timely as preparations were underway for the national meat rationing scheme, which began on 7 April. As with previous rationing schemes there was a vast amount of work involved, with more than 140,000 individual meat cards produced and distributed by volunteers in Derby and its district alone. The efforts of women and schoolteachers were particularly valuable. When the national scheme began local schemes across the county ceased.

A Business Men's Week was held across Derbyshire during March to obtain more funds to buy war vehicles and equipment. Each town or village was expected to raise varying amounts dependent upon its population. Chesterfield was expected to fund a submarine at £100,000, Alfreton to fund nineteen aeroplanes, Belper twelve aeroplanes, Buxton fourteen aeroplanes, Derby one monitor, Glossop twenty-two aeroplanes, Heanor twenty aeroplanes, Ilkeston one submarine, Long Eaton nineteen aeroplanes, Ripley twelve aeroplanes and Swadlincote nineteen aeroplanes.

In late March 1918 the war news looked bleak. During what was described as the 'World's Greatest Battle', but is more popularly known as the Spring Offensive, British troops were attacked by 'overwhelming' numbers of Germans. The fate of the British Empire was in the balance, the *Derbyshire Times* reported, 'for the full weight of the German armies has been thrown on to the British line on a Front of 30 miles'. A positive spin was put on the news, with it being said that some German divisions had been annihilated and that French planes were dropping bombs, with French reinforcements coming to the assistance and British soldiers 'doggedly fighting'. The *Derby Mercury* described a 'German onrush', causing 'anxiety' and 'great stress'.

On 3 March, Russia finally exited the war, upon signing a peace treaty with Germany and its allies, losing approximately one million square kilometres of its land. Fighting had ceased on the Eastern Front weeks earlier, enabling Germany and its allies to concentrate almost all their efforts on advancing on the Western Front.

Huge losses on the Western Front as a result of the Spring Offensive resulted in a further Military Service Act being introduced, allowing men up to the age of fifty-one to be compelled to join the army.

During April, F.C. Arkwright appealed for Derbyshire folk to give hospitality to Anzac soldiers. He pointed out that overseas dominions provided hospitality to English in peace time so we should make a greater effort in war time to those who have come to help our forces.

During the Whitsun holiday a mock battle was held on the Monday as part of the Whitsuntide camp of the 2nd Battalion Derbyshire Volunteers. The 'battle' was fought in the open countryside between Brimington, Calow and Chesterfield. Later that day there was much merriment at the sight of approximately 200 men standing in footbaths.

Merriments elsewhere included sports on the Baseball Ground in Derby and a carnival at Bolsover Castle where the Bolsover Colliery Silver band, comic costumes, decorated perambulators, Scouts and girl guides. Corporal Norburn's Follies, decorated cars and women in the national costumes of the Allies and sports all provided such an enjoyable day that memories were evoked of pre-war celebrations.

In Derbyshire, shops were closed and people flocked to entertainment venues, with packed trams heading into Derby town centre. Refreshment caterers were said to have done a 'roaring trade'.

The Whitsuntide holidays were kept to a minimum, however, as was the earlier Easter break, with factories instructed to produce more tools and weapons for the Western Front in order to make good the losses encountered during the Spring Offensive.

In June, Matlock raised nearly £35,000 to buy aeroplanes. The intention had only been to raise half that amount and when the total was revealed there was a mass demonstration in Matlock Park to celebrate.

Towards the end of that month, Matlock Bath and Buxton had cause to celebrate when the Duke of Connaught, the Duke of Devonshire's predecessor as Governor General of Canada, visited the Canadian hospitals in both towns. In Matlock Bath he praised the hospital and the scenic beauty of the area. Residents turned out in large numbers in both towns to welcome the visitor.

The health of the county's children became a serious concern during June, when Dr Barwise, the Medical Officer for schools in Derbyshire, reported to the County Council. There was a lot of heart disease and other common afflictions included ear disease, enlarged tonsils and adenoid growths (affecting between 1 in 5 and 1 in 10 of all children), rheumatism and tuberculosis. In terms of tuberculosis, sixty-six children had been sent to the sanatorium in the previous twelve months and 1,032 had been referred to the tuberculosis dispensaries. Indeed, it was the doctor's belief that in terms of health the situation in Derbyshire was so hopeless that it could not be put right.

Few would have been aware of the health concerns, although they were well reported in the Derbyshire newspapers, with greater concern about food supplies. Despite the meat rationing scheme in Chesterfield there was no fresh meat for a short period in June. Generally, however, the food situation had improved so much that it was decided to close the communal kitchens for the summer. The meat situation countywide had also shown signs of improvement.

Following the success of the local schemes, most notably in Chesterfield and its district, rationing came into being in July 1918 for all parts of Derbyshire, and the whole country, for sugar, butter, margarine and lard, as well as new ration allowances for meat. It was decided not to ration tea nationally at that time, but local authorities were allowed to impose their own local scheme. Due to the partial failure of fruit crops in the summer of 1918, and the shortage of sugar, provision was also made for jam to be rationed on a local scale should Local Food Control Committees decide it was needed. Jam was much needed by the military and so priority was given to supplying the army. In June strawberry stocks were commandeered in Derby to make the preserve and a large scale campaign of blackberry picking was initiated across the county during the early autumn months in order to try and obtain sufficient fruit, though heavy rain spoilt the crops, with only 12 tons picked of an anticipated 150 tons.

To accommodate the dietary requirements of Jews and vegetarians, they were allowed to interchange their meat and fat allowances. Those suffering from medical problems such as diabetes and tuberculosis were provided with supplementary meat rations, as were those engaged in heavy industry and farming. The rules applied to all civilians as well as soldiers and sailors on leave.

Tobacco shortages led to long queues at shops in Derbyshire in June and July. However, it was thought genuine customers were not going short, with 95 per cent of people in the queues actually intending to buy up tobacco to sell at a profit. In order to try and reduce this problem people were reminded it was illegal to congregate in crowds and illegal to hoard tobacco and sell it without a license.

In addition to food and tobacco, coal and fuel had to be rationed from 1

July. Each household was allowed one ton of fuel, per occupied room, per year. The wording of notices regarding fuel rationing caused confusion because people assumed only coal was being rationed because of the reference to the 'ton' measurement, and so they thought they were free to use as much of the other fuels as they pleased. In fact the ton measurement was equal to one ton of coal, 1½ tons of coke, 15,000 cubic feet of gas, or 800 Board of Trade units of electricity. People were free to take their allowance with any combination of the different fuels, provided they did not exceed the one 'ton' per room limit.

The price of coal continued to be alarming, at 31s 6d per ton and in July, for a time, there was no coal available in Ashbourne.

The supply of fuel led to the exploration for oil in Derbyshire. Oil had been found at Pye Bridge near Alfreton years earlier and so hopes had been high of its discovery once again in the county. Prospectors began boring in Derbyshire shortly before the armistice but it was not until May 1919 that they located an oilfield at Hardstoft, six miles from Chesterfield. Its discovery led to the belief that Chesterfield would fill the dual position of metropolis for both the oilfield and coalfields of Derbyshire and that it would be a tremendous boost for industry in the county.

Although the shortages of food and fuel were at the forefront of people's thoughts as 1918 progressed, there remained the problem of the shortage of men in the army. With this in mind H.A.L. Fisher, President of the Local Government Board, wrote to the Derbyshire recruiting tribunals in June pointing out the extreme importance of tribunals deciding upon cases as soon as possible. Many more men were needed without delay, he added, and that exemptions were not justified unless there were fully adequate reasons. After reading the letter the tribunal at Chesterfield considered a number of cases including that of Thomas Soar. His wife applied for exemption on his behalf because her first husband had been killed in Ypres two years earlier and she could not bear for the same to happen to her second husband. The claim was disallowed. Walter Worthington, a forty-three-year-old brush maker from Staveley also applied on the basis that he provided brushes to the munitions factories and therefore was carrying out important war work. His claim was also disallowed and he was given coastal defence duties.

Although the tribunals in Derbyshire had been rather harsh with their decisions, it would appear there had been some slackening in the East Midlands by July 1918. In that month a letter from the county headquarters of the National Service Ministry was sent to the Chesterfield Borough Tribunal, pointing out that during the period 11 May to 8 June the percentage of refusals of exemptions in the East Midlands region was below the average for the country. The letter asked that something be done to improve this position. At the Chesterfield tribunal, following the consideration of the letter, many exemptions were given to the men who attended, mostly due to their work in industries in particular the James Pearson's Ltd pottery company and the Barker Pottery Company, with some of the applicants being granted exemption until 1 February 1919, which would mean they were never to participate in the war.

The letters of H.A.L. Fisher and the Derbyshire headquarters of the National Service Ministry further shows that recruitment was influenced by the need to meet targets even if the individual's circumstances ought to have resulted in an exemption being granted.

More funds for weapons were needed. In Derby, a War Weapons Week began on 8 July to raise £500,000 in sales of War Savings Bonds and Certificates. Money was greatly needed because nationally sales had fallen. A large marquee in the Market Place formed a temporary bank, and a motor bus lent by the Trent Motor Traction Company, which was decorated with flags and had a miniature tank on its roof, visited places of work to encourage buying. The Midland Railway and Rolls-Royce each contributed £100,000 and a total of £576,585 was raised during the week. Due to the sum raised it was recommended by the National War Savings Committee that two tanks be named Derby.

There was less success in Belper where its War Weapons Week, which was also held in July, raised only £5000 of the £30,000 needed.

In early August, a YMCA Hut Week was held to raise £5,000 to fund huts which were used on the Western Front; and to provide comforts, games, concerts, and a place where men could rest when not in the trenches. A range of events were held to raise the money.

YMCA Hut Week coincided with the Clowne Rural District War Weapon's Week. Creswell contributed to the effort, with the Duke of Portland and Mr J.P. Honfton JP of Mansfield addressing a big crowd.

The Duke said on many occasions Creswell people had been asked to show their support for the war and 700 Creswell men had joined the army. Now he was asking them for money. They may have heard rumours that by subscribing to War Bonds they were prolonging the war, but he wanted them to know this was not true. Instead the more money they contributed, the more rigorously the war would be waged and the sooner it would be brought to an end.

Mr Honfton said they should not be satisfied until every town and city behind the Rhine were bombed and until Berlin itself had experienced the horrors of war. He hoped Creswell was going to find the money for that purpose.

War weapons weeks helped the troops advance. In the first week of August there had been a 'great advance by the Allies', with 7,000 prisoners and 100 guns taken. The Germans had been taken completely by surprise, it was said.

There were grounds for a slightly more relaxed attitude towards the prospects of the war and it with this in mind that people enjoyed an unusual spectacle in Queens Park in Chesterfield on 10 August, when American troops stationed in the town, having arrived in England in March, played baseball. A reporter for the *Derbyshire Times* described the crowd's curiosity towards the game and the unusual manner in which it was played. The troops had yet to complete their training and it was remarked that given the skill with which they pitched balls, and their other abilities in the game, they would turn into a very fine body when their training was complete. Baseball was not new to the county, with efforts having been made by Francis Ley in Derby, with the baseball ground being created. Additionally, Matlock Bath had witnessed baseball matches due to the presence of Canadians recovering in the town's Canadian Convalescence Hospital.

On the fourth anniversary of the war, which had become known as Remembrance Day, special intercessionary services were held across the county. There was a crowded congregation at All Saints' Church for prayers and thanksgiving. Reverend W.H. Green said he hoped 4 August would be a national day for the British, a day of solemn remembrance and prayer.

At a united service at the Central Hall in Derby, Archdeacon Noakes said the nation had accepted many changes over the past four years and it was with courage and hope that they renewed their determination to see the good fight through to the end.

A civic church parade overshadowed a demonstration organised by the Derby branch of the National Federation of Demobilised and Discharged Soldiers some of whose members assembled in Unity Square with a banner appealing to 'Help Your Own Local Heroes.'

According to the editor of the *Derby Mercury*, Derbyshire entered the fifth year of war strengthened in its determination to fight. He added that changes in the fortunes of war, especially on the Western Front, had 'brightened the outlook to a degree which seemed hardly possible a few weeks ago'. Quoting Lloyd George, it was said readers should 'Hold fast' because 'our prospects of victory have never been so bright as they are today'.

In Belper, Reverend J.A. Cooper spoke of how they now felt more convinced going to war was right and that the English race had never shone brighter than during the past four years. With their determination, and the Americans, he was sure of victory.

Resolutions in various towns and villages pledged loyalty and ongoing determination to see the war through to a full victory.

In Chesterfield, to mark the anniversary, a meeting was held in the Corporation Theatre, but such was the demand to attend that a second meeting had to be held in the Hippodrome.

A resolution was passed stating: 'That the citizens of Chesterfield here assembled on Remembrance Day, 4th August 1918, silently paying tribute to the Empire's sons who have fallen in the fights for freedom on the scattered battlefields of the world war, whether on sea or shore, and mindful also of the loyalty and courage of our sailors, soldiers, and men everywhere and those who are working on the munitions of war and helping in other ways for the preservation of civilisation, unanimously resolve to do all that in their power lies to achieve the ideals on behalf of which so great a sacrifice has already been made.'

Addressing the main meeting, the Mayor reiterated that the outcome of the war depended as much on their efforts as the efforts of the soldiers on the Front.

Councillor Edmunds said that the previous year they had met under heavy dark clouds, but that now there was a break in these clouds. However, he stressed that victory was not now inevitable and that meetings such as this were needed more than ever so that they remained determined to carry on the war to a successful conclusion rather than agree to peace terms with Germany that would be unfavourable to the Allies. Such a peace, he argued, 'would be the blackest treachery to our gallant lads who had fallen'.

Mr Handel Booth, MP for Pontefract, said the allies were now on the highway to a great success, but it would be slow. He warned them of the danger of a premature peace, which would lead to a second war which would in all probability be waged on British soil and might find us without allies.

At the overflow meeting, which also had a very large audience, Chesterfield's Vicar spoke of the determination to continue the war and the graves in different parts of the world where crosses stood over the bodies of British boys, and the families at home who were grief stricken. An appeal for economy was also made and those who could not fight were encouraged to give their money so weapons could be bought to hasten the end of the war.

People were beginning to realise that the dark cloud of war would pass, although when that would happen they could only speculate and the hardship was to continue in the meantime.

A special effort to sell War Bonds and Savings Certificates was made on 30 August in Great Longstone, with a short event well advertised (a poster advertising the event forms part of the Derbyshire Record Office archive: reference D307/M/9).

By the beginning of October, Chesterfield's war bonds had exceeded £900,000 and people were asked to make a special effort to reach £1million in sales. There were also appeals for £25,000 for the Comrades Club to provide care to soldiers and sailors who had been made disabled in the war.

A need for better care was recognised in Derby in September when Charles Hooper, who had been discharged in February suffering from shell shock, committed suicide. People were beginning to realise that war could affect psychological, as well as physical, health.

In Derbyshire in October there were 4,356 discharged men on the register of the Derbyshire War Pensions Committee of the County Council suffering from a range of disabilities including heart disease, chest complaints, amputations, other wounds, tuberculosis, blindness, deafness, rheumatism, epilepsy, neurasthenia and other mental afflictions.

At the end of that month a Derby County committee was formed for the King's Fund for the Disabled. Major Herbert Evans, Chief Inspector of the Ministry of Pensions, said it was common to find an ex-serviceman in the workhouse or requiring parochial support and so action was necessary. Conscription had made it the duty of the nation to ensure that just as it had been easy for a man to enter the army, so it ought to be made easy for a man to enter civilian life without suffering any consequence of having served his country.

In October, one of the largest dairy companies suddenly discontinued deliveries in Wirksworth because it was prevented from selling milk at 7d per quart. The local Food Control Committee took over the supply, with lady clerks from the Food Control Office, with special constables, distributing the milk to eager buyers at 5d per quart.

Jam rationing was introduced in November 1918 and the sale of milk became controlled by the government. Tea was also again rationed in parts of Derbyshire, having been suspended in August.

On the war front, news brightened significantly in October and early November with rapid developments. On 18 October it was reported in the *Derby Mercury* that there had been 'events of foremost importance to the future peace of the world' with Germany having appealed to President Wilson for an armistice, and the surrender of Turkey, as well as successes on the battlefields.

Two weeks later the same paper reported that there were signs to encourage high hopes. 'The end of the war, it has been prophesied, is not only in sight but is at hand', the editor noted, with peace terms being drawn up by Britain and its allies.

Anticipation and emotions began to build up as the war news looked extremely positive, with the headline of the *Derby Daily Telegraph* on 6 November reading: 'Germany and Peace – delegates leave Berlin to meet Foch' and 'The Great British Victory – German defences Broken on Thirty Mile Front'.

Austria-Hungary signed an armistice agreement on 3 November and when negotiations with Germany began on 7 November it was believed to be only a matter of time before the fighting ceased altogether.

On 9 November the *Derbyshire Times* reported on what was fast being realised to be the closing stages of the war. The headlines for the 'magnificent news' were:

ALLIED ARMIES SWEEPING ON
GERMANS IN FULL RETREAT
TURKEY AND AUSTRIA OUT OF THE WAR
GERMAN'S WHITE FLAG DELEGATES
REPORTED MUTINY IN THE GERMAM ARMY

Despite the retreat of the German army, and peace negotiations beginning, efforts were still made in Derbyshire to raise money for weapons. Whittington and Newbold Gun Week began on 4 November to raise £70,000. A howitzer gun was placed at the junction of the Sheffield and Station Roads.

Alongside the news of the German retreat an advert in the *Derbyshire Times* attempted to persuade people, as part of the Gun Week, to 'Bombard the Hun defences with your money!' The advert ended, 'Lend ALL you can – and when the "Cease Fire" sounds on the day of final Victory you will have the right to claim a share in the triumph of our Great Cause. Feed the Gun with War Bonds and help to win the war.'

With that cease fire occurring just two days later, the contributors from Whittington and Newbold did not make a difference to the war, but the enthusiasm they gave to 'feeding the guns' certainly made them feel like they were helping achieve victory.

A Derby Gun Week was advertised to commence on 18 November to raise £600,000 but it was acknowledged the fighting could have ended by then.

CHAPTER 22

The End of Hostilities

With encouraging news being reported, as Monday 11 November 1918 approached people across Derbyshire, as elsewhere, believed the war was coming to an end very soon.

The Armistice was signed at 5am French time and came into effect at 11am; and before that time the first editions of the daily newspapers had announced the imminent end of hostilities. Unfortunately false reports of an armistice prior to 11 November had led to cynicism. Indeed, when the official announcement was made, and celebrations began, there were some in Derbyshire who did not believe it.

On the whole, however, when the news reached Derbyshire there was, as the *Derbyshire Times* put it, 'a spontaneous outbreak of rejoicing' with Derbyshire folk giving themselves up to 'healthy, reasonable celebration of the great event', with jubilations and rejoicing throughout the county, lasting for several days.

The last time parts of Derbyshire had seen jubilation was in June 1914 during the royal visit. Now the entire county, and what a different county it had been transformed into since those relatively carefree days of early summer 1914, had cause to engage in one of the greatest celebrations ever witnessed. It is not possible to describe the reaction in every town and village of Derbyshire but the following accounts, based on information from the *Derby Mercury* and *Derbyshire Times*, on 15 and 16 November 1918 respectively, give a flavour of the atmosphere and how the news was celebrated.

In Derby, the announcement was received 'with feelings of great thankfulness and joy'. Shortly after 10:30am, the Mayor and other 'notable citizens' were informed. A special edition of the *Derby Daily Telegraph* went on sale with the headline, 'The End of the war – hostilities are to cease on all fronts at 11am today'. That newspaper was quickly sold out. Flags of the Allies appeared on all public buildings, soon followed by flags and ribbons on residences. Hand-flags and tricolour ribbons, bearing red, white and blue were also quickly sold out as the town adopted a 'gay and animated appearance'.

Business came to a standstill in many of the works and workers left the factories and marched the streets, obtaining ribbons, flags and makeshift decorations. Soldiers, including those wearing hospital blues, were 'infected' with the holiday spirit and where possible joined the processions. As the afternoon wore on people donned their Sunday best and flocked to the centre of town for the main festivities of music, processions, cheering and speeches from local dignitaries. Before long it was impossible to traverse the streets due to the volume of people. 'All over the district the rejoicings were universal', the *Derby Mercury* later reported, though there was an equal amount of sorrow in the hearts of those who had lost loved ones to make that day possible.

The church bells across Derby rang out merry peals and the churches opened their doors for the swarms of people to offer prayers of thanksgiving, especially at All Saints' Church. Ad-hoc services were held, with more formal ceremonies arranged for subsequent days.

The Chief Constable received a telegram from the Commander in Chief of the Northern Command informing him that with no threat now existing the lighting restrictions could be lifted and that fireworks and bonfires would be permitted as part of the celebrations.

Elsewhere in the south of the county adults and children alike paraded the decorated streets and church bells rang, with thanksgiving services held.

In Chesterfield, news of the Armistice was signalled, shortly after 11am, by continuous sounding of the factory 'bulls'. Immediately, people left their places of work, not caring whether there was consent, and before long the streets were packed. All public buildings became adorned with the Union Flag and the flags of the allies. A public house in Brampton made its own flag bearing the words 'Welcome Home', though celebrations would be limited at that establishment, because beneath the flag there was a note stating 'No Beer.'

Although there was much joy and 'gaiety' on the streets of Chesterfield this was modified out of consideration for those who would not be able to welcome home loved ones. In Chesterfield Market Place, the Mayor and Archdeacon Crosse addressed a crowd of thousands and throughout the day the Town Band played music.

The bells of the parish church rang out a 'joyful peal' and in the evening the church was opened up for those who wished to give silent prayers of thanksgiving. Within quarter of an hour the church was packed and an impromptu service given. A special service of thanksgiving was arranged for Sunday morning. Thanksgiving services were also held at other churches in the town. At night Chesterfield was a blaze of light. Fireworks produced colourful displays in the sky, in part compensating for some of the street lights that could not be lit due to coal shortages.

On Whittington Moor the factory buzzers delivered the news. Work ended and before long the streets were filled with excited crowds, although most people headed to Chesterfield town centre, and 'bunting of all descriptions' was displayed everywhere. Whittington Moor was almost entirely deserted by the evening, with festivities in full swing in the town just two miles away.

In Staveley, the news was received with a 'general feeling of thankfulness and rejoicing'. People realised the fighting had ended when the buzzers of the works and collieries all sounded. It was not long before the parish church and houses across the town were draped with flags and bunting. During the afternoon there was a united service on The Cross. The following day, 'quite a holiday spirit' was present. Staveley Grammar School reopened but there were no lessons as such. The headmaster, Mr A.R. Blackburn, spoke to the boys about the war, and at the conclusion of his address the pupils gave cheers for the Allies, the Empire and the flags.

In Clay Cross, an announcement was made prior to the Armistice coming into effect. Perhaps it was because of previous false announcements that celebrations did not begin until it was almost noon. Before long there were so many flags and buntings on display that there were very few businesses and houses without any type of decoration. At the local schools the pupils 'jubilated lustily' and no more lessons were held until Wednesday. With the schools closed, 'happy bands of youngsters' paraded the streets singing patriotic songs. Work also ended until Wednesday in order to make merry the occasion. Merriment was provided by women of the Long Rows who arranged an impromptu open air concert. The church bells also provided a 'joyous peal' before a special united service of thanksgiving was held. With no school or work on the Tuesday 'local people absolutely gave themselves up to unprecedented rejoicing'.

In Heath and Holmewood, a thanksgiving service was held in the parish church in the evening. This was followed, on the Tuesday evening, with a United Service in the Primitive Methodist church, Holmewood.

The management at Glapwell Colliery received the news at around 11:30am. Its workers were informed when the large colliery flag was hoisted on the headgear at the pit top, resulting in outbursts of cheering by the surface workmen and officials who continued working until 2:45pm.

Doe Lea was 'gay with flags and bunting' and the Glapwell Colliery Brass Band paraded the village on Monday night and headed a procession of school children the following day. Although they were supposed to return to the colliery on Tuesday, none of the men showed up.

The people of Bolsover learnt the news when the colliery buzzers began to sound. People soon flocked to the parish and Wesleyan churches, where feelings of sorrow and joy were clearly evident as solemn prayers of thanksgiving were offered. The younger residents of Bolsover expressed happier emotions by marching through the streets singing patriotic songs whilst tapping away on improvised drums. Despite feelings of sorrow there were also feelings of happiness and relief, and demand for flags and other decorations far exceeded supply and so 'make shifts were the order of the day'.

In Clowne, the news was met with 'unbounded enthusiasm'. Flags were hung everywhere 'with bewildering profusion'. The local schools were closed for the whole week and the miners decided to down tools and have a two-day holiday. On Tuesday, school children, carrying flags, and headed by the Clowne Silver Prize Band, marched through the village singing patriotic songs. Discharged soldiers made a tour of the village on a lorry, and sang lustily *Old Soldiers Never Die*.

The men who worked at the Southgate Colliery in Clowne were supposed to return to work on the Tuesday morning but refused to do so, deciding instead to take another day's holiday to continue the jubilation. On learning this, the agent of the Shireoaks Colliery Co., Mr R.E. Jones JP, ordered the flag, which had been raised on the headstock to mark the occasion, be removed. This caused much resentment amongst the men, who held a meeting at which it was agreed that Jones' action was a national disgrace, and that unless the Union Flag was replaced they would not return to work until Monday. Jones backed down and had the flag replaced on Wednesday morning and work was resumed on Thursday.

In Whitwell, Barlborough and Creswell there were similar scenes of decorations and joy. The bells of the Barlborough parish church rang out merry peals.

In Pleasley, the news was learnt by the colliery management at around 11am, who duly sounded the hooters to alert the wider community. The village was quickly decorated. A thanksgiving service was held at the Old Cross the following day.

In Eckington, celebrations were mixed with sorrow for the dead. Whilst flags adorned many of the houses, and were carried by children in the streets, there was no cheering and no excitement, although the church bells rang throughout much of the day. However, well attended services of thanksgiving were held in the parish church and in the United Methodist Church.

Very soon after hearing the news, the village of Mosborough, which was at this time part of Derbyshire, was adorned with flags and the church bells rang. Patriotic songs were sung in the school before it was closed for the day. With the school closed, throughout the afternoon 'troops of children' paraded the village waving their flags. The following afternoon a fancy dress parade, headed by the Eckington Prize Band was held.

Upon the news reaching Renishaw, 300 cadets at Mount St Mary's paraded the streets, accompanied by their bugle and bagpipe bands. In the evening, a whist drive and social was held at the Renishaw Council School.

In Killamarsh, the pits closed upon the news being heard and some did not return to work until Friday. The children arrived at school, following a fortnight's break, to be informed they were to have the afternoon off to celebrate the armistice. That evening the church bells rang out and prayers of thanksgiving took place. On Thursday the local prize band paraded the main streets.

In Beighton (part of Derbyshire until 1967), the news was announced by the colliery buzzers and was received with 'great joy and thankfulness'. The pits were closed for the rest of the day. Flags soon flew from the church, school and from the windows of nearly every house. Children paraded the streets waving flags and singing patriotic songs. In the evening the church bells rang out 'joyous peals' and prayers were said. The following day a short, well attended, thanksgiving service was held, with members of all the religious denominations present.

In Dronfield, the works' buzzers heralded the good news and work stopped. Flags soon appeared on buildings and before long the town 'assumed a holiday appearance'. The bells of the parish church rang out loudly. The RAF personnel stationed at the Coal Aston aerodrome marched round the town, with happy spectators cheering, and scenes of 'great gaiety'. A well-attended thanksgiving service was held later in the day.

'Intense joy' greeted the news of the armistice in Holmesfield. The news was announced by the hoisting up of the Union Flag on the church, and the ringing of the church bell. Within half an hour the church was filled with thankful residents of the village and surrounding hamlets.

In South Normanton, the news was quickly followed by joy and celebration, with the town soon 'beflagged from end to end'. During a thanksgiving service the rector urged the congregation not to forget the men who had laid down their lives to make that day possible.

In Pinxton, the news was celebrated in 'a somewhat quiet way', though it too made merry. At around 11am the news reached Messrs Coppee's Works and the buzzers passed the glad tidings to the workers and the community. Within a few minutes buildings began to be decorated with the Union Flag and flags of the Allies and soon presented a 'a gay appearance'. The local school was closed until Wednesday.

In Alfreton and its district, it was remarked that news arrived 'within an amazingly short period of the terms of the armistice being signed' and immediately it underwent 'a meteoric change', adopting a 'festive mood'. The town was decorated with thousands of flags and patriotic emblems. Some of the works closed immediately, and the pits closed early, remaining closed until Wednesday. A thanksgiving service was held at Alfreton Parish Church, with a large congregation. The Swanwick Collieries Silver Prize Band provided musical entertainment in the Market Place. During the evening a 'liberal' supply of fireworks lit up the sky.

At Blackwell a united service was held on the cricket ground. In the evening there was a thanksgiving service at the parish church.

Thanksgiving services were also held at other locations in the Alfreton district, including the Tibshelf Parish Church, and at Somercotes and Riddings parish churches.

In Sheldon, Gyte wrote in her diary that there were a few flags flown, 'but some had no heart for joy'.

It was a time of mixed emotions for those who had lost loved ones, but there was, arguably, a greater cruelty in the timing of some of the deaths of Derbyshire men. There was no cause for celebration in the home of Mr and Mrs King of Chapel Road, Grassmoor. Whilst jubilations raged across the county they were consoling themselves with the news, received that day, that their oldest son Albert had been killed in France. He was one of the last to go to war, enlisting in April 1918 and arriving in France at the beginning of August. It is a sad irony he was also one of the last to die.

Three Derbyshire men are known to have died on Armistice Day itself as a result of enemy action, although news of their deaths would not be revealed until some time later: Private Francis James Eyre of Eyam (2nd Battalion, Machine Gun Corps (Infantry); Private Robert Bernard Stead, of Driffield (10th Battalion, East Yorkshire Regiment); and Private W. Gough, of Caldwell (3rd Battalion, Sherwood Foresters).

CHAPTER 23

Memories That Will Not Fade

Thanksgiving services were held across the country in the weeks following the Armistice and a Day of Thanksgiving took place on Sunday 17 November.

The service at Chesterfield is a typical example. Chesterfield people queued to gain admission to the parish church where Canon Shaw spoke of how much people had to be thankful for now that this unparalleled victory had been achieved thanks to God's work. It was He who inspired the leaders in the war, He who filled the hearts of the men with such superb courage and He who had upheld the morale of the country. The country would never forget those who have lost their lives, he remarked, saying their memories would never fade.

In order that memories of the men and their sacrifices should never fade memorials were planned across the majority of the county. As a temporary measure wooden crosses were erected whilst details were finalised for permanent structures.

It was an issue that dominated public discussions, with meetings being organised and the correspondence columns of local newspapers featuring suggestions. One suggestion put forward by Mr W.M. Greaves, was for avenues of trees along the main routes through towns and villages, with each tree representing a soldier or sailor who had died, and bearing a plaque commemorating that individual.

Another suggestion was that cots should be purchased for hospitals, with each one dedicated to the memory of a killed serviceman. At the Royal Hospital in Chesterfield a cot had been bought in the name of Lieutenant Bower and a suitable inscription was written on the wall next to the cot. Entire hospital wards could be named in honour of the killed, as well as streets being named in their honour.

In Derby, it was decided to produce a bronze figure of a woman holding a baby in her arms, representing a war widow, stood in front of a large cross. The Midland Railway Company created its own memorial, costing £10,958, for the 2,833 of its employees who lost their lives.

The First World War memorial dedicated to the men of Derby who lost their lives.
The Author

A memorial dedicated to the 2,833 workers of the Midland Railway Company in Derby, who were killed during the First World War. *The Author*

In Bolsover, the council decided to restore the market cross as a memorial and incorporate a captured German gun and a tablet bearing the names of the fallen. One councillor wanted the memorial to take the form of public baths. 'If we have been able to find so much money for the war we ought to be able to find money to keep people healthy and well', he argued.

During a two-day sale of work in aid of the Chesterfield Parish Church Curate's Fund, where the Mayor spoke of the happy circumstances and his hope it would encourage people to buy what they did not want at double the price it was worth, discussions took place for Chesterfield's memorial. The vicar suggested a monument in the form of a calvary on which would be inscribed the names of the local soldiers who had fallen.

A proposal for a 'first-class public hall' in Chesterfield to commemorate the end of the war, and those who lost their lives during the conflict, was seriously considered but was never constructed. Chesterfield's war memorial consists of the calvary in the graveyard of the parish church and a stone memorial for both world wars opposite the Town Hall, immediately adjacent to the large gardens dedicated to the memory of Chesterfield's war mayor, Ernest Shentall.

The most impressive memorial in the county is that known as Crich Stand, which can be seen for many miles as a prominent feature on the landscape and was built in memory of the men of Derbyshire and Nottinghamshire who fought and died with the Sherwood Foresters.

Matlock's memorial was erected at Pic Tor so that it too could be seen for miles around. It was an apt location because High Tor and the surrounding hills had been stripped of trees for timber for the war effort.

Individual parishes had their own memorials, usually in churchyards. The one village in Derbyshire without a memorial is Bradbourne, which was one of only fifty-three civil parishes in England and Scotland whose servicemen all returned home, and therefore no memorial was

Crich Stand, the memorial to the Sherwood Foresters, soon after it was built in 1923. *Courtesy of Derbyshire Libraries and www.picturethepast.org.uk*

The memorial to the men of Bakewell killed during the First World War. *The Author*

required. A grave for Private Daniel Holmes lies within the village but Holmes died in England during training and never saw active service.

It was well into the 1920s before many of the war memorials were erected, following years of fund raising and planning. Indeed, a memorial tablet for the men of Youlgreave, Alport, Middleton and Harthill was unveiled and dedicated on 9 November 1925 (an invitation to the unveiling forms part of the Derbyshire records Office archive: reference D1190/254). Solemn ceremonies were held when the memorials were officially dedicated.

The unveiling of the Ilkeston War Memorial in January 1922. *Courtesy of Derbyshire Libraries and www.picturethepast.org.uk*

The unveiling of the war memorial in Creswell in 1921. *Courtesy of Derbyshire Libraries and www.picturethepast.org.uk*

There was anger in Matlock Bath where it was hoped to display four war guns captured by the Sherwood Foresters. However, the government demanded money for them. The chairman of the Urban Council condemned the government for wanting to sell the weapons. 'Our boys fought and bled for those guns', he remarked, 'We do not mind paying the cost of the carriage but it is too much to ask us to buy them.' However, it was later agreed if they had to pay they would.

Appeals were made in Derby for more money for what was planned as a war weapons week but became regarded as a means of paying towards the cost of national reconstruction and was dubbed a 'peace loan'. During Derby's War Weapons Week, which began on 18 November, a total of £915,328 was raised, far in excess of the £600,000 required.

As 1918 came to a close people began to commence the slow process of returning to peace.

In December a winter carnival and fun fair was held at Chesterfield's ice skating rink, with special guests Jack Oliver and his famous war dog; the dog 'with a human brain'.

What was described by the Mayor of Chesterfield as the 'brightest day in the town's history' was enjoyed in the run up to Christmas, when a contingent of the 1st/6th Battalion of the Sherwood Forester were given a heroes welcome. On 11 December, the battalion colours, which they had left for safekeeping in the parish church, were returned to the men in a 'memorable' ceremony.

Following the ceremony, a civic procession led to the Market Place where there were 'memorable scenes' with music, singing and loud cheers. The men of the 1st/6th Battalion returned to France the following day, where they remained for Christmas prior to demobilisation in January 1919.

Two days later there was joy in Derby when the colours of the 1st/5th Battalion of Sherwood Foresters, who had entrusted them to All Saints' Church for safekeeping, were returned to a delegation of the battalion during a moving ceremony.

Following the ceremony there was a procession to the Market Place where the Mayor congratulated the men on their courage and bravery. He asked them to tell the men in France that Derby was proud of them. 'May you go back and finish your work for a glorious and lasting peace, and may we at home so do our duty, whether in the municipality or in parliament, as to make our land in the words of our great Prime Minister, one "fit for heroes to live in!"'

For the first Christmas of peace restrictions were lifted on some of the foods that had been rationed, with turkeys, geese, ducks, fowls, chicken and game to be freely available between 16 December and 4 January. An increased ration was made available for other types of meat for the same period. In parts of Derbyshire jam was not available at all until the very end of December. However, tea was freely available and in such quantities that rationing was not necessary.

Although the fighting had ceased, and some loved ones were able to return on leave for Christmas, it was considered too soon to enjoy a traditional Christmas, although it was regarded as the most sacred and the most memorable for many years. There were more absences from the dinner table but those whose loved ones had survived the war had feelings of joy and optimism that they would soon be returning for good.

During the Christmas period there was some discussion about the General Election held on 14 December in which tens of thousands of women of thirty years of age and older, and more men than ever before, placed their vote. Counting of votes did not begin until 28 December and the results were not known until the very end of the year when it was announced Lloyd George was to form another coalition government.

CHAPTER 24

The Influenza Outbreak

'We are experiencing a fresh bout of influenza, but it is not as bad as some which we have endured within the memory of the present generation', the *Derby Mercury* reported on 1 November 1918. How wrong those words would be proven to be. In the same article it was suggested that by not thinking or talking about the illness, the chances of becoming a victim would be greatly reduced. Yet within days it would become impossible not to talk, think and indeed greatly worry about the scourge of influenza.

In the weeks leading up to the armistice, and in the weeks and months which followed, hope and jubilation were replaced with gloom and despair in homes across Derbyshire. Just as Derbyshire was beginning to look to the future approximately 3,000 people lost their lives within the county.

Indeed, in some households the armistice celebrations could not be enjoyed at all, as an increasing number of people were struck down. The illness spread due to poor sanitation and living conditions, including overcrowded homes, and because the population had become weakened by poor nutrition as a result of food shortages and rationing.

The God-fearing who had given 'heartfelt thanks to the Almighty' (as the *Derbyshire Times* had described the flocking to churches following the cessation of hostilities) when fighting ceased on 11 November, must surely have questioned the divine plan which now saw civilians being struck down at home, as bullets had struck down men abroad.

As men began to return from overseas where they had been lucky to escape death, they faced the risk of illness and death at home. Private Fred Margereson of the Royal Engineers, who hailed from Barlow, became seriously ill with pneumonia following influenza. Whilst being treated at Wareham Hospital, his sister Nellie was summoned to visit him. Dutifully she hurried to his bedside and in doing so contracted the illness. Both sister and brother died.

Fred Holmes of Buxton served with the 1st/6th and the 21st battalions of the Sherwood Foresters, prior to being discharged through ill health in March 1917. In late 1918 he contracted influenza which led to pneumonia, from which he died in December that year.

Private John Goodwin of Staveley arrived home on leave following the cessation of hostilities and ironically returning home was what led to his death. He contracted influenza and when he arrived back in France he was seriously ill and died two days later.

Private C.W. Fishlock, of the 20th Company, Labour Corps, died of pneumonia, presumably following influenza, at his home in Long Eaton on Armistice Day.

Another Derbyshire soldier died of influenza on Armistice Day, although his death took place in Egypt. Private William Pooler, a native of Glossop, served with the 2nd Battalion, Royal Welsh Fusiliers.

Although news of influenza dominated the press and public thoughts from November 1918 into the early months of the following year, the illness had its roots during the summer of 1918. During the summer months there had been requests to close certain entertainment venues in the Chesterfield district. However, Dr Herbert Peck, Medical Officer of the Chesterfield Rural District, refused to do so unless all churches, chapels, theatres, 'cinematograph' shows, most works, passenger trains and other public conveniences were similarly closed. However, after making its presence known in July 1918 there was a short abatement in recorded incidences of the disease, until September when it became more prevalent, reaching its peak in the second half of November, when almost 400 people died in the county during the course of a week, with most deaths taking place in the rural communities.

It was on 7 November, the day that negotiations between the allies and Germany began, that the need for action was identified and it was decided in Chesterfield that in order to help prevent the disease from spreading children aged fourteen and under were to be prohibited from places of entertainment, such as cinemas and theatres.

Mr Welshman, the manager of the Corporation Theatre and Hippodrome, was concerned what effect the ban would have on his establishments. A large proportion of his customers were children, he said, and the same was true for other entertainment venues. The restriction was applied to the whole of the area of the Chesterfield Rural District. Cinemas in and around the town were disinfected and ventilated before each performance.

Many schools were closed, not just to prevent the disease being spread among the children, but mainly because so many of the teachers were ill from influenza it was often not possible to have lessons. By the end of November more than half of the county's 380 schools were closed. During December some schools briefly reopened, only to close again as it was realised that their reopening was making matters worse.

Children could attend cinemas in any district that schools were open. Most schools in Derbyshire remained closed until after the Christmas period, however, and consequently the ban on children in most cinemas also continued for the remainder of 1918.

It was not until the end of November that precautions were taken in Derby, with cinemas closing between 5:30 and 6:30pm for disinfecting; and further disinfecting taking place during the evening. Smoking was believed to help minimise the risk of contracting the disease.

On 23 November, the 'scourge of influenza' was described as raging across the country, with hardly a home being spared. Unlike many illnesses the influenza, which was at this time also being called 'the plague', particularly affected the young and 'strong middle-aged'. The virulent nature of the disease caused great strain to doctors and nurses who could not cope with the number of patients, and the high mortality rate was causing a strain on grave diggers who could not prepare graves fast enough, with funerals being delayed. The *Derbyshire Times* advised people to 'keep calm' and take every precaution by keeping warm and avoiding visiting places where large number of people congregated.

There was anger and frustration from the medical community, as well as the patients and their families, about the lack of medical help available.

Dr J.A. Magee of Clowne, wrote to Lord Burnham, the chairman of the Liquor Control Board, demanding more brandy be made available. With the lack of effective medicines, whisky and brandy were used as a 'stimulant' to help combat the symptoms of influenza. However, there was a scarcity of spirits available. In his letter, which was reproduced in the *Derbyshire Times*, Dr Magee wrote that 'People are dying for the want of stimulant.' He described telephoning a grocer and wine merchant asking for brandy, in order to treat a young man who, in the doctor's opinion, was dying. It was his belief that the only hope for the young man was a plentiful supply of liquor. He pointed out supplies of food and coal were being affected by workers being struck by the illness. He was outraged that the 'good and sober citizens' could lose their lives or be confined to bed for lengthy periods of time, when whisky or brandy would help their chances of recovery, simply because a minority of people had been convicted of drunkenness. His letter ended with a direct plea to make the spirits more readily available: 'If you had been in a house where I was today and saw a young miner collapse from a severe attack of influenza, and his friends trying to obtain a supply of stimulant, I am sure you would see that such a condition of things was altered…'

In the run up to Christmas 1918 an increased ration was made available for sugar, so that chemists could make cough mixture. Medical officers were instructed to give special certificates to their patients so that they could obtain necessary sustenance without having to worry about restrictions.

Doctors, priests and other religious ministers were at high risk of catching the disease, as they visited its sufferers. Reverend Father William Long, of the Annunciation Roman Catholic Church in Chesterfield, visited a parishioner suffering a 'serious case' of influenza and contracted the illness. He died on 13 November, aged just thirty-three, from pneumonia caused by influenza. Reverend William Bunting of Crich died of pneumonia following a bout of influenza, also in November.

In December 1918 there was anger at a Chesterfield Town Council meeting when Councillor Varley suggested not enough was being done to combat influenza. In response to a question about the situation, Councillor Edmunds responded that the medical fraternity did not understand the illness and that everything possible had been done. There were, he acknowledged, insufficient numbers of nurses to treat patients, despite nurses from Penmore Hospital being released to help treat patients. All that could be done now, he said, was wait until the disease gradually abated on its own. This angered Varley who shouted: 'Have we to sit down like fatalists and say it has to be?' The council's refusal to do any more was further shown when Varley was told he should not have raised the matter in that meeting and instead should have waited for the next meeting of the General Purposes Committee.

Following the decision to close the schools for the remainder of 1918, and until the disease abated, it was agreed to also contact churches in order to recommend the closure of Sunday schools. At a meeting of the Chesterfield Rural District Council on 7 December it was also suggested that all public gatherings should be ended. Election meetings for the General Election (which was held on 14 December) were attracting large crowds and, it was believed, they helped spread the disease.

At the same meeting there were also plans to effectively cancel all Christmas festivities. Reverend J.L. Blake, of Clay Cross, said festivities, such as parties and teas would have to be abandoned. It was also decided to ask promoters of dances to discontinue them. Messrs J. Simpkin and H. Sykes argued that if schools and cinemas were to be closed, and election meetings and Christmas parties cancelled, because they were places where people congregated, then churches and chapels should be closed. It was not a popular suggestion and one which was not given further consideration.

The disease in Derbyshire began to abate in December 1918, before experiencing another, albeit lesser, wave during the spring of 1919, before finally abating in May 1919 shortly before the peace celebrations.

Adults aged between twenty and forty were the most at risk from influenza. Pregnant women and their unborn children were especially at risk, with an increased likelihood of still birth and premature births. If the mother and child survived the full term of pregnancy, according to a study by Dr Alice Reid of the University of Cambridge, the child's early health would have suffered as a result of the mother's inability to provide infant care due to her illness, which would potentially have had long-term implications on the health of the child, with a significantly higher possibility that they would die before their first birthday than those babies whose mother had not contracted the illness, as well as an increased probability of the child contracting the disease itself from his or her mother.

It is not possible to say exactly how many people died of influenza in Derbyshire, although it is believed by Reid that 2,993 succumbed. The true figure is likely to have been higher. The disease contributed to a number of illnesses, most notably pneumonia, and the official records would only state pneumonia as the cause of death despite pneumonia being the direct result of influenza. Additionally, in the early months of the pandemic accurate records were not kept of the incidence of the disease because it was not considered necessary to do so. Furthermore, diagnoses were not always accurate, especially in the early stages, and it can be expected that some deaths directly due to influenza were misdiagnosed. Regardless of how many died this indiscriminate killer, like the war which had largely preceded it, robbed communities of Derbyshire, who had already suffered loss, of a large part of their lifeblood.

CHAPTER 25

Peace Celebrations

Having been demobbed earlier in 1919, the servicemen were given heroes' welcomes, especially the Sherwood Foresters.

On 10 April the 2nd Battalion of Sherwood Foresters returned to Derby, approximately only seventy of the men having survived. When they arrived in the town they formed part of a procession leading from the Midland Railway station to the Market Place, with the streets lined with enthusiastic spectators. In the Market Place, which was densely packed with people, they were welcomed home by the Mayor of Derby.

The 1st Battalion of Sherwood Foresters returned home on 18 May and received a similar welcoming party, as did the Derbyshire Imperial Yeomanry when they too returned to the county.

On 21 June, the 6th Battalion were given an enthusiastic reception when they paraded through Chesterfield, and, on a smaller scale, when the men who did not hail from the town of the crooked spire returned to their towns and villages. The men of the 5th Battalion received a rapturous reception in Derby. On 12 July, the 1st/5th Battalion held a reunion in there, with a dinner in the Drill Hall attended by approximately 600 men bearing the 'honourable scars' of their service. No matter how disfigured some of them happened to be, they were fortunate because thirty-seven officers, two CSMs, one staff sergeant, twenty-six sergeants, ten lance sergeants, twenty-four corporals, sixty-six lance corporals and 500 privates had laid down their lives to make that happy reunion possible.

Lieutenant Colonel Clifford T. Newbold said that those who had survived the war now had a duty to make sure the mothers and wives of their fallen comrades were looked after and that those who had been maimed as a result of active service were given the assistance they required. He hoped that the men would be welcomed back into civilian life and that they would be able to return to their old jobs. He added that the territorial forces were to continue and he hoped the men present would consider signing up once again.

On 7 July a Victory Loan Week began in Derby to raise £1,000,000 towards paying off the war debt. Meetings were held, with local dignitaries urging the town's folk to be generous. The Mayor of Derby was unwell on account of the great stress he had been under in organising the forthcoming Peace Celebrations, and had been forced to take a two-week holiday in Llandudno. Bands played throughout the week and soldiers and sailors paraded in the town. On the opening day an aeroplane flew over Derby, causing great excitement. The week's events enabled the target to be surpassed, with £1,161,000 being raised.

When the Treaty of Versailles was signed the war finally came to an end, on 28 June 1919. To mark the joyous occasion peace celebrations were held across the land, usually on 18 and 19 July, although some places, such as Mickleover, held their events weeks later. It is not possible to describe the events held in every town and village in Derbyshire, but the following examples give a good representation of the festive spirit. For those places not mentioned, they too held events with the general theme being one of services of thanksgiving followed by sports, tea (usually for children and pensioners), more sports, music and dancing, victory parades by servicemen and during the night bonfires, flares and fireworks although often the celebrations were cut short by heavy rain.

In Derby on 18 July, it was Schoolchildren's Day, an event immediately preceding the main peace celebrations. Twenty-five thousand medals were handed out by the Mayor to the town's youngsters to award them for their endurance of war on the Home Front. Following the medal ceremony there was a substantial tea for all the children in their schools. The day witnessed a 'whirl of juvenile joy' and one girl was so happy that she asked her teacher 'When will there be another war?' because she wanted another peace celebration.

That evening there was 'revellery' at Normanton Barracks, where a victory dance and social was held. The entertainment included comedy, impersonations and ventriloquism.

On 19 July the main day's events began with an angling 'victory match' before the bells of All Saints', St Peters and St Andrews; and St Aldmund's started to ring out merry peals at 8am.

Derby town council held a special meeting in the morning to pass a resolution: 'On this day, set apart nationally to celebrate the restoration of peace, this meeting of the Derby Town Council, specially convened, places on record its deep appreciation, and that of the inhabitants of the county borough of Derby, of the patriotism, heroism and self-sacrifice of all those

Derby men who served in any branch of His Majesty's forces during the great war, and especially of those who made the supreme sacrifice.'

At the meeting criticisms of pensions for those disabled by war were also raised, but could not be discussed because the issue was not on the agenda. As the celebrations got under way it was remarked the 'smiles and buoyancy that vanished five years ago surged forth volcanically' across the town.

Public buildings were well decorated and of the residential streets the inhabitants of Norman and Eagle Streets had made notable efforts, with streamers and garlands displayed in 'great and artistic profusion'. Effigies of the Kaiser suffered 'death without formal trial' in Clive Street, Crowton and Dale Road, Derby.

Sports, including tennis, golf, bowls and athletics, were held at the Arboretum before a large crowd.

A spectacular parade drew crowds so large that it was said the whole of Derby must have turned out, along with their 'country cousins'. The parade consisted of a procession of individuals, organisations, servicemen and decorated vehicles and floats in what was described as 'pageantry of the most attractive and beautiful character'.

The Deputy Mayor and his wife threw rolls of red, white and blue ribbon, flowers and confetti as they drove and it was 'the object of a confetti storm'. People threw the ribbons, flowers and confetti at each other with 'real wedding morn glee and vivacity'. One of the floats consisted of an R34 airship upon a Trent motor bus. The spectacle was dubbed 'The Latest on the Road' on account of the R34 being the most up-to-date air vehicle and the Trent bus the latest on the road. People in fancy dress costumes featured prominently in the parade, as did decorated prams containing the children born during the war years. Mr O.H. Abrahart took his son into the procession in a decorated chair. It was his child who had been born without legs, apparently due to shock from the 1916 air raid.

A victory march of the demobbed servicemen led from the Cattle Market to the racecourse and county cricket grounds, where the war heroes were entertained with sports including running, cycling, a tug of war and boxing, the latter being particularly popular. They were treated to lunch and liquor and were given 10s worth of tickets to spend. Coconut shies, refreshment tents, roundabouts, dolly stalls, houp-las and shooting galleries added to a carnival atmosphere. Music and dancing also helped entertain the men. In recreation grounds across Derby there were open-air concerts and, at night, flares and firework displays.

At Darley Park approximately 8,000 people enjoyed entertainment

Chesterfield's Armistice Celebration Arch forming part of the decorations to mark the end of hostilities. *Courtesy of R. Shemwell and www.picturethepast. org.uk*

including athletics, a regatta of illuminated boats, concerts and fireworks at night.

In Chesterfield there were 'memorable scenes' in Queen's Park, where 2,500 Chesterfield servicemen marched through the park in front of a crowd of 20,000. Late into the night and early hours fireworks and bonfires lit up the town.

On 27 July, 15,000 to 20,000 people enjoyed a musical festival at Queen's Park was given by a choir of 500 singing to an orchestra of 120 instruments.

In Ashbourne the streets were well decorated and a joyous peal from church bells started the day. A minute's silence for the dead was held in the Market Place whilst the bugler sounded the *Last Post*. A resolution was then passed stating, 'That the inhabitants of the town of Ashbourne, in solemn conclave assembled to commemorate the restoration of the peace, hereby places upon record their undying appreciation of the heroic part played by their sons and daughters in the great European War, and whilst tendering to the relatives of the fallen their heartfelt sympathy, welcome with pride and gratitude the return of the men and women of the Allied campaign on behalf of the liberty, the peace, and the morality of the world.' A short united service was then held before a great procession then marched through the town. In the afternoon sports were held for children, followed by tea in their schools.

Children then had games in the Paddock. In the evening there was music and dancing before a grand carnival went through the streets, consisting of decorated lorries, drays and cars, with horses and pedestrians, though it was somewhat spoilt by heavy rain. The celebrations were brought to a close with a huge bonfire in the Cattle Market.

At Barrow-on-Trent a procession of parishioners through the 'gaily decked village' was led by servicemen, to the parish church where a service was held. A substantial dinner was provided for the men, with a ham tea for women and children. Sports were played for the children in the afternoon and for adults in the evening.

There were no great efforts to decorate Belper, though some individual streets made efforts. Festivities began with photographs taken in the River Gardens before a united service was held in the Market Place. This was followed by a dinner for the over 60s and sports for past and serving servicemen, which included tug of war, wheelbarrow races and obstacle races.

The Belper Prize Band headed a procession of children from the Market Place to the parks where they entered 'wholeheartedly and with the zest of youthful optimism into the day of days that will leave its imprint on their memories for years to come'. In the park the 4,000 children sang and said prayers before heading to their Sunday schools for a tea. Dinner was also provided to about 1,400 soldiers and sailors with their wives, mothers or sweethearts in the marquee at the River Gardens, widows of soldiers and sailors also being welcome. A band provided dance music in the pavilion in the evening and sports were held. A bonfire was lit on Cow Hill while illuminations in Milford also served Belper. Flares and electric lights from Denby could also be seen.

In Brailsford a dinner was provided to the servicemen. A procession through the village was led by the Brailsford band and children were transported on vehicles by the Brailsford Dairy Farmers' Association to Ednaston Lodge where they were entertained and given a commemorative mug. At 6pm they were taken to Brailsford Hall where festivities were held. In the meantime the adults had been given a tea. Dancing, sports, and other amusements followed, with a large bonfire at the top of Common Side ending festivities.

At Dalbury Lees an excellent tea was given to the women and children and a supper provided for the men and women. In the afternoon the children assembled on the village green each carrying a Union Flag and wearing decorated victory caps. A memorable scene was when a German prisoner working on a local farm paid a visit and accepted a victory cap and placed it on his head. Children then moved to Wood House where they sang and played games. The adults had a 'most substantial dinner' followed by sports and races before rain brought the sports to an end. A concert and fireworks were later enjoyed and as a memento of the day the boys received a mug and girls were given a cup and saucer.

Kirk Langley presented a very festive appearance. A ladies versus gents cricket match was played, the ladies being victorious. Other sports were also enjoyed, as was a meat tea in the schoolroom for the whole village. Due to the rain the fireworks display was postponed.

At Repton, sports were held at the Hall for the children, followed by tea, with each child given a mug. Servicemen had a meat tea and were welcomed back by Reverend J. Solwyn. Further sports were played by the adults and there was a fancy dress costume parade and a parade of decorated bicycles and prams.

Heage and Ambergate enjoyed a substantial programme of events although no details were recorded. At night the villagers observed the bonfires of Crich and Matlock, which could be seen in the distance.

In Spondon an outdoors thanksgiving service started the day's events. A cricket match was followed by a procession to the Spondon House School, where Captain J. Drury addressed 150 demobilised Spondon men and medals were given to the children. There was music and sports, including maypole dancing. In the afternoon 600 children had tea and when the soldiers arrived they (the soldiers) gave their wives and mothers an ovation. A 'monster' bonfire ended the festivities.

In Melbourne a public welcome was given in the Market Place to approximately 250 returned servicemen. The Admiral of the Fleet, Lord Walter Kerr, addressed the men. He had been there in 1914 to appeal for recruits. A short united thanksgiving service was followed by a procession with the servicemen going to the public hall for luncheon and entertainment and the children to their schools for a tea. At the public hall, soldier songs were lustily sung and cheers given for the nurses, doctors, Lord Walter Kerr, Major J.D. Kerr, and the women who kept the home fires burning. Band music and sports were held, though proceedings were cut short by rain.

In Matlock the day was 'royally celebrated'. The prize band played from the kiosk in the morning, with a concert and sports in the afternoon, followed by a tea for children and the aged and more sports. The Matlock servicemen's homecoming celebration was originally planned for the same day as the peace celebrations but the men refused to attend because their wives and partners had not been invited. As such a separate event was held on 23 August with the authorities agreeing to extend the celebrations to loved ones.

In Matlock Bath the day was celebrated with 'commendable energy'. Luncheon was provided at the Albion restaurant for the returned servicemen, followed by a procession of residents to the Old Pavilion where a short thanksgiving was held. The day also featured sports, a regatta, music, a cinema performance at the Pavilion, and a ball. Heavy rain prevented the illuminations from taking place but flares could be seen emanating from neighbouring districts and some fireworks were displayed later in the evening.

In Cromford, Scarthin and Darley Dale there was tea and sport for the residents, with a bonfire and fireworks in North and South Darley.

At Milford there were streams of flags and evergreens, and lots of enthusiasm. A parade of demobilised soldiers and sailors, about 150 in all, marched to the recreation ground where there was a thanksgiving service and a short address of welcome and appreciation. A substantial dinner was then provided to the servicemen. Children were given a substantial tea before being presented with victory medals. In the afternoon the grounds of Milford House were the scene of sports including a football match in fancy dress between married men and single men. There was also a victory dance before fireworks and flares were set off, lighting up the sky so much so that they were visible from several miles away.

Ockbrook and Borrowash were well decorated and were the scene of a united service, followed by sports and a 'splendid tea' for the children. Further sports were cut short by rain in the evening.

Wirksworth entered 'wholeheartedly' into the celebrations with a pageant procession, which lined up at Old Land End and was headed by the Wirksworth town band and the Derby Cadets band. It consisted of decorated vehicles and floats, along with pedestrians in fancy dress. The procession paraded the main streets of the town and assembled in the Market Place where songs were sung and cheers were given for the returned men. The parade then led to the recreation ground where there were sports for the children, who were also given a tea. A jazz band performed in the evening despite the rain, with a procession to Allport Heights where a beacon fire was lighted at 11pm and a pyrotechnic display concluded the programme. The fire had been advertised the previous night when a 'practical joker' brought the whole town out of their homes with the frantic ringing of the town hall's fire bell. When asked where the fire was, he responded it would be at Allport.

Teas and sports were held at Bolehill and Steeple Grange. At Gorsey Bank tea was given to all the inhabitants of that hamlet and the children played sports before a bonfire was lit. At Middleton by Wirksworth the villagers were treated to a tea, with sports for the children. Flares and fireworks ended the day.

In Starkholmes and Riber there were sports, and tea was provided for children and the over 60s.

Buxton, having been home to the 2nd/6th Battalion placed great emphasis on its parade, led by the Burbage Silver Prize Band and the Lime Firms Women's Legion band. The parade consisted the police, fire brigade, other local organisations and discharged servicemen who received cheers from the crowds that lined the town's streets. Prior to the parade a meeting was held in the Market Place. The town was well decorated, especially Bennett Street which was reported in the *Buxton Advertiser* to have been a 'blaze of colour'. During a speech that day the Mayor, Alderman W.F. Mill, spoke of how he hoped the Great War would be the war to end all wars. Again there were sports and teas.

The streets of Buxton lined with spectators of the Peace Day parade in Buxton. *Courtesy of Derbyshire Libraries and www.picturethepast.org.uk*

A photograph to commemorate the Peace Day celebrations in Whitwell. *Courtesy of Derbyshire Libraries and www.picturethepast.org.uk*

In Bugsworth, Chinley and Whitehough there were 'joy rides' for the children, followed by a procession, including a fancy dress parade and decorated vehicles, followed by a remembrance ceremony. The service was followed by sports and entertainments, teas for all, a balloon display and presentations to the children of souvenirs. There was a supper for serving and former servicemen in the evening, before a torch-lit procession led to Cracken Edge where rockets and fireworks ended the day's events (the programme for the day's events can be viewed at Derbyshire Record Office: reference D1219/17/2-3).

In Whitwell there were sports and a tea. As in many other places a photograph was taken of the children of the village as a lasting reminder of the joyous occasion.

In Glossop, in addition to sports and teas, there was a parade which included war babies in decorated prams. The town was prettily decorated with flags, bunting and banners. Concerts were held and the mayor planted a tree in Glossop Park. An impressive display of flares brought the festivities to a close.

In Sheldon, Gyte noted there were a few flags and a garland on display, but she could not comprehend 'how people can think of the sorrowing hearts

Mothers with prams containing war babies, forming part of a Peace Day procession in Glossop. *Courtesy of Mrs E. Bennett and www.picturethepast. org.uk*

of those who have lost their loved ones being expected to look on or join in any festivities'. Certain people, in her opinion, were more interested in food and festivities: 'Some people have had a deal to say (to Mr Stephenson) because there was not something at Sheldon for today. Miss Grover is proving an excellent tea (ham etc) for every one next Thursday, grown up and children as well, but I should think some of them wanted two gorging do's.'

On 24 July in Sheldon, a game of cricket was held with men playing against women, following which there was a tea for all, and children were given mugs. A memorial service was held for those who had died.

Returning to a Land Fit for Heroes

When the servicemen were demobilised in 1919 they returned to a Britain that was very different to that which they had been fighting for. Industrial expansion, changes to the status of women, changing attitudes to the class system, changes to the supply of food and liquor (with rationing continuing after the war), plans for major housing developments to replace the overcrowded and derelict homes that were not fit for human habitation, were among the most notable changes.

Men had difficulty adapting to those changes, especially having lived by a military lifestyle for up to four and a half years. They had to adapt to civilian life, and society had to adapt to meet the needs of its returned heroes. Men who had experienced the horrors of warfare often could not speak of them and carried their terror to their graves. Shell shock and other psychological disorders were all too common and little understood by the medical community let alone the friends and families of the sufferers of such afflictions who expected life to return to normal once their loved ones came home.

Physical disabilities were also prevalent and there was a need for good pensions for those who could not work, and long term support and health care. Some men who survived the war had health problems which led to their deaths months, and sometimes years, after returning home. For example, my great grandmother's brother, Patrick Kelly, who was gassed in the trenches in 1916 and was later shot through the shoulder. He survived the war but died in his Chesterfield home in January 1922. These later victims of the war are all too often overlooked, their names usually absent from war memorials yet their deaths no less sacrificed for their country, although in the case of Patrick Kelly he received a full military funeral which brought large parts of Chesterfield to a standstill.

Whether they died during, or in the aftermath of, war the loss of human lives saw the most important change in Derbyshire. Sons, brothers, husbands, fathers and friends were lost. The effect was also felt on businesses and industry with large numbers of skilled employees having been killed, resulting in a skills shortage which was to affect the future industrial success of the nation. Their absence was felt for decades and families faced extra financial hardship as well as the trauma of bereavement.

It is apt to end these chapters with a poem, titled 'Perhaps', written by Vera Brittain in memory of a man whom she loved, who was killed during the war, which eloquently sums up the sorrow felt in homes across Derbyshire in the years that followed the war:

Perhaps some day the sun will shine again,
And I shall see that still the skies are blue,
And feel once more I do not live in vain,
Although bereft of you.

Perhaps the golden meadows at my feet
Will make the sunny hours of spring seem gay,
And I shall find the white May-blossoms sweet,
Though you have passed away.

Perhaps the summer woods will shimmer bright,
And crimson roses once again be fair,
And Autumn harvest fields a rich delight,
Although you are not there.

Perhaps some day I shall not shrink in pain
To see the passing of the dying year,
And listen to Christmas songs again,
Although you cannot hear.

But though kind time may many joys renew,
There is one greatest joy I shall not know
Again, because my heart for loss of you
Was broken, long ago.

'Picture the Past'

'Picture the Past' is a not-for-profit project that aims to make historic images from the library and museum collections across the whole of Nottingham, Nottinghamshire, Derby and Derbyshire available via a completely free-to-use website.

In the past, anyone wanting to view these collections would have to travel many miles to track down the ones they were interested in. This proved to be frustrating and time consuming for researchers and a barrier to anyone from further a field. It was also damaging to the more fragile images from all the handling (the collections include hundreds of thousands of photographs, slides, negatives, glass plates, postcards and engravings).

Thankfully senior staff in the four local authorities got their heads together to solve the problem and came up with the idea of conserving them using

digitisation and making them accessible via a website, which also opened the collections to anyone anywhere in the world.

Work on digitising the images started in 2002 and by 2014 over 100,000 photographs, postcards, engravings and paintings had been added to the website. Photographic copies of the images can also be purchased online and, as a non-profit making project, money raised from these sales goes back into conservation of more pictures.

You can visit the website for free at www.picturethepast.org.uk

Index